Homeplace Geography

D1594486

Homeplace Geography

Essays for Appalachia

Donald Edward Davis

MERCER UNIVERSITY PRESS
Macon, Georgia
2006

ISBN 0-88146-014-1
MUP/P331

© 2006 Mercer University Press
1400 Coleman Avenue
Macon, Georgia 31207
All rights reserved

First Edition.

Library of Congress Cataloging-in-Publication Data

Davis, Donald Edward.
Homeplace geography : essays for Appalachia /
Donald Edward Davis.--1st ed.
p. cm.
Includes bibliographical references and index.
ISBN-13: 978-0-88146-014-8 (pbk. : alk. paper)
ISBN-10: 0-88146-014-1 (pbk. : alk. paper)
1. Appalachian Region, Southern—History. 2. Appalachian Region,
Southern—Geography. 3. Appalachian Region, Southern—Environmental
conditions. 4. Environmentalism—Appalachian Region, Southern.
5. Natural history—Appalachian Region, Southern. 6. Mountain
life—Appalachian Region, Southern. 7. Appalachian Region,
Southern—Social life and customs. I. Title.
F217.A65D38 2006
974—dc22
2006001478

For Appalachia

Introduction

Acknowledgments

While this body of work is not representative of all I have written about the Appalachian region, nor does it reflect my most recent efforts, the collected essays are testament to my lifelong love for the Appalachians and for those who have called the mountain region home. I owe many thanks to those who helped edit these and other writings or who offered encouragement and helpful suggestions over the years on how best to put pen to paper. Special mention goes to Marc LaFountain, who supported my writing early on, as did Alan Drengson and Eugene Hargrove, the respective editors of *The Trumpeter* and *Environmental Ethics*. Clayton Jones deserves special mention for his mastery of the written word and for numerous editorial suggestions. Lastly, I must thank my great-aunt Virgie Ross Dailey for teaching me, as a young child, the importance of homeplace. To her and others of her generation, I am forever indebted.

Introduction

The following essays, arranged chronologically in the order they were first written, represent my twenty-year career as a writer, environmental activist, and scholar of all things Appalachian. Several of the essays were published in independent journals with somewhat limited audiences, while others were never formally submitted for publication. A few of the writings were reprinted in several different works, including the opening chapter, "Homeplace Geography." Nominated for the prestigious Pushcart Prize, this essay was originally published in 1989 in *Mescechabe*, one of America's first bioregional publications. A year later, it found a home in *Now and Then: The Appalachian Magazine*. Reprinted here, "Homeplace" speaks of a rural landscape lost but not forgotten.

The second essay, "On Building Ecological Fences," was printed in the Canadian journal the *Trumpeter* in 1988. Edited by philosopher Alan Drengson, the *Trumpeter* was the principal voice of the North American Deep Ecology movement for nearly two decades. The essay is based upon a morning encounter with Kentucky environmental activist Hazel King and speaks of the irrelevance of ecological philosophy to rural residents, especially those living in the more remote areas of the mountain region. In Appalachia, grassroots environmental activism is often the result of events that threaten the people's way of life, actions initiated by corporate interests such as large coal-mining and timber companies. In the mountains, environmental problems are social problems. Local residents must pragmatically solve them, but within the context of an imbalanced, or even corrupt, community power structure.

"The Greening of Appalachia" is a substantially revised paper that was delivered in fall 1989 at the Southern Sociological Society's annual meeting in Norfolk, Virginia. As a former student of social theorist Murray Bookchin, whose scholarly work inspired the formation of the German

Green movement, I was hopeful at the time that the Green Party might one day improve the environmental conditions of the mountain region. I was also aware that the success of the movement depended ultimately on a more inclusive and forthright community organizing approach. Today, the Green Party is known mostly as the party that made Ralph Nader a national political force as opposed to one that truly represents local community or environmental interests. Although in many municipalities across the United States the Green movement has been successful at challenging the political status quo, few, if any, Green Party groups exist in the Appalachian region today.

Parts of the fourth chapter, "The Politics of Wilderness in Appalachia," were first read at the fourteenth annual Appalachian Studies Conference held in Berea, Kentucky, March 1991. I argue throughout the now updated essay that wilderness in Appalachia is a social construct that means different things to different stakeholders in the region, each of whom possesses institutional or cultural biases about how best to manage the mountain landscape. For rural Appalachians economically dependent on natural resources found in wilderness areas, making public lands off-limits to all human uses is not always a good thing. On the other hand, rural mountain residents know that turning vast areas over entirely to commercial interests can be equally devastating to mountain ecosystems. In order to preserve the wild and scenic landscapes of Appalachia, a more serious and ongoing dialogue among all concerned groups is needed.

Essay five, "Community Organizing in Appalachia," was first written for a roundtable session of the American Sociological Association held in Cincinnati, Ohio, in 1991 and was based upon research I did while attending a graduate seminar at the University of Tennessee. Environmental sociologist Sherry Cable was the seminar instructor; her research on the Yellow Creek Concerned Citizens of Middlesborough, Kentucky, forced me to reconsider the question of how group structure might influence the long-term success of grassroots environmental organizations in the region. Professor and author Stephen Fisher later asked me to revise the essay for his book *Fighting Back in Appalachia* (Philadelphia: Temple University Press, 1993), but a late submission meant it was not formally considered for publication.

"Gore in the Balance" was first published in the *Southern Reader* in spring 1992, a now-defunct regional journal that featured original essays and book reviews. This review essay points out the contradictions in the then-future vice president's environmental words and political deeds, anticipating the nationwide campaign that literally had hundreds of readers of Gore's *Earth in the Balance* (New York: Houghton Mifflin: 1992) mailing the book directly to Senator Gore's office with the personalized inscription "To Al Gore: Read this Book!"

Essay seven, "Feist or Fiction?: The Squirrel Dog of the Southern Mountains," was first published in the winter 1992 issue of the *Journal of Popular Culture* and is reprinted here with permission. Written with the editorial assistance of sociologist Jeffrey Stotik of the University of South Alabama, the finished article was the culmination of our four-month ethnographic study of the American Treeing Feist Association and its members. Based in east Tennessee during the early 1990s, this association attempted to make the feist dog a standard breed. The essay documents the group's efforts at accomplishing that task. The updated narrative also attempts to show the importance of the breed in Appalachian subsistence culture, as feist dogs have been used for hunting squirrels and other game in the region for more than two centuries.

"Roads to Ruins," the eighth essay, was first presented at the 1993 Appalachian Studies Conference in Johnson City, Tennessee, and was edited heavily in its original form by historian Margaret Lynn Brown of Brevard College. The piece was inspired by a three-month investigation of the hiking trails in the Great Smoky Mountains National Park, a research stint funded by the Great Smoky Mountains Natural History Association. The research led to the publication of the regionally best-selling book *Hiking Trails of the Smokies* (Gatlinburg: Great Smoky Mountains Natural History Association), a work published in 1994 that featured me as a "historical consultant" and "hiker-writer" for six individual trail narratives. While documenting the historical sites and folklore of the Great Smoky Mountains National Park, it became obvious to me that the hiking trails have a history that mirrors the history of the mountains themselves.

The ninth selection is a brief review essay of Shelby Lee Adams's *Appalachian Portraits* (Oxford: University Press of Mississippi, 1993), a book that has received high acclaim by art critics but was not generally well received by longtime Appalachianists. My review appeared in the spring 1994 issue of *Appalachian Heritage*.

The tenth essay, "Grassroots Movements and Rural Policy in Appalachia," was submitted for publication in *The State, Rural Policy, and Rural Disadvantage in the Late Twentieth Century*, a book that was to be compiled and edited by the late sociologist Fred Buttel of the University of Wisconsin. Although the original essay underwent several revisions, Buttel's collected volume was never formally approved for publication, and so only a handful of individuals, including John Gaventa, who made several editorial comments, have seen the final draft. An earlier version of the paper was presented to the State and Rural Policy Working Group of the Rural Sociological Society's Task Force on Rural Poverty, which met in 1994 and was also chaired by Fred Buttel. The updated essay summarizes the history and principal activities of several Appalachian organizations, all of which claim to have represented the grassroots, or least a grassroots perspective, in their public missions. My position throughout the narrative is that ordinary rural citizens, when given the opportunity and proper resources, can in fact shape their own destinies, even when federally- or state-sanctioned programs are designed to work against their interests.

The next selection, "Before Albion's Seed," was presented in 1994 at the seventeenth annual Appalachian Studies Association Conference at Virginia Polytechnic University in Blacksburg, Virginia. With only minor revisions, the paper was published a year later in volume 7 of the *Journal of the Appalachian Studies Association*, the official publication of the well-respected regional organization. Much of the material was derived from research I did while completing my dissertation at the University of Tennessee, a massive project that surveyed environmental and cultural change in southern Appalachia from 1500 to 1800. While a great deal of scholarly attention had focused on the Scots-Irish origins of mountain culture, my thesis was that Appalachian culture is derivative of many cultural traditions, including Native American ones. The version reprinted here has many of the endnotes and original bibliographic references deleted.

"The Forest for the Trees" was first presented at the University of Wisconsin Land Tenure Center's conference "Who Owns America?" that was held at Madison, Wisconsin, in summer 1995. The essay surveys community opposition to US Forest Service timber management practices in the mountain region, which at that time included efforts to stop clear-cutting, extensive road building, and the proliferation of pine-plantation monoculture. The narrative was largely informed by my organizing work with the Armuchee Alliance, a grassroots group formerly incorporated in the state of Georgia. During the mid-1990s, the Armuchee Alliance was at the forefront of forest activism and received national recognition, including substantial coverage in Suzanne Marshal's important book, *"Lord, We're Just*

Trying to Save Your Water": Environmental Activism and Dissent in the Appalachian South (Jacksonville: University of Florida Press, 2002).

Selection thirteen, "Living on the Land: Blue Ridge Life and Culture," was printed in the official publication of the Georgia Wildlife Federation in spring 1997. The federation's beautifully illustrated magazine, titled simply the *Blue Ridge*, featured numerous essays on the North Georgia mountains by noted environmentalists, ecologists, and environmental historians. My essay provides an overview of the cultural and environmental history of the Blue Ridge Mountains, from the Mississippian period of the sixteenth century to the creation of the Appalachian region's first national forest reserves during the second decade of the twentieth century. Endnotes have been added to this version that reference the many direct quotes found in the original essay.

Chapter 14, "Razing Appalachia," was written for the journal *Techné*, which is published occasionally by the Jacques Ellul Society. Headquartered in Washington, DC, the society was formed in 1996 to bring together thinkers, writers, and activists devoted to the ongoing struggle against "mega-technologies"—that is, technological contrivances so enormous that they threaten life on earth. This brief essay, published in the journal's second issue in 1998, concisely and directly discusses the phenomenon of mountaintop removal, perhaps the single most ecologically destructive force in the Appalachians today. At that time, I was regularly taking students to mountaintop removal sites in West Virginia to witness the destruction firsthand. The commentary is based on those many on-site observations.

The fifteenth chapter, "A New Beginning," consists of several journal entries taken from a yet unpublished memoir, *My Place on Earth: A Gordon County Almanac.* I wrote the diary entries mostly in 1999 as I struggled to save a marriage and reconnect with the hundreds of undeveloped acres that surrounded my John's Mountain home in northwest Georgia. For more than a year, I lived entirely alone. My companions were most often the many deer, turkey, barred owls, and wildflowers that inhabited my hillside sanctuary. Though the daily entries are often deeply personal, the writings provide important documentation of the comings and goings of the area's rural people and native wildlife. Writers such as Wendell Berry, Annie Dillard, and Aldo Leopold inspired the narrative style. The selections printed here cover two consecutive weeks of journal entries, mostly from January 1999.

"Medicinal and Cultural Uses of Plants in the Southern Appalachians" was presented at the European Institute of Ecology in Metz, France, during summer 1999. The paper was immediately accepted for publication and appeared in the bulletin of the French Society of Ethnopharmacology, titled *Ethnophamacologia*, later that same year. Written with the editorial assistance of Penelope Lane, then of the Tennessee Humanities Council, the study surveys 400 years of medicinal plant use in southern Appalachia and ends with a brief discussion of how plant collecting in the region for medicinal purposes might irrevocably impact mountain ecosystems.

Chapter 17, "A Whole World Dying," was published in the *Journal of the American Chestnut Foundation* in 1999 and is based on materials found in the concluding pages of my book *Where There Are Mountains* (Athens: University of Georgia Press, 2000). For more than two centuries, American chestnuts may have been the single most important living thing in the Appalachians as the abundant trees were used for numerous wood products and were an important food source for both humans and livestock. The loss of the trees due to an exotic blight during the 1920s, I argue, ensured the end of a truly forest-dependent way of life for those residing in the Appalachian region. The essay is reprinted here with permission from the University of Georgia Press and the *Journal of the American Chestnut Foundation*.

Essay eighteen, "The Land of Ridge and Valley," was excerpted from the introduction to my book by the same title. *The Land of Ridge and Valley* was published in 2000 by Arcadia Publishers of Charleston, South Carolina, an international press specializing in local and regional photographic collections. Though the book is now out of print, I maintain copyright to all written materials in the volume, including this selection, which surveys the environmental history of the Northwest Georgia mountains from pre-settlement to the early twentieth century.

"The Great Smokies" is a review essay of historian Daniel Pierce's study of the Great Smoky Mountains National Park and its immediate environs. Pierce's book, titled *The Great Smokies: From Natural Habitat to National Park* (Knoxville: University of Tennessee Press, 2000), was based on his dissertation at the University of Tennessee and is thus well documented and researched. The book is not without its flaws, however, as it includes little treatment of the pre-nineteenth-century Smokies landscape. My review appeared in the spring 2001 issue of the *Appalachian Journal* and is reprinted here with permission.

The final and concluding essay, "Mountains of Culture: Environmental History and Appalachia," was an invited public address delivered at Berea College in September 2001. Berea's Appalachian Center, which annually presents a symposium on themes related to Appalachian history and culture, sponsored the event. The paper contains considerable unpublished research, some of which was gleaned from portions of my doctoral dissertation. The narrative's central theme revolves around the idea that the natural environment in Appalachia played a key role in shaping culture, a theoretical position not always embraced by social scientists or historians. For centuries, humans and nature have had a symbiotic relationship in the mountains, although certainly one of lesser magnitude as the twentieth century came to an end. My entire career has been spent trying both to document and celebrate this evolving human/nature relationship.

Chapter 1

Homeplace Geography

Every environment encourages a special mythology.
—Frederick Turner, *Beyond Geography*
A whole history remains to be written of spaces.
—Michel Foucault, *Power/Knowledge*

On hot summer days, through ocher sedge and aromatic rabbit tobacco, my brother and I would often walk to Flatrock to fish or swim. Flatrock is a half-mile to the west of my north Georgia homeplace, the community name for a stretch of slow-moving water on West Chickamauga Creek, a tributary of the Tennessee River. Layers of smooth limestone form the creek's bank and bottom at Flatrock, making it the preferred site for swimming, fishing, or wading.

At the south end of Flatrock was the principal fishing hole, in the deep shade of two ancient silver maples. There, in the sharp bend of the creek, one could catch a variety of freshwater fish, the kind and number generally depending on four variables: time of day, season, type of bait, and method of angling.

On summer mornings, a cane pole baited with larvae from a pillaged paper-wasp nest might land a black crappie or red-eye bass. We caught brown bullheads or mudcats on warm spring days, usually with the aid of store-bought spinning reels and red worms gathered from my grandmother's compost pile. Sauger, or "jack" as my daddy called them, were our catch in colder winter months; they would sometimes bite anything resembling small minnows. On one occasion, a Jack even latched on to a shiny, baitless treble-hook.

In May 1960, Daddy's trotline—a series of hooks tied to a long cord stretched diagonally across Flatrock's slow-moving waters—netted a 28-pound shovelhead. The monstrous catfish was the cause of much excitement in the Davis family as everyone had their picture made with it, including the dogs, us kids, the neighbors and their kids.

Trotlines in southern Appalachia were traditionally baited with young bullfrogs or salamanders known as "spring lizards" and then stretched diagonally across a creek just before dark. This method of fishing and variations of it are still practiced in many parts of the Tennessee and Mississippi River valleys.

Earlier in the twentieth century, communities used fish baskets as their primary means of catching fish on West Chickamauga Creek. Basket users not only increased the numbers of fish caught and fed to their community, but also the varieties of species harvested from the creek. Like trotlines, fish baskets in southern Appalachia were generally baited at dusk and checked early the next morning before or at sunrise. According to my maternal grandmother, several families in the community sometimes shared the fish basket on West Chickamauga Creek as usufruct. For example, one family might use it on Tuesday, another on Wednesday.

I remember Grandmother saying that in the late 1920s, her family had the basket on Saturdays and Sundays. Before sunset, her mother would bait the basket by crumbling cornbread, made especially for the occasion, into the square center of the long wooden trap. The next morning, my great-grandfather brought home the basket and its contents—usually bream, small catfish, drum, and bass. He cooked and cleaned the fish, and the family ate them with biscuits and hominy grits before Sunday's church service.

In late spring when I was a child, schools of large carp would come to Flatrock to lay their roe in the sandy residue covering the limestone creek bottom. Carp were introduced to North America from Europe in 1870. Considered trash fish by most members of our community, they were generally treated with contempt. Because carp are course browsers of submerged plants, they often muddy the water, rendering it uninhabitable for most native species. However, at the time, African Americans in the nearby community Happy Top prized carp as a food source and had a number of creative ways for catching and preparing them.

I remember a warm, sunny day in June in which my brother and I thought it necessary to wrestle, with bare hands, several of the carp from the creek's blue-green water. With the help of a few friends, we were successful and also fortunate because no harm came to the fish—or to us. After close inspection of our formidable opponents, we returned the fish to the creek and perhaps a more ecological fate.

The practice of catching fish with one's hands, or grappling as it is more properly called, was a common skill possessed by the earliest inhabitants of the Chickamauga Creek watershed. Both the native Creek and Cherokee Indians were practitioners of this virtually lost art. It is quite probable that the Creek or Cherokee taught the grappling technique to the first white settlers who came to the area in the late 1700s. Even as late as the 1920s, when the rivers and creeks in the region supported larger populations of fish, grappling was a common, if not essential, survival practice. A skilled grappler would work the creek's slick banks by placing his hands among tree roots in underwater holes. As he felt a fish, usually a catfish, he immediately rendered it immobile by grasping it around the gills and pectoral fins. Then, using both hands simultaneously, he pulled the fish forcefully from the hole and tossed it high on the creek bank away from the water. The grappler performed this maneuver swiftly in a sweeping singular motion, and if successful, he likely accompanied it with loud woops of delight.

A favorite boyhood haunt, Flatrock was also the reference point for all events on West Chickamauga Creek. If a flock of wood ducks was seen during a day's outing, the location of the sighting was described as being either south or north, upstream or downstream from Flatrock. If a more exact description was needed, we broached other natural landmarks. For example, some fifteen years ago I described the location of a hummingbird's nest to my older brother like this: "south of Flatrock, just beyond that old beech tree, across from the canebrake on Mr. Rodger's place." Simply put, events were located according to a recognized physical proximity to other landmarks; activity on the creek bottom was never defined in terms of exact or measurable distances.

In many ways the calendar of our family's homeplace was marked not by the passing of days or weeks, but by what author David James Duncan has called the "barely perceptible shiftings, migrations, moods and machinations of its creatures, its growing green things, its earth and sky."[1]

---

[1] D. J. Duncan, *The River Why* (New York: Bantam Books, 1983) 54.

The repetitious song of the whippoorwill and the foxfire-like glow of lightning bugs marked the beginning of summer; the southerly migration of nighthawks, or "bullbats" as Daddy called them, meant summer's end. Fall was signified by the gathering of mast—hickory nuts or black walnuts. Winter was the time for turning loose the dogs, for hunting bobwhite quail, rabbits, and ducks on the ridges and creek bottoms. In these ways, natural cyclical forces shaped the calendar of our lives; the rhythms of seasonal change dictated the order and execution of our daily activities.

Union Grove

No purely Thoreauvian landscape, our homeplace was also a peopled one. Our own kin had settled the West Chickamauaga Creek Valley in the early 1870s, leaving subtle yet visible traces of their existence upon the land. Not unlike the once homeless clans of Faulkner's *The Hamlet*, our forebears came to West Chickamauga Creek through the Tennessee and North Carolina mountains "by stages marked by the bearing and raising of children…. They brought no slaves and no Phyfe and Chippendale highboys…[and] what they did bring most of them could [and did] carry in their hands."[2]

My ancestors came to the West Chickamauga Valley seeking the freedom and material security offered by a newfound geography of possibility. Their settlements and communities quickly inscribed the land with appellations like Flatrock, Cross-Roads, Daffron's Ford, Pleasant Hill, Pond Spring, Dyer's Bridge, and Union Grove. Some of the original Creek and Cherokee names given to local areas were consciously replaced or unconsciously forgotten. However, the county name "Catoosa," Cherokee for hill or mountain, was retained, as were several other Indian names for various local sites.

The first detailed maps of the area, drawn in the early 1860s, reveal a landscape sparsely dotted with homesteads, mills, woods, and bottomland—all connected by a complex web of roads, fords, footpaths, and springs. These early maps show a community closely bound by its topography. Roads running "north-south" followed the curvature of the valley's creek bottom; roads crossing "east-west" took travelers through gaps in the ridges or shallow fords on West Chickamauga Creek. Centers of

---

[2] William Faulkner, *The Hamlet* (New York: Vintage Books, 1956) 4.

activity were farms, mills, and stores, most of which were located directly on or in proximity to fertile bottomland.

In the late 1870s, my great-great-grandfather Lemuel Ross built a home on hillside property, north of what was once known as the Coleman Place. After completing the house, he deeded property for a school and church near Dailey Hill Road, about a mile from Daffron's Ford on West Chickamauga Creek. Because the school and church was undenominational, it was named Union Grove.

A one-room structure, Union Grove was built solely with monies from community members. People made additions as time and money allowed, so it was several years before the school got a ceiling. When completed, two wood-burning stoves heated the classroom using fuel cut by both patrons and schoolboys, the latter chopping wood during recess or after school. Each side of the frame structure bore large windows, and a single door opened at the back of the building. Between the two front doors were narrow shelves for lunches. According to a passage in Susie Blaylock's *Official History of Catoosa County*, it was common for all members of one family to eat from a basket or pail during lunch. Water was passed around in a bucket "during books." Everyone used a common dipper.[3]

My grandmother and great-aunt, Janie and Virgie Ross, were pupils at the school and later taught there in the early 1900s. In my possession are several texts used at Union Grove, including a worn blue-back speller, dated 1880, and *Frye's Higher Geography*, printed in 1904. The school served students for approximately thirty-five years before it was sold in the late 1920s to Mr. F. E. Rodgers, a dairy farmer who owned adjoining land.

Today, Union Grove has escaped all physical and mental maps. No part of the structure is visible, and no one seems to remember exactly where the building was located on the Dailey Hill Road. Constructed of lumber cut from local hardwoods, the building has decayed back into the humus out of which it originally grew. When questioned about its exact location, contemporary Dailey Hill residents look at me in disbelief, as if the one-room schoolhouse and grounds were invented for the purposes of selling them insurance policies or funeral plots. Like many people, they cannot imagine that such a place ever existed, that the landscape they inhabit has a history older than their own, even as I remind them that Dailey Hills is the geographic namesake of my great-uncle John Dailey, who built his own

---

[3] Susie Blaylock McDaniel, *Official History of Catoosa County, 1853–1953* (Dalton GA: Gregory Printing and Office, 1956) 183–85.

homeplace above Union Grove in the late 1930s. His small stone house can still be seen high on a nearby knoll, across from a recent subdivision development known as "Dailey Hills."

Although Union Grove is no longer a recognized structure or place, it manages to persist, if only in the memory of a few elderly individuals. Largely unconcerned with history, modern life ensures the fate of places such as these. Because the present defines the past as an unproductive or primitive one, we are encouraged for the sake of "progress" to forget. Unfortunately, with the lost of these historical artifacts, the possibility of creating a future lived harmoniously with the natural world becomes increasingly remote and distant. And since "humans beings cannot create what they cannot imagine," as Stephen Fisher once wrote, the reconstruction of a former way of life, indeed an entire physical geography, remains for the most part a cultural impossibility.[4]

Homeplace Geography

Modern cartography tells us little about a landscape or its people. Remotely photographed, mapped, and surveyed, today's landscapes are transformed into hectares and grids in lifeless, two-dimensional space. The contemporary map is not the territory. We should remember this dictum when deciphering the plans and projections of our municipal planners, who interpret and project a world based on representations found outside the realm of our own lived experience. The Rand McNally Commercial Atlas, for example, states that Catoosa County is a now a "metro area," a commercial satellite of the city of Chattanooga, Tennessee. In the projections of Rand McNally, my land has value only as a future site for industry or business.[5]

Landscapes are themselves deceptive, even when experienced firsthand. No one traveling along the roads surrounding my birthplace could be expected to know the full history of the land or its people. Modern development projects, strip mine sites, industrial parks, expressways, and subdivisions transform the countryside overnight, erasing all known signatures of past geography. In this sense, as John Berger writes in *A Fortunate Man*, a landscape is "less a setting for the life of its inhabitants

---

[4] Quoted in Rodger Cunningham, *Apples on the Flood: The Southern Mountain Experience* (Knoxville: University of Tennessee Press, 1987) 157.

[5] Rand McNally, *Rand McNally Commercial Atlas and Marketing Guide* (Chicago: Rand McNally and Company, 1989) 65.

than a curtain behind which their struggles, achievements, and accidents take place. For those who, with the inhabitants, are behind the curtains, landmarks are no longer geographic but also biographical and personal."[6]

The landmarks of my homeplace are personal and evocative. There is deep history written in the bends and oxbows of West Chickamauga Creek. An ancient beech tree near Flatrock has carved into its smooth bark the names of blood relatives, many long since dead and buried. The Dailey homeplace, designed and built by those who where to live within its four walls, represents a dwelling in the purest sense of the term. The home suggests permanence—a place where one dwells. Gathering moss, the structure is made entirely from ridgerock, a common construction material of post-1920 homes in the northwest Georgia area. This masonry technique required the collective gathering of thousands of loose rocks and stones, usually in a wagon or pickup truck, which were then glued together using a thick homemade mortar. Ridgerock construction was generally used to build the foundations of larger frame houses or to make smaller outbuildings such as wells, springhouses, garages, and sheds. Other landmarks have vanished entirely, suggesting that the preservation of my homeplace requires more active intervention and a more direct assessment of the powers that are presently reshaping our American countryside.

In my assessment of the drastic changes that have occurred around my homeplace, I am at once reminded of the two interpretations of the Cherokee word *chickamauga*. Most historians agree that the word literally means "river of death," citing numerous stories of tribes who supposedly died of epidemics along the banks of the stream. Others say this meaning is erroneous, that the name comes from the Cherokee words *chucama*, meaning "good," and *kah*, meaning "place"—thus "Good Place."[7]

For obvious romantic reasons, it is difficult not to choose the latter interpretation. It is becoming increasingly harder to do so, however, as each return visit to Chickamauga Creek reveals a new commercial development— a new business, an outlet mall, a convenience store. With the completion of each project, a part of our family's past is erased, our very being thrown into

[6] John Berger, *A Fortunate Man* (London: Writers and Readers, 1976) 13, 15.

[7] John P. Brown, *Old Frontiers: The Story of the Cherokee Indians from Earliest Times to the Date of Their Removal to the West* (Kingsport TN: Southern Publishers, 1983) 3–5; cf. Gilbert E. Govan and James Livingood, *The Chattanooga Country, 1540–1962: From Tomahawks to TVA* (Chapel Hill: University of North Carolina Press, 1963) 12.

doubt. All that remains are unforgotten images and the possibility that an entire way of life—a way of talking, eating, working, and playing—is forever lost.

With bottomlands and ridgetops,
my memory plays games with pokeweed and honeysuckle—
snake-doctors and field larks.

I remember my grandma—
Mamada we called her
berry picking with sulfur-filled shoes…
a blackberry betty.

Canecutters as big as beagles,
and canebreaks cagin' in the creekbank reappear,
as trips to childhood fishin' holes recall…
a slow, less nervous day.

Waterdogs, trotlines, and spring lizards,
the peahen's cry, and a harlequined feather of a nervous guinea
trick me into believing I never left the world of
well-water and crawdads…
rabbit tobacco and huckleberries.

As the memories of winesap apples drying on
the hood of a '39 Plymouth chase images of
telephones and walkmans
into holes of limestone ridgerock…

I see her apparition in a scarred grey beech.

Chapter 2

On Building Ecological Fences

To be a philosopher is not merely to found a school, but to love wisdom so as to live according to its dictates a life of simplicity, independence, magnanimity, and trust. It is to solve some of the problems of life, not only theoretically, but practically.
—Henry David Thoreau

Route 38 takes me slowly out of Evarts, Kentucky, a coalmining camp nestled precariously in the long, narrow valley between the two ridges known as Big Mountain and Little Black Mountain. The morning air is dry and cold, with temperatures in the low 20s. Translucent cirrus clouds drift slowly across the cobalt-blue sky, and a northwest wind scarcely stirs the newly fallen oak leaves that line the road's narrow or absent shoulders. Inside the car, a 1979 Ford Fairmount, my poorly shod feet grow numb as the vehicle's heater has lost entirely its warming function. My breath becomes visible on the windshield ahead and, like the Cumberland Mountains above, blocks the warming rays of a late-morning November sun.

Several hours earlier, my own body had provided the warmth needed to endure the November cold. I had been to visit Hazel King, a sixty-six-year-old native of Evarts, who led me on a 2-mile hike up and down and around the steep mountain slopes she has called home for more than forty years.[1] In front of her brother's three-room house, Hazel greeted me warmly as we

---

[1] For a more detailed account of Hazel King's views on Harlan County and coal production, see her "Member Interview" in KFTC's *Balancing the Scales* 6/10 (22 October 1987): 3.

stood on a wooden footbridge that stretches across the creek and separates her land from a paved state road. After our obligatory "good mornings" and general comments about the brisk weather, she announced with almost child-like enthusiasm that she had just seen a dozen wild turkeys outside her kitchen window. "If we're lucky we might see them again," she whispered, as if the birds were in earshot at that very moment.

Hazel, like many of her friends and neighbors in Evarts, knows a great deal about the natural history of her mountains. She has harvested ginseng. "I do it as a pastime, not for profit," she says. Hazel is also well versed in the region's flora and fauna and understands all too well the ecological imbalance caused by the introduction of coalmining into her community.

Our morning outing included a tour of "subsidence sites," where long-abandoned coal mines have caved in, causing snake-like crevices in the earth 100 yards long, 200 feet deep, and occasionally more than several yards wide. While most of the subsidence sites on Hazel's ridge have been "reclaimed" by the Office of Surface Mining, deep new fissures have recently appeared. In the cold morning air, steam rises through narrow rifts while the noxious smell of natural gas permeates from pools somewhere down deep below.

Although Hazel has witnessed firsthand the perennial exploitation and debasement of her mountainside community, she knows little about the growing "Green Party" movement in North America. If she knows anything about deep ecology, social ecology, bioregionalism, ecophilosophy, or the radical environmental group known simply as Earth First!, I am too afraid to ask, not knowing what her response might be. No, she has not heard of Edward Abbey, Arne Naess, Murray Bookchin, Dave Foreman, Kirkpatrick Sale, and George Sessions.[2] She has, however, heard of Al Fritsch, the director of Appalachia—Science in the Public Interest and the author of *Renew the Face of the Earth* (Chicago: Loyola University Press, 1987). Hazel says she reads Fritsch's books because they speak to her needs as both a Kentuckian and as a Christian. The words are both familiar and comforting and ring not of philosophy but of spiritual faith, commitment, and mystery.[3]

---

[2] An excellent summary of each of these individual's views can be found in Brian Tokar, *The Green Alternative: Creating an Ecological Future* (San Pedro CA: R. & E. Miles, 1987).

[3] Writes Fritsch, "The environmental movement is divided into various factions. Some groups disregard the efforts of the other members of the movement and overemphasize their own activities. The struggle for unity among the Christian

Hazel deeply understands that the successful protection of her local environment and the animals that live there requires more than an ecological lifestyle acquired from reading books about the virtues of environmental awareness. She is also an active member of one of the state's most successful organizing groups: Kentuckians for the Commonwealth (KFTC). KFTC is a membership-based citizens' action group that works on a variety of environmental and social justice issues throughout the coalfields.

KFTC also practices direct-action tactics that might cause more radical environmental organizations like Earth First! to take notice. In the October 1987 issue of *Balancing the Scales*, KFTC's self-published newspaper, author and KFTC member Denise Giardina announced her organization's plans to form a "Citizens Action Team" that would be involved in direct action protests, including demonstrations, boycotts, and sit-ins at strip mine sites.[4]

What separates groups like KFTC and SOCM (Save Our Cumberland Mountains) from most other environmental groups is the truly grassroots level at which local members participate. Hazel knows everyone in her Harlan County chapter on a first-name basis; she knows who is active and who is not, who is good at certain organizing tasks, and who is likely to miss the next meeting because of Monday Night Football. According to KFTC bylaws, chapters are formed at the county level but send representatives to a larger governing body known as a steering committee. Active participation in the decision-making process is vital, as is the political education the participants receive in organically facilitating this process.

Among the various local chapters, alliances and affinity groups are regularly formed; a history of common experience and of shared successes and failures ensures a group commitment to sustainable and reachable goals. To prevent paternalism, hired organizers are not permitted to chair any chapter meetings and are reprimanded if their name or photograph appears in any publication. For members of KFTC, the shared fruits of their collective organizing activities are most important. Collectively, they are

---

communities has resulted in a learned experience which is useful within the environmental movement.... Forms of Christian celebration may offer the means of holding the emerging environmental movement together" (*Renew the Face of the Earth* [Chicago: Loyola University Press, 1987] 209–10).

[4] Denise Giardina, "KFTC Preparing Tactics for Broad Form Deed Emergencies," *Balancing the Scales* 6/10 (22 October 1987): 8.

taking part in what social ecologist Murray Bookchin has called "the new municipal agenda," a body politic that acts locally but thinks globally.[5]

As organizational models for environmental and social change, KFTC and SOCM are exemplary. Both are situated in bioregional milieus, yet each works politically on regional, state, and federal issues. Each group sees intrinsic value in working directly with grassroots members on their own terms with problems they identify themselves. KFTC and SOCM recognize the effectiveness of direct action protest without embracing "ecotage" or "monkeywrenching" as a fundamental or necessary practice for their group. Each acknowledges the need for a transformation in the dominant collective consciousness but realizes this transformation cannot occur overnight without systematic assaults on the industrial system and those who govern it.

Hazel sadly tells me there are fewer and fewer individuals in Evarts who share her ecological sensibilities as well as her personal commitment to political activism. Despite KFTC's successful track record, Hazel's grassroots organization is hardly the citizens' group that wins all battles or has problems with organizational bureaucracy. Many of the old-timers who do share her heartfelt appreciation for the environment are stricken with black lung and physically unable to participate in organizing activities. Others have reconciled themselves with the fact that they will never in their lifetimes see environmental or social change—in Evarts, Harlan, Hazard, or in any community where coal is king.

A car without a heater is a car without a window defroster, so somewhere in the vicinity of Flat Lick, Kentucky, the condensation on my Fairmount windshield freezes, making visibility near zero. In order to see through the 3 remaining inches of unfrozen glass, I crane my neck high and to the left, the top of my head touching the car's ice-cold ceiling. Suddenly, an 18-ton coal truck roars by, its horn blowing and driver undoubtedly shouting loud obscenities.

With one hand on the steering wheel and both eyes squarely on what I imagine is the road, I nervously find the thin, nubby bath towel brought purposely for the occasion. I swiftly, with several squeaky, circular swipes, render the road partially visible. After a heavy sigh and a few of my own profane utterances, the journey continues—toward a higher sun and what I willfully hope are warmer temperatures.

---

[5] Murray Bookchin, *The Rise of Urbanization and the Decline of Citizenship* (San Francisco: Sierra Club Books, 1987) 225–88.

Oddly, my preoccupations with the cold, the difficult driving, and the icing windshield do not interfere with my early morning memories of Evarts or Hazel. As I drive northward toward Lexington—my ultimate destination—I recall Hazel's vividly constructed memories of her region's past. I hear her tell about the enormous American chestnut trees that once provided an ample food source for the area's early settlers, then see her point to our only remaining vestiges of those once formidable hardwoods—a few decaying stumps, some easily 4 feet across, rise noticeably from the forest floor. The chestnut blight, like Dutch elm disease, was a European introduced fungus, and by 1930 it had infected all healthy trees in southern Appalachia. I see Hazel staring at an old creek bed that prior to strip-mining ran straight and true, and I watch her mentally reconstruct the trout that once swam in the stream's pre-acidic waters.

I see the bleak images of tired worn buildings, the coal-dust-stained company houses that no longer belong to the company but are nevertheless inhabited by those indentured to it. I recall the "Battle of Evarts" in which hundreds of striking miners fought courageously against car loads of company deputies on 5 May 1931...Kennedy and Johnson's "War on Poverty"...the controversy surrounding the Kentucky Supreme Court ruling that in 1987 reinstated the provisions of the antiquated broad-form deed, a document that awards virtually all mineral rights claims to coal companies and not to landowners...Alan Sondheim's concept of "environmental forgetfulness"...the 1987 movie *Matewan* about the coal wars of the 1920s...the documentary *Harlan County U.S.A*...Dwight Yokum's ballad "Readin', Ritin', Route 23"...the role of Appalachian Mission Schools in changing the cultural integrity of the mountain settlers...John L. Lewis's UMWA...the fact that one-fourth of all land in Harlan County is owned by absentee corporations...

As the noon sun defrosts my window on the Appalachian countryside, I think about my morning in Evarts and about the rural activist's place in the environmental movement in general. I think about the heated debates over deep, social, and bioregional ecology that took place at the Green gathering at Hampshire College in Amherst, Massachusetts, last July. And then I try to imagine how Hazel King would address those in attendance there. "What is all the fuss about?", Hazel would likely ask the spokespeople of the various factions. "Why build fences around your ecological ideals? Who are you trying to keep out? Keep in? If you really want to do Green politics, come to the Kentucky coalfields. We'll put your theories to the test real fast."

In all honesty, the recent Green conference at Hampshire College did not fully represent folks like Hazel King. While a few activists like Grace Lee Boggs and David Haenke argued that a more authentic Green future might emerge from constituencies similar to KFTC's and SOCM's, there was generally a lack of grassroots representation at the meetings. Indeed, the language was by and large an urban, intellectual one; it was certainly not the discourse Theodore Roszak describes in a postscript to his book *Person/Planet* as coming from "an intelligent ecology"—that is, an ecology that speaks the wisdom of traditional folkways and authentic ecological experiences.[6] Since Hazel already practices an ecumenical version of Green politics, bioregionalism, and deep and social ecology, these various "eco-movements" would probably appear unserviceable to her.

As I slowly steer the car onto the entrance ramp to interstate I-75, I begin to notice a distinct change in both terrain and temperature. The sun is high and the landscape less austere. The heart of the coalfields behind me, I tell an unknown voice on the car's radio that there is much we in the environmental movement can learn from Hazel and others just like her in rural Appalachia. The majority of rural Tennesseans and Kentuckians know too well the subtle and not so subtle distinctions between power and powerlessness, the role industrialization and modern technology play in uprooting a way of life that is by its very nature tied to the Earth and its rhythms. Through conventional though no less effective means, Kentuckians for the Commonwealth and other similar organizing groups are beginning to preserve the rural and ecological heritage of their membership by actively restructuring the political agendas of not only their local communities but their respective geographic regions as well. While other environmental groups are clouded in controversy, their self-appointed leaders involved in often petty name-calling debates, groups like KFTC and SOCM are making environmental history. And if Appalachia can be successfully organized, so can the rest of North America.

From the grassroots grows a green movement.

---

[6] Theodore Roszak, *Person/Planet: The Creative Disintegration of Industrial Society* (Garden City NY: Anchor/Doubleday, 1978) 272.

Chapter 3

The Greening of Appalachia

In 1979, thousands of West German citizens formed a coalition of feminists, environmentalists, and peace and community activists in order to fight environmental abuses and an escalating nuclear arms race in Europe. This coalition, *Die Grunen*, or "The Greens" as they are called in the United States, is an official political party in the German *Bundestag*, representing more than 10 percent of the popular vote in that country. Successful in shaping environmental and social policy in West Germany for nearly a decade, the German Greens are continuing to pressure parliament into adopting their more ecologically sound and socially responsible political agenda. Recent articles in the *New York Times* report that a coalition of Greens and Social Democrats are forming to run the entire city of West Berlin.[1]

Since 1984 the Green movement has also become a growing political force in North America. The North American Greens now consist of more than 100 official local groups, known internally as "Committees of Correspondence" or COCs. In some regions of the US, Greens have become a major political force: in New Haven, Connecticut, for example, Greens have become an official political party. In Vermont, New Hampshire, and Maine, Greens have worked with their local town meetings to stop the federal government from locating high-level nuclear waste dumps across New England. In college towns such as Madison, Wisconsin,

---

[1] Serge Schememann, "For West Berlin, Is Socialist-Green Rule Coming?," *New York Times*, 8 March 1989, A8; Serge Schememann, "West Berlin Social Democrats and Greens in Pact," *New York Times*, 11 March 1989, A28.

and Ann Arbor, Michigan, Green candidates poll 10 percent in local municipal elections.

Strongest in New England, California, and the upper Midwest, the North American Green movement is starting to experience organizational prominence in the American South. There are, at present, more than twenty-five Green organizations in the Southeast, representing nearly one-fourth of the nation's total number. These organizations range from loosely organized study groups to well-managed community assemblies. The study groups, which serve largely as educational forums, are represented by the Woodland Greens of Nashville, the Auburn Greens of Auburn University, the Cumberland Greens of Middle Tennessee, and the Charlottesville Greens of the University of Virginia.

These smaller, newly formed Green groups, including those in Appalachia, are generally comprised of college students, community organizers, or environmental activists who have come together in order to educate themselves about the larger North American Green movement or perhaps explore the possibility of becoming an official Green Committee of Correspondence. The basis for initial Green activity, these learning groups, as we will see momentarily with the Shocanage of east Tennessee, often evolve into the more structurally organized and theoretically sophisticated COC, which has the status of being recognized at major conference gatherings and is able to send delegates to interregional and national meetings.

The most politically active of Green COCs in the Upper South are the Orange County Greens of North Carolina and the Ozark Greens of Arkansas/Missouri. Unlike learning or study groups, the more formative Committees of Correspondence are comprised of experienced organizers or activists and are generally situated outside a major university system. However, it should be pointed out that the majority of Southern Green COCs, at almost every stage of their organizational development, serve both political and educational functions. Southern Greens as a whole are involved in a variety of activities, ranging from developing waste management plans and recycling projects to protesting the transportation of hazardous materials. In addition, like many other North American Green groups, Green COCs in the South participate in both direct action protest and local municipal politics, educating themselves and others, they argue, about the political benefits of both strategies.

One of the better examples of Southern Greens combining both conventional and radical political approaches is found in eastern Texas. The Lone Star Greens of Austin have demonstrated against the use of 345-kilovolt power lines by holding under them ordinary fluorescent tubes, that, due to electromagnetic fields generated by the lines, glow brightly. This highly publicized action, which was done in conjunction with presentations to the city council on the negative health effects of electrical pollution, ultimately resulted in the halting of the proposed 345-kilovolt lines in the Austin area. Since that time, the Lone Star Greens have prepared a proposal for decentralized, environmentally sound alternatives to high-voltage power lines that was reviewed and acted upon by Austin's city council.

Most COC members strongly believe that participation in grassroots politics simultaneously educates Green Party members to the processes of local government and local government to the virtues of socially and ecologically responsible public policy. One of the most politically active and successful Green COCs using this approach is the Orange County Greens of North Carolina. In 1985 the Orange County Greens organized to run veteran community organizer Wes Hare for mayor of Chapel Hill. Although the attempt was unsuccessful—Hare came in third in a field of six—a Green candidate was elected in 1986 to a county commissioner seat on a platform of environmental protection, recycling, balanced community development, and no nuclear energy. After learning that having representation on the county commission was not effective without a strong activist base placing issues before the commission, the Orange County Greens began building support with other activist groups in the area. In 1989, the Orange County Greens drafted a platform for the local election, working with a number of activists and community organizing groups in the planning process.

Also involved in municipal politics, though to a lesser degree than the Orange County Greens, is the Ozark Greens of Northern Arkansas, the oldest COC in the southern region and perhaps one of the oldest Green COCs in North America. Since 1984 the Ozark Greens have been active in a number of community-based, alternative lifestyle projects encouraging the use of solar energy, waste recycling, composting, and holistic health care.[2]

The dual-organizing strategies used by groups like the Lone Star and Ozark Greens also create new and important challenges to social movement analysis. On the one hand, Green Party activists participate directly in

---

[2] Brian Tokar, *The Green Alternative: Creating an Ecological Future* (San Pedro CA: R. & E. Miles, 1987) 50.

municipal politics, yet at the same time they attempt to retreat from dominant institutions promoting a "hegemonic worldview." As social movement theorist Carl Boggs has argued, the Green political strategy represents a revival of Gramscian notions of counter-hegemony but at the same time provides a unique synthesis of social democratic and anarchist political strategies.[3] In their view, Green Party members exhibit both a capacity for theoretical self-analysis and deliberate, self-initiated political activity, making them creators, rather than creatures, of social change.

The Shaconage (Shock-a-naja) Greens of east Tennessee are perhaps a case in point. In September 1988, a small group of activists, professors, and graduate and undergraduate students met on the third floor of the University of Tennessee's campus library in Knoxville. The purpose of the initial meeting, publicized only through a campus newspaper box ad, was to form a "Green Party Study Group." Led for the most part by two activist graduate students, within several weeks the study group emerged as a Green group/organization with aspirations of joining the larger COC network. After only five weeks, the local group had grown to more than forty members and had received favorable coverage by the local media. By late October, they decided to call themselves the Shaconage Greens, a name derived from Cherokee lore, and began work on a series of Green presentations to educate high school and elementary school students. They also sent several delegates to a regional Green Party meeting in New Jersey. By March 1989, the group had made several Green Party presentations to local elementary and high schools, participated in several direction-action protests, and exposed a Knoxville Metal Finishing Plant to state officials for illegally dumping toxic waste into the Tennessee River.

Inspired by other Green Party groups in the United States, many of the members had come to the early meetings having either heard of or participated in prior Green-type political activity. Several had been actively involved in the Oak Ridge Environmental Peace Alliance, a group that has been highly successful in publicizing the relationship between environmental hazards and the Department of Defense's development of a strategic nuclear arsenal. Some members had read about the success of the Greens in Europe or in other parts of North America. A few others had friends or relatives who were active in Green politics elsewhere and simply

---

[3] Carl Boggs, *Social Movements and Political Power: Emerging Forms of Radicalism in the West* (Philadelphia: Temple University Press, 1986) 186.

wanted to learn more about the movement in Knoxville and elsewhere in the Appalachian region.

During the group's formative period, outreach was deliberate but limited: bright green flyers displayed strategically around the UT campus were the extent of recruitment during the first four weeks of activity. Many people were simply informed of the group's existence by word of mouth, which by the four and fifth weeks had accounted for the majority of the group's collective recruitment. Some members privately discouraged publicizing the meetings, insisting that the group was growing too large too quickly.

From the initial meeting, the Shocanage Greens also exhibited a keen interest in direct action protest. One group member, a twenty-six-year-old male, wanted to publicize the destruction of the world's rainforest by engaging the group in "guerrilla theater" at a local fast-food establishment. As one of the group's founding members, he sought direct action protest as a way to provide an incentive for group activity as well as a way to build morale. He also appeared concerned with members getting bored with group process, policy procedures, and other organizational business. Privately, he expressed a keen interest in the group becoming more politically active as he did not want the Shocanage Greens to remain a study group or, in his words, "an alternative social club."[4]

In terms of group process and political structure, the Shocanage Greens quickly adopted the meeting format and working guidelines of the Woodland Greens of Nashville. These guidelines, adapted from standard North American Green meeting procedures, suggest that the group, "for the purpose of unity and solidarity," strive for informal consensus in all group deliberations. Under those working guidelines, the group assumes informal consensus unless an individual member requests a "point of clarification." When and if informal consensus cannot be reached through simple clarification, formal consensus is used to help clarify the points of consideration or to air grievances of those in disagreement with group decisions or process. The meetings are also chaired by rotating facilitators who are responsible for making sure all individuals are heard as well as keeping the discussion centrally focused.[5]

---

[4] Anonymous student respondent, author's survey of Shocanage Greens, University of Tennessee, Knoxville, 14 April 1989.

[5] "Working Guidelines," unpublished internal document, Committees of Correspondence, New Orleans, March 1988, 1.

The consensus process of the Greens is certainly nothing new and has been used in the alternative community in America since at least the 1960s, and particularly in the anti-nuclear movement of the late 1970s. In many ways, Green groups operate as "affinity groups"; that is, a collection of individuals actively and directly participating in the decision-making process of the larger movement or organization. In theory at least, affinity group process ensures that all minority views are heard: "any individual who objects in principle to a direction the group is taking can block the group's decisions; thus the group is compelled to fully accommodate individual concerns."[6]

Historically, the affinity group and its organizational structure can be traced back to the *groupos de afinidad* of pre-Civil War Spain. The *groupos de afinidad* comprised the broadly popular anarchist movement of the 1920s and 1930s that actively confronted the institutions of the Spanish monarchy and helped people organize communities according to cooperative principles.[7] Even though the informal consensus mechanisms adopted by the Shaconage Greens are reminiscent of the organizational strategies of the Spanish anarchists, they still preserve group autonomy and identity outside any formal political system. Likewise, Green groups tend to organize in decentralized networks of small primary groups. "The stress is rather on personal development and direct participation. The organization is seen as the means and the ends at the same time."[8]

Because the affinity group encourages direct participation, individual members become personally empowered by the recognition that their own voice makes a difference within the context of the group's broader political agenda. Ironically, this becomes even more apparent in meetings where younger Green members become involved in the decision-making process. In a questionnaire I distributed to approximately thirty Green members, one twenty-year-old male undergraduate student stated that he was pleased with his role in the group "because everyone listens to what I have to say." This response was typical of the younger members who had little or no

---

[6] Brian Tokar, *Green Alternative*, 104.

[7] Murray Bookchin, *The Spanish Anarchists: The Heroic Years, 1868–1936* (New York: Harper Colophon Books, 1977) 195–98.

[8] M. Friberg and B. Hettne, "The Greening of the World: Towards a Non-Determinstic Model of Global Processes," in Hodder and Stoughton, eds., *Development as Social Transformation: Reflections on the Global Problematic* (Denver: Westview Press, 1985) 259.

organizing experience or of those who had never participated in consensual forms of group process.[9]

The creation of democratic institutions that promote direct, face-to-face participation is indeed a fundamental goal of the Green movement. In this sense, the North American Green Party views direct action protest and practices as the logical extension of the direct democracy they exhibit in their own group structure. Likewise, many of the Shocanage Greens argue that the use of direct action tactics ensures each individual has a chance to participate in the formulation of social policy. Murray Bookchin, a leading spokesperson for the North American Green movement and a longtime political activist, agrees: "to exercise one's powers of sovereignty—by sit-ins, strikes, nuclear-plant occupations—is not merely a 'tactic'...it is a sensibility, a vision of citizenship and selfhood that assumes the free individual has the capacity to manage social affairs in a direct, ethical, and rational manner...a form of ethical character building in the most important social role that the individual can undertake: active citizenship."[10]

As the Shaconage Greens evolved into an important player in Knoxville environmental politics, it was easy to get the impression that Appalachian Green groups are not substantially different from any other Green organizations in the United States. It does appear that even though Green COCs are located in a variety of demographic regions and work on a variety of local issues, they persistently, with few exceptions, maintain a conventional Green identity and focus. How does one account for the homogeneous nature of Green movement activity in the United States?

One simple explanation is that built into Green philosophy and politics is the insistence upon local political control. Green COCs must be organized and maintained at the local level before becoming affiliated with regional or interregional committees. This "bottom-up" approach gives each COC member a sense of responsibility and ownership as suggested by the Green National Clearinghouse statement:

> Grassroots people fall away when they feel the organization is not really theirs; when they are needed only periodically, not as people whose ideas and initiative are valued, but merely as bodies at

---

[9] Anonymous student respondent, author's survey of Shocanage Greens, University of Tennessee, Knoxville, 14 April 1989.

[10] Murray Bookchin, *The Rise of Urbanization and the Decline of Citizenship* (San Francisco: Sierra Club Books, 1987) 259.

a demonstration or voters on election day. Such organizing breeds passivity and apathy. It will never create the grassroots strength, substance, and consciousness that we need to make fundamental change in this country, change that will take power from the institutions that now grind on toward extermination, change that will empower people in local communities to construct humanistic, ecological alternatives.[11]

Obviously, organization ownership is important in creating a feeling of group solidarity among individual COCs, but this fact alone does not explain how such groups mobilize around local issues while simultaneously maintaining a collective identity with the larger Green movement. In their important article, "Identity Incentives and Activism: Networks, Choices, and the Life of a Social Movement," Debra Friedman and Doug McAdam point out that social movement theories either ignore the larger structural factors surrounding group mobilization or avoid asking questions of the individual activist's role in initiating and maintaining group solidarity. According to Friedman and McAdam, a "collective identity model" provides both structural and individual reasons for the emergence of collective action. By locating the social movement actor in a larger supportive network of identity incentives, a wider range of political activity can be explained.[12]

Applying the collective identity model to the Shocanage Greens of east Tennessee, one can see how members received personal rewards not only through individual participation in local meetings, but also by being part of a more visible national, indeed international, social movement. The collective identity process is one borne out of rewards gained individually as a member of a local Green COC and structurally by the identification of oneself and others to the larger, more politically viable national organization. At this point in their eight-month history, the Shocanage Greens do appear to be carrying on the ideological vision of the Green platform as originally adopted in Minneapolis in 1984. The question of whether Greens in the southern Appalachians can continue their commitment to the broader

---

[11] Green National Clearinghouse statement, internal document, New Orleans, March 1988, 2.

[12] Debra Friedman and Doug McAdam, "Identity Incentives and Activism: Networks, Choices, and the Life of the Movement," working paper presented at the annual meeting of the American Sociological Association, Chicago, 18 August 1987, 12.

Green philosophy and political platform while maintaining a relatively autonomous identity—with feelings of group ownership and a strong commitment to grassroots organizing—remains to be seen. The success of the entire North American Green movement may in fact depend on whether grassroots groups in the region can continue to mobilize and cultivate their own organizational and political identities without ideologically alienating themselves from other Green groups across the United States.

Author's Note: By the late 1990s, it became apparent that Green Party activism would lose most if not all of its grassroots focus, as the most active members in the movement shifted their energies toward influencing national elections. To my knowledge, no formal Green groups exist in Appalachia today, although many individuals in the mountain region regularly support Green candidates.

Chapter 4

The Politics of Wilderness in Appalachia

The year 2004 marked the fortieth anniversary of the signing of the Wilderness Act by President Lyndon B. Johnson. Since that time, our nation's wilderness areas have grown to include more than 106 million acres of federal lands in 677 units of national parks, national forests, and wildlife refuges in 44 states. In 1980 alone, 10 million acres were added to the national forest wilderness system, more than doubling the amount of land set aside by the 1964 Wilderness Act. More recent additions to the national park system include the Gauley River National Recreation Area, a 24-mile stretch of river that winds through the Allegheny Mountains of the southern part of West Virginia, and the Hagerman Fossil Beds National Monument, a 4,400-acre archeological site in southern Idaho. In the late 1980s, Congress also designated additional wilderness lands within the National Park System, including 1,729,000 acres in Washington's three national parks—Olympic, North Cascades, and Mount Ranier—and 15,000 acres in South Carolina's Congaree Swamp National Monument.[1]

Without question the passage and implementation of the Wilderness Act has inspired an entire generation of environmental activists who have sought to preserve the environment from population pressures, encroaching development, and industrial pollution. Today's environmental movement has been shaped by the ideals and inspiration embodied in the twentieth-century wilderness movement. Because of this fact, the Wilderness Act remains one of the most important documents of US environmental

---

[1] National Parks and Conservation Association, "100th Congress Adds New Parks," *National Parks* 632/1–2 (January/February): 8–9, 1949.

history.[2] In the twenty-first century, the Wilderness Act endures as a reminder to environmentalists that conservation and preservation interests are politically achievable.[3] In fact, as Samuel Hays and others have noted, the Wilderness Act was the first act to provide for citizen involvement in the formulation of national environmental policy. However, as I will argue momentarily, the passage of the Wilderness Act has never ensured that those government agencies assigned to carry out the wilderness preservation mandate will faithfully do so, or that the full concerns of the public will be adequately addressed. The Wilderness Act has always been wrought with political controversy, its proper implementation the subject of heated debate among environmentalists, anti-environmentalists, politicians, and concerned citizens.

Since the passage of the Wilderness Act in 1964, one of the most theoretically significant issues surrounding wilderness preservation politics is the interpretation of the term "wilderness" itself. As historian Roderick Nash has stated, "one man's wilderness is another's roadside picnic ground...."[4] Oddly enough, our contemporary definition of wilderness is the product of a civilization that has historically sought refuge from wild lands and uninhabited landscapes. As Paul Brooks points out in *Speaking for Nature*, it was not until the Romantic movement of the late eighteenth century that Western literature and sentiment regarded wilderness or wilderness landscapes as something less than ugly or crude. Conversely, Native Americans had no comparative concept of wilderness since it made

---

[2] As Samuel P. Hays has noted, "Citizens aroused in behalf of wilderness extended their interest and action to other segments of the American landscape, to the countryside, the wildlands, and the cities themselves. Wilderness areas were the base from which thought and action were launched into wider environmental concerns" (*Beauty, Health, and Permanence: Environmental Politics in the United States, 1955–1985* [New York: Cambridge University Press, 1987] 121). For an excellent historical overview of the creation of the 1964 Wilderness Act, see T. H. Watkins, "Untrammeled by Man: The Making of the Wilderness Act of 1964," *Audubon* 91/6 (November 1989): 74–90.

[3] The 1980s saw the largest percentage of wilderness areas designated by the four Interior Department agencies: the US Forest Service, National Park Service, Fish and Wildlife Service, and Bureau of Land Management.

[4] Roderick Nash, Wilderness and the American Mind (New Haven CT: Yale University Press, 1982) 1.

no sense for them to distinguish "wilderness" from "civilization" or "wild" animals from "tame" ones.[5]

Today the term has a variety of different connotations. For example, the rural residents of Cocke County, Tennessee, near the Great Smoky Mountains National Park, do not perceive any of the surrounding park area as wilderness. They instead refer to it as a place where parents and grandparents once lived or mention specific landmarks that have personal significance—for example, a favorite hunting site, a large ginseng patch, a familiar stream, or a frequently visited mountaintop. For the local natives immediately surrounding the park lands, the concept of wilderness has no meaning other than perhaps the mythical place where "outsiders" come to take pictures, ski, feed the bears, or spend important tourist dollars.

Unlike the local natives' definition of wilderness, the Wilderness Act of 1964 sees wilderness as any area where nature and its living community remain "untrammeled by man." To quote at length from the act itself, wilderness is

> an area of undeveloped Federal land retaining its primeval character and influence, without permanent improvements of human habitation, which is protected and managed so as to preserve its natural conditions and which (1) generally appears to have been affected primarily by the forces of nature, with the impact of man's work substantially unnoticeable; (2) has outstanding opportunities for solitude or a primitive and unconfined type of recreation; (3) has at least five thousand acres of land or is sufficient size as to make practicable its preservation and use in an unimpaired condition; and (4) may also contain ecological, geological, or other features of scientific, educational, scenic, or historical value.[6]

In its most ideal form, the Wilderness Act definition of wilderness implies that such landscapes are foremost biological constructs, self-sustaining entities that must be essentially free from human intrusion. However, as a number of environmental historians have pointed out, there is virtually no area on Earth that has not been inhabited by humans or altered

---

[5] Paul Brooks, *Speaking for Nature: How Literary Naturalists from Henry Thoreau to Rachel Carson Have Shaped America* (Boston: Houghton Mifflin, 1980).

[6] The Wilderness Act, public law 88-577, *United States Statutes at Large*, no. 78 (Washington, DC: US Government Printing Office, 1964) 890–96.

in some way by humankind.[7] Moreover, the Wilderness Act definition presupposes some form of recreational use, which paradoxically encourages human intervention into these so-called "primeval" areas. Wilderness, as defined by the most powerful political document protecting its use, must be perceived as an entity ultimately regulated by human values and human interests. Therefore, as Alston Chase correctly argues in his perceptive, albeit controversial book *Playing God in Yellowstone*, wilderness is never fully a biological construct or independent ecosystem void of human content and meaning. Wilderness is a social construct, and all interpretations of wilderness in some way circumscribe its intended use or method of management.[8]

The idea that commonly held notions about wilderness are ultimately mediated through competing knowledge communities, by social actors and stakeholders who have vested interests in defining wilderness in a particular way, brings us to the more political question of how wilderness areas are presently defined and managed by the land agencies and individuals ultimately responsible for preserving them. A brief discussion of each of these agencies' management practices should give us a better understanding of how they interpret and implement their own wilderness preservation agendas. At present, four national agencies are responsible for managing federally owned wilderness areas: the United States Forest Service, the National Park Service, the Fish and Wildlife Service, and the Bureau of Land Management. While it is assumed that these federal agencies would perceive Wilderness Act objectives in a similar light, a closer inspection reveals four different wilderness management systems and protocols.

---

[7] See especially Daniel Botkin et al., *Managing the Global Environment: Perspectives on Human Involvement* (New York: Harcourt, Brace, Jovanovich, 1989); Alfred Crosby, *Ecological Imperialism: The Biological Expansions of Europe, 900–1900* (New York: Cambridge University Press, 1987); Donald Worster, ed., *The Ends of the Earth: Perspectives on Modern Environmental History* (New York: Cambridge University Press, 1988).

[8] Chase, for example, charges that our national parks, "unimpaired for future generations," are being destroyed "by the very people assigned to protect and enjoy them" (Alston Chase, *Playing God in Yellowstone: The Destruction of America's First National Park* [New York: Atlantic Monthly, 1986] 6). For a more constructive discussion of the National Park problem, see his "How to Save Our National Parks," *Atlantic Monthly* 260/1 (July 1987): 35–44.

Wilderness: Four Federal Views

Of all the federal agencies responsible for protecting wilderness, the US Forest Service manages the largest number of wilderness areas in the National Wilderness Preservation System, holding more than 35 million acres in 406 wilderness "units."[9] Historically, the Forest Service has given their conservation mission a "multiple-use" criterion; they strive to produce in the forest "the greatest good for the greatest number." This utilitarian management philosophy has of course been the US Forest Service's since 1905, when Theodore Roosevelt appointed Gifford Pinchot head of that government agency. In practice, the multiple-use concept simply means specific areas in national forests may be zoned for a number of separate uses, including timber-harvesting, hunting, fishing, backpacking, primitive camping, bird-watching, and mountain biking.[10] However, in most instances the implementation of the Wilderness Act in 1964 initiated few changes in overall US Forest Service policy and management. In fact, many Forest Service managers saw the wilderness designation as a way of defining simply another non-consumptive use for the forests. Therefore, only those areas within the national forests that were designated as "wild" or "wilderness" actually saw changes in management policy because of the newly implemented Wilderness Act protocols. In those areas, wilderness "zones" were to be determined by all interested parties and then managed according to specific Wilderness Act guidelines. However, in the much larger areas immediately adjacent to wilderness area boundaries, the forest service continued its utilitarian policy of providing both open access to tourists and recreationists and natural resources to commercial interests like timber and paper companies.

Within the proposed wilderness boundaries of our national forests, the management guidelines of the Wilderness Act have, by and large, been faithfully implemented and strictly enforced. In nearly every instance, national forest wilderness areas are managed in accordance to Wilderness

---

[9] Wilderness Society promotional map, "The National Wilderness Preservation System, 1964–1989" (Washington, DC: Wilderness Society, 1990); available online at <http://www.wilderness.net>.

[10] Peter Matthiessen, in his classic book *Wildlife in America*, states that the Tennessee Valley Authority was one of the earliest examples of government resource management using the "multiple-use" concept, which, he claims, is "practiced not according to dogmatic rules but according to the mutual, balanced interests of the local community and of the land" (New York: Viking Penguin, 1987, p. 219).

Act guidelines so as to maintain what Linda Graber and others have called "wilderness purity."[11] The wilderness purity policy of the National Forest Service not only limits human intervention into these areas, but even dictates minimum interference from natural damage, including fires, insects, and disease.

Once zoned as such, wilderness is then "managed" by the Forest Service as a relatively self-contained biological entity that must be preserved in its "purist" ecological state. This type of wilderness management may, paradoxically, create more environmental problems than it actually solves, as these areas often become prime destinations for literally thousands of campers and hikers. In fact, the purity form of wilderness management—as envisioned by a long line of wilderness enthusiasts, including Aldo Leopold—has long been the subject of heated debate in environmental literature. A growing number of commentators are going so far as to claim that purity wilderness management is actually responsible for the ecological crisis in many of America's National Parks.[12]

The National Park Service, as the principle holder of wilderness acreage in the US, manages the largest portion of federally designated wilderness land, with more than 38 million acres in 43 preserves. Unlike the Forest Service, the National Park Service has not hesitated to define wilderness areas as lands existing primarily for human use and enjoyment. In fact, the agency's wilderness philosophy has historically *encouraged* public access to wilderness areas, even to the degree of building roads and lodging to accommodate tourists. In many ways, the National Park Service has viewed the Wilderness Act as a threat to public enjoyment of wilderness and therefore has been less interested in implementing Wilderness Act policy. This fact perhaps better explains the deterioration of many of our national parks; forty-two populations of mammals are in danger of extinction, and other mammals, like the gray wolf and grizzly bear, have disappeared altogether in all but three national parks. Clearly, the management plans of the National Park Service have largely ignored the wishes of the environmental community, who have persistently sought radical preservation over public use.

---

[11] Linda Graber, *Wilderness as Sacred Space* (Washington, DC: Association of American Geographers, 1973) 16–29, 76–79, 82–110.

[12] A review of the popular literature on the subject can be found in Lynette Lamb, "U.S. National Parks in Trouble," *Utne Reader* (November/December 1989): 10–11.

The US Fish and Wildlife Service (FWS), another Interior Department Agency, has for the most part viewed the Wilderness Act as a way for its agency to secure and protect more habitats for fish and wildlife. Because the provisions of the act did not make wilderness areas wildlife sanctuaries, the FWS has used the Wilderness Act "as a tool to control more effectively the use of refuge areas for the benefit of protected species." For the FWS, wilderness simply means wild lands appropriated for hunting and fishing, so the Wilderness Act ensures managing officials that such areas will be secured and protected. Presently, there are more than sixty-six wilderness areas under FWS management, comprising more than 19 million acres in twenty-one states.[13]

The Bureau of Land Management is the smallest government agency controlling wilderness areas in the US. Originally formed in 1946 to provide a more permanent land management framework for western grazing lands, the BLM currently is responsible for protecting more than 466,000 acres of federal wilderness. Like the Forest Service, the BLM has historically been concerned with promoting multiple-use land management practices—mining, ranching, drilling, and some recreational use. However, with the passage of the Federal Land Policy and Management Act of 1976, the BLM took up wilderness concerns with a new, albeit short-lived enthusiasm. In the end, the BLM under both the Carter and Reagan administrations tended not actually to be committed to developing and maintaining new wilderness areas under the BLM system. As the BLM reviewed potential sites, limitations such as location and proximity to human development reduced the agency's long-term commitment to wilderness planning. The Pentagon has permits to use more than 16.7 million acres of Bureau of Land Management land and is seeking another 4.6 million acres for additional training facilities and bombing ranges.[14]

---

[13] Craig Allen, *The Politics of Wilderness Preservation* (Westport CT: Greenwood Press, 1982) 147.

[14] Groups from Nevada, Utah, Idaho, and Mississippi—as well as officials from the National Cattlemen's Association—have recently testified against the Pentagon's plans to expand its bombing ranges and training grounds into US wilderness lands. The US military's claim for using public lands include, among other plans, (1) increase an Air Force bombing range in Salyer Creek, Idaho, from 100,000 to 1.5 million acres; (2) establish an army national tank training range on 700,000 acres in central Nevada; (3) expand by 200,000 acres a navy bombing range at Fallon Naval Air Station near Reno; and (4) build a state National Guard bombing range and training ground on 970,000 acres in Montana.

The Bureau of Land Management's failure to expand substantially its wilderness protection program because of lack of what they considered appropriate land is a good example of how preconceived conceptions of wilderness may actually limit the federal government's ability to protect wild lands. Since the passage of the Wilderness Act in 1964, all four federal agencies have been hampered in fulfilling their role as wild land protectors because of the assumption that wilderness areas must always comprise "at least five-thousand contiguous acres" or exhibit "outstanding opportunities for solitude." These criteria make wilderness something it can never fully be—a completely isolated, geographic entity void of sustained human intervention. Although officials representing the Bureau of Land Management, the US Fish and Wildlife Service, the National Park Service, and the US Forest Service may identify wilderness using Wilderness Act criteria, their respective management practices clearly demonstrate that "human intervention" in wilderness areas is ultimately determined by human values that must be mediated politically at federal, state, and local levels.[15]

Wilderness: State Lands and Perceptions

Within each governing federal agency, managed wilderness areas tend to share general characteristics in terms of their size and degree of isolation. State-owned wilderness areas, on the other hand, vary not only in size but also with respect to their proximity to large population centers and urban development. In most instances, state agencies do not even view their wild lands as "wilderness" *per se* but instead use appellations like "natural area" or "state recreation area." In terms of land classification, state wild lands are often a mixed bag of second- and third-growth forests, rural pasture and woodland, lakes, streams, and rivers. This fact often places a different set of demands upon state-owned wild lands and those responsible for governing their use. Excluding Alaska, there are more than 100 million acres of state-owned lands in the United States, most of which have historically been acquired from private landowners and returned to the states via federal land grants. In the West, state land amounts to more than 35 million acres, while in the North and East, states like New York, Pennsylvania, Michigan, and Minnesota manage large tracts of wilderness land, most of which have been classified as state forests or recreation areas.[16]

---

[15] The Wilderness Act, public law 88-577, *United States Statutes at Large*, no. 78, pp. 890, 891–93.

[16] Samuel Hays, *Beauty, Health, and Permanence*, 103–104.

In the southern Appalachians, the amount of state-owned wilderness is relatively small compared to other regions of the United States. This regions' wild lands, Albert Cowdrey reminds us in *This Land, This South*, have historically been owned by the federal government or by private corporations or single individuals.[17] In North Carolina, for example, the federal government now owns 7.1 percent of the total land in that state (about 1.2 million acres), of which all but 100,000 acres is under the jurisdiction of the US Forest Service, the National Park Service (467,000 acres), and the Pentagon (314,192 acres including 111,330 held by the Army Corps of Engineers).[18] Owning an almost equal portion of land in North Carolina are the top nine timber companies, holding more than 2,130,000 acres (6.8 percent of the total). By contrast, state lands—most of which are maintained as state forests or recreation areas—comprise only 450,000 acres, or 1.4 percent of land in the state.[19]

Of course, the acquisition and management of forest lands varies from state to state and from region to region. In southern Appalachia, state forests are on the whole managed in a way similar to the way national forests are managed. By and large, utilitarian, multiple-use management criteria influence all southern Appalachian wilderness management agendas. A ten-year management plan for the Prentice-Cooper State Forest, a 25,000-acre mountaintop preserve on the Cumberland Plateau in southeast Tennessee, for example, explicitly stated that forest managers must "attempt to strike a delicate balance among uses and benefits to satisfy as many [users] as possible."[20]

In terms of actual wilderness use regulations, the Prentice-Cooper State Forest is zoned according to three distinct land classifications, each allowing or restricting certain kinds of user activities: (1) unregulated scenic

[17] Albert E. Cowdrey, *This Land, This South: An Environmental History* (Lexington: University of Kentucky Press, 1983) 111–20; see also Thomas D. Clark, *The Greening of the South: The Recovery of Land and Forest* (Lexington: University of Kentucky Press, 1984) 47–53.

[18] The US government owns 1 acre out of every 15 in the state.

[19] Bob Hall, "Who Owns North Carolina," in Bob Hall, ed., *Environmental Politics: Lessons from the Grassroots* (Durham NC: Institute for Southern Studies, 1988) 10621. See also Appalachian Land Ownership Task Force, *Who Owns Appalachia?: Landownership and Its Impact* (Lexington: University of Kentucky Press, 1983) 1–13.

[20] Tennessee Department of Conservation, "Management Plan for Prentice Cooper State Forest, 1989–1999" (Nashville: Tennessee Department of Conservation, 1989) 2–3.

zones established adjacent to all hiking trails, primary roads, and secondary roads; (2) regulated scenic zones, which can be harvested for select timber; and (3) natural areas, the most protected land classification. The forest is further subdivided into four management units, the largest being "unit 1," a 16,470-acre tract of land that offers the full range of multiple-use activities, including hunting, target shooting, timber harvesting, and hiking. "Unit 2," the Hicks Gap Natural Area, is the smallest zone in the entire forest and is also the only unit managed as "wilderness" in terms of having restrictive use. This 350-acre "natural area" was created by the Tennessee General Assembly and approved by the governor during spring 1989 largely because the site contains a population of large-flowered skullcap (*Scutellaria montana*), a federally designated endangered species.[21]

In terms of timber harvesting in the Prentice-Cooper Forest, all regulated scenic zones within the 16,000 acres of unit 1 are potentially open for clear-cutting activities. Local citizens have protested the state's decision to allow clear-cutting in this section of the forest but have not been given an official public hearing. In fact, the citizen environmental organization Save Our Cumberland Mountains (SOCM) protested the state's draft plan during the late 1980s by holding a Public Acceptance Hearing that brought considerable media attention to the proposed management agenda. While state foresters claimed the plan would be a "radical departure" from previous forest management agendas, the members of SOCM insisted it was "business as usual" in the Tennessee State Forest.[22]

As previously noted, most state conservation departments have historically perceived wilderness planning as a way to preserve natural areas for as many users as possible. However, during the 1990s, national, state, and local environmental interests groups increasingly challenged this view as a lowest common denominator form of land management. While state-owned wild lands may be smaller and less pristine than areas under federal control, regional environmental groups like Save Our Cumberland Mountains have been successful at questioning, if not redirecting, the management policies of many state-managed natural areas. Public participation in environmental policymaking does appear more successful at the state level, though no less difficult in terms of challenging decades of utilitarian management practices. Whereas the management of federal

---

[21] Ibid., 8.

[22] Anonymous, "Prentice Cooper Acceptance Hearing," *SOCM Sentinel*, Save Our Cumberland Mountains monthly newsletter (9 March 1988): 8.

wilderness areas is directed by the more purist demands of the Wilderness Act—and those agencies interpreting it—the management policies of state-owned wild lands appear, in the final analysis, to be influenced greatly by citizens' or other interest groups operating at the local or state level.

Wilderness: Public Interest Groups

Environmental interest groups have been an important part of wilderness planning in the United States since the late 1800s. Today, the Sierra Club is perhaps the best-known wilderness advocate and the most ardent visible supporter of the kind of wilderness management promoted by the provisions of the 1964 Wilderness Act. In fact, one could argue that the Sierra Club's ability to generate mass political support for the act in the 1950s and 1960s had a great deal to do with its eventual passage. Of course, the number of environmental organizations openly supporting the preservation of wilderness has increased tremendously since 1800 and now includes such groups as the Wilderness Society, the Nature Conservancy, and the Natural Resources Defense Council. By the 1990s, many of these interest groups also had state and local branches that have given them the ability to work on the wilderness planning issue at both national and state levels.

One of the best known of the wilderness planning and protection groups is the Nature Conservancy, which owns some 1,177,000 acres in the United States, Canada, Latin America, and the Caribbean. Since 1951, the Nature Conservancy has been involved in both identifying and cataloging wilderness areas for government agencies as well as acquiring and managing wild lands privately (its 1,340 preserves make the conservancy the largest owner of nature sanctuaries in the world). The Nature Conservancy has more than 900,000 members, including more than 200 corporate associates, and a land preservation fund of $1 billion. Latest agency figures show that the Nature Conservancy has protected or helped protect more than 10.5 million acres of North American wild lands.[23]

As an environmental interest group, the Nature Conservancy is highly successful in promoting the public value of wilderness and wilderness areas. Unlike other wilderness preservation organizations like the Sierra Club, the Nature Conservancy avoids the explicit use of the term "wilderness,"

---

[23] "Background Information," internal document, Nature Conservancy, Department of Communications, Arlington VA, n.d., p. 1; available online at <http://www.undueinfluence.com/nature_conservancy.htm>.

referring instead to its land holdings as "natural areas" or "sanctuaries." Staff conservationists, trained primarily as ecologists, zoologists, and botanists, appear to embrace fully the idea of biological diversity as a criterion for wilderness, yet they argue that biological diversity is not achievable within single tracts of land—regardless of size.

For this reason, the Nature Conservancy began promoting the idea of preserve "networks," which include areas as small as 1/2 acre. This conservation philosophy, says Robert Jenkins, has the Nature Conservancy actively involved in the acquisition of lands "adjacent to already existing preserves, establishing clusters of related preserves, or connecting preserves with natural corridors." Under this land management philosophy, wilderness is protected by the agency securing a interconnected network of large and small preserves in order to create larger regional landscapes or ecological "megasites."[24]

The Nature Conservancy, like most other national environmental organizations, has tremendous membership support, which gives it a great deal of lobbying power at the level of state and federal government. Politically, however, groups like the conservancy are weakest in terms of working directly with individuals or local communities on issues surrounding appropriate land use or private land acquisition. In response to my characterization of their organization as one that simply acquires "lands,"[25] the Nature Conservancy responded in writing by stating that "[r]ather than land, or even habitat, the Conservancy focuses on life—on protection of rare, threatened, and endangered species and natural communities through protection [of] their habitat and ecosystems. To do so, we work with many partners, two of the most important being governments (state and federal, here and abroad—the Conservancy is an international non-profit) and corporations."[26] The Nature Conservancy's focus on the protection and acquisition of "natural communities" rather than "land" suggests a "biocentric" bias against humans, particularly rural folk who are often dependent upon natural communities for their daily survival.

---

[24] Robert Jenkins, "Long-Term Conservation and Preserve Complexes," *Nature Conservancy Magazine* 39/1 (January/February 1989) 5.
[25] In Donald E. Davis, *Ecophilosophy: A Field Guide to the Literature* (San Pedro: R. & E. Miles, 1989) 124.
[26] Nature Conservancy, letter to the author, 21 February 1989, parenthesis theirs.

Because of the national and indeed international scope of the larger environmental organizations, it is not too surprising that the voices of local citizens are often among those least heard in wilderness management debates. Despite the fact that many local residents are conservation minded, the organizational structure of pro-wilderness groups often prevents them from participating in wilderness planning processes. Local residents thus perceive the concerns of national wilderness interest groups as being the same as those of the federal government, which often places the residents in a position of opposing pro-wilderness legislation.

In public participation programs concerning wilderness management in Tennessee's national forest in the late 1970s, local response was overwhelmingly opposed to designating additional wilderness in the forests. As a citizen from Elizabethton, Tennessee, put it, "Upper East Tennesseans do not want anyone in Congress to tell us what is wilderness. I am opposed to it."[27] Not surprisingly, during the government's RARE (Roadless and Undeveloped Area Evalutation) II wilderness assessment hearings in the late 1970s, which dealt with twenty-one roadless areas in the national forest, more than 92 percent, or 24,500 of the respondents, expressed opposition to more wilderness.[28] Part of the conflict is due to the simple fact that wilderness interest groups view use in purely biological or recreational terms, whereas local citizens see use as related to both recreation *and* resource extraction activities, including hunting, fishing, and logging.

Wilderness: The Grassroots

During the early 1990s, an increasing number of grassroots citizen organizations were involved in the wilderness planning issue. In the southern Appalachian region, citizen groups like Save Our Cumberland Mountains, Tennessee Citizens for Wilderness Planning, the Western North Carolina Alliance, and Kentuckians for the Commonwealth have, in varying degrees, involved themselves in wilderness use planning and politics. However, unlike the larger national environmental organizations just mentioned, these regionally based groups perceive wilderness preservation in terms of power conflicts among users and interest groups rather than

---

[27] Roadless and Undeveloped Area Evaluation (RARE) II oral comment, Cherokee National Forests Headquarters, Cleveland TN, 13 September 1978.

[28] US Department of Agriculture, Forest Service, *Mountaineers and Rangers: A History of Federal Forest Management in the Southern Appalachians, 1900–1981* (Washington, DC: US Government Printing Office) 169.

simply a question of habitat conservation. Their organizing strategies are generally reactive rather than proactive; these citizens' groups are not so much interested in the expansion of wilderness areas—with the possible exception of Tennessee Citizens for Wilderness Planning—as they are with the proper management of already designated areas. Moreover, groups like the Western North Carolina Alliance and Kentuckians for the Commonwealth do not embrace the purist definition of wilderness outlined earlier since their membership consists largely of individuals who live within or adjacent to national forests and national parks.

Also, individuals in these citizens' groups are often economically dependent on the natural resources found in the preserved areas and have financial—rather than purely ideological—interests in maintaining the environmental integrity of their communities. This is not to say that some individuals would be against defining their local communities as remote, isolated, or even as a wilderness area. What it does mean, however, is that for these citizens the wilderness designation by an outside group or agency will inevitably result in some kind of discrimination against their own individual or community interests, many of which may be viewed as anti-environmental by nonresident, pro-environment observers. Rightly or wrongly, in the eyes of local residents, the designation "wilderness," "natural recreation area," or "wild and scenic river" by a federal, state, or environmental agency generally means the interests of a select few—namely tourists, recreationists, and large land-holding timber or coal companies—will receive priority over their more immediate local interests.[29]

The Wilderness Society, on the other hand, which represents wilderness enthusiasts and recreationists, argues that both community interests and the interests of preservationists can be served by adopting more aggressive wilderness management agendas. The Wilderness Society's vision for the southern Appalachian national forests, for example, states that "conserving the [national] forest's exceptional biological diversity" ensures a healthy economic base for the region and its communities.[30] For the Wilderness Society, the US Forest Service's planned timber-cutting practices in the region will greatly limit profitable recreation opportunities, which, according to the Southeastern Forest Experiment Station in Athens,

[29] Laura E. Jackson, *Mountain Treasures at Risk: The Future of Southern Appalachian National Forests* (Washington, DC: The Wilderness Society) vi.
[30] Ibid.

Georgia, accounts for more than 188,000 jobs in the rural areas surrounding national forests.[31]

In the final analysis, both the Southeastern Forest Experiment Station and the Wilderness Society argue that there are strong positive ties between recreation- and wilderness-related tourism and adjacent local economies. In fact, US Forest Service figures show that in the late 1980s, economic activity worth more than $6 billion was generated annually by recreation and wilderness activity on Forest Service lands. And in a draft document supporting their 1989 Resource Planning Act Assessment, the US Forest Service found that ecological impacts on natural systems from most outdoor recreation and wilderness uses are minimal compared to more consumptive uses such as lumbering or mining. Not surprisingly, the report recommends that protection of wilderness and wilderness-like areas should be given dramatically greater emphasis in the management of the National Preservation System.[32]

Although wilderness preservation does appears to have considerable economic impact on local rural economies, economic indicators like those cited above may be misleading to outside observers. Environmental interest groups should note the *kinds* of jobs created by wilderness preservation as well as the ultimate benefactors of the wilderness-generated income. In many instances, tourist and recreation economies benefit only a small population in terms of generated wealth, and in some cases these same recreational economies can encourage further environmental degradation. For example, Cocke County, Tennessee, adjacent to the Great Smoky Mountains National Park, has one of the highest unemployment rates in Tennessee. While spring, summer, and fall months generate an enormous amount of work for area teenagers, off-season unemployment in the area often exceeds 20 percent. In fact, a study of eighty-four rural counties in twelve states argues that the communities with the highest levels of tourism actually fare *worse* than neighboring areas.[33]

---

[31] Miles Tager and Jeff Fobes, "Recreation and Wilderness Good for Local Economy," *Greenline* 3 (Fall 1990): 1.

[32] H. Ken Cordell et al., *An Analysis of the Outdoor Recreation and Wilderness Situation in the United States, 1989–2040*, general technical report RM-189, US Department of Agriculture, Forest Service, Rocky Mountain Forest and Range Experiment Station, Fort Collins CO (Washington, DC: US Government Printing Office) 1–112.

[33] Michael Smith, *Behind the Glitter: The Impact of Tourism on Rural Women in the Southeast* (Lexington: Southeast Women's Employment Coalition, 1989) 23.

Canoe and rafting outfitters operating in the national forests of North Carolina, Georgia, and Tennessee, for example, employ only a handful of individuals, many of whom are nonresidents with little or no community ties to the area. Moreover, these outfitters are only profitable if a large number of individuals are exposed to the water, which often puts increased pressures on the rivers and surrounding landscape. The Chattooga River on the Georgia/South Carolina border now supports more than 40,000 whitewater rafters annually. Traffic on the river has increased to the point that local fishermen have taken rifle shots at passing rafters. Increased traffic, garbage, noise, and billboard advertisements are all byproducts of wilderness-generated economies, as are jobs that often pay no more than minimum wage to the local residents.

Another critique offered by local residents concerns wilderness development projects financed by private landowners and/or corporations. Landowners who own large tracts of land adjoining wilderness areas benefit highly from federal wilderness legislation since their land is more valuable to tourists who want to take advantage of the nearby wilderness area. The privately held land thus becomes a prime target for high-end resort development, which generally requires the construction of modern facilities such as convention centers and amenities like RV hookups and golf courses. Though profitable to developers, the resort areas are virtually inaccessible to local residents. In Jackson County, North Carolina, for example, membership at a local resort costs more than $12,000 a year. In this particular instance, the wilderness-generated economy discriminates against local citizens who likely viewed the resort area as an undeveloped public commons, accessible to all.

Wilderness: A Sociological Analysis

To my knowledge, only a handful of environmental sociologists have critically discussed the wilderness issue, especially in terms of how human values and perceptions have influenced, if not redirected, wilderness use politics in the United States.[34] In general, environmental sociologists appear to have accepted the *de facto* wilderness idea that permeates federal and state wilderness management agendas. For this reason it should not be surprising that the sociologists who study the wilderness issue often do so from a

---

[34] See, for example, Bill Devall and George Sessions, *Deep Ecology: Living as if Nature Matters* (Salt Lake City: Gibbs Smith, 1985) 109–29.

utilitarian resource management and/or recreation perspective. However, the preservation of wilderness is ultimately possible only by understanding the social structures and organizations that give wilderness its fuller meaning. The sociological approach, I would argue, not only allows the researcher to illustrate how perceptions of wilderness can vary from interest group to interest group, but also provides information about how wilderness is ultimately used—and misused.

A sociological analysis of wilderness also allows for a better understanding of how environmental problems associated with wilderness use are embedded in management agendas enforced by human values and organizational controls. Even if one accepts the idea that humans can recreate a biologically independent natural area, the fact remains that wilderness land will always be subjected to both internal and external human pressures. For example, when rainforests in the Amazon are destroyed by multinational logging companies or local cattlemen, migratory bird populations in North American wilderness areas are directly impacted. Thus in terms of future wilderness development, environmentalists should be aware that all wilderness sites—be they a nature conservancy natural area or a federally designated wild and scenic river—must also be able to withstand pressures generated by human influence.

To date, the multiple-use criteria guiding federal and state conservation practices have created little more than pragmatic, utilitarian attitudes toward preserving the natural environment. Not only does this pragmatic philosophy represent bad ecology in the narrower biological sense, it also underestimates the extent to which human beings can alter the environment by their sheer presence. As Alston Chase points outs, the so-called preservationist approach of the federal government sometimes destroys wilderness by promoting it and indeed using it.[35] The greatest good for the greatest number simply means more people will use wild lands. Ironically, this policy desideratum also jeopardizes most opportunities for wilderness "solitude," another Wilderness Act mandate ignoring the multitude of historical and sociological dimensions of wilderness use and experience.[36]

---

[35] Alston Chase, *Playing God in Yellowstone*, 328.

[36] In defining wilderness, the Wilderness Act states that "[a] wilderness...has outstanding opportunities for solitude..." (public law 88-577, in *United States Statutes at Large*, no. 78, sect. 2a[2], pp. 890–96). See also Jay Hansford Vest, "The

Environmental sociologists should also be aware that humans do not always alter the landscape in ways that are necessarily harmful to the larger environment. Persistent use of any given environment will always affect the landscape, but the effects will vary from culture to culture, region to region, and according to type of use (mountain bikes obviously alter the terrain in ways different from hunters on foot). Obviously some uses are more harmful than others, and some uses, such as strip-mining or clear-cutting, may do irreversible damage to fragile ecosystems. On the other hand, history is replete with social groups who have interacted with the natural world in such ways as to minimize ecological "dislocations."[37] Groups like the Native Americans, for example, had sophisticated methods for harvesting nature's bounty without substantially altering biological diversity. And nineteenth- and twentieth-century rural Appalachians, who themselves borrowed many native American subsistence techniques, also did relatively little damage to their local environment. Even today we find that rural communities in the Appalachian south are less likely to alter their local environment if these communities are economically stable and their citizens have fair and equitable access to the land and its resources. It is little wonder, then, that the wilderness politics of groups like the Western North Carolina Alliance and Save Our Cumberland Mountains are inspired by a grassroots interest in securing local control over wilderness management as much as by an intrinsic interest in preserving wilderness areas.

If wilderness is indeed a social construct whose definition varies from interest group to interest group, the discovery of human values and social structures mediating wilderness management policy is vital to preserving wilderness itself. Wendell Berry, aware of artificial dichotomies created by contemporary wilderness management agendas, proposes that we preserve wilderness areas by creating economies and values in a *culture* that promotes wise use of all natural resources. Though Berry is not entirely opposed to establishing what Edward Abbey has called "absolute wilderness" (wilderness tracts that through general agreement "none of us enters at all"), he is suspicious of wilderness proponents who do not address the issue of preservation as it relates to our domestic economy and collective behavior. According to Berry,

---

Philosophical Significance of Wilderness Solitude," *Environmental Ethics* 4 (Winter 1987): 303–30.

[37] See, for example, F. Berkes et al., "The Benefits of the Commons," *Nature* 340 (13 July 1989): 91–93.

if we do not have an economy capable of valuing in particular terms the durable good of localities and communities, then we are not going to be able to preserve...[wilderness]. We are going to have to see that, if we want forests to last, then we must make wood products that last, for our forests are more threatened by shoddy workmanship than by clear-cutting or fire.... We could say, then, that good forestry begins with the respectful husbanding of the forest that we call stewardship and ends with well-made tables and chairs and houses, just as good agriculture begins with stewardship of the fields and ends with good meals.[38]

However, the question of giving local communities more management control of public lands further clouds the wilderness debate. Even if one can prove that the masses of urbanites annually descending upon wilderness areas do more damage than a handful of local residents extracting resources from the wilderness in order to maintain their rural lifestyles, the issue of what constitutes proper long-term use must still be addressed. Broader criteria for what constitutes "minimum impact" should be developed by policy makers and resource management professionals so as to include the needs and wants of local wilderness users, even if this means restricting non-local use. Of course, giving use primacy to local communities and their residents ultimately means reversing decades of wilderness management philosophy. On the other hand, if the only alternative is to allow unlimited access to as many wilderness users as possible, we are not only proposing the end of wilderness, we are also proposing—to quote from best-selling author Bill McKibben—"the end of nature."[39]

---

[38] Wendell Berry, *Home Economics* (San Francisco: North Point Press, 1987) 143–44.

[39] Bill McKibben, *The End of Nature* (New York: Random House, 1989).

Chapter 5

Community Organizing in Appalachia

In the decades of the 1980s and 1990s, an increasing number of studies addressed the issue of community resistance in Appalachia. During this period, writers such as Kathy Kahn, Helen Lewis, and John Gaventa documented numerous community struggles in the region, adding critical and important insights to understanding of Appalachian protest and dissent. Although helpful in understanding the political forces that have oppressed particular mountain communities or individuals, these studies did not anticipate the groundswell of grassroots activism that would occur across the region during the late 1980s and early 1990s. In fact, the growth and success of community activism during these years has forced many commentators in the region to rethink several political assumptions about the nature and extent of community organizing in the Appalachian region.

At the same time, mainstream journalism has provided the general public with little more than cursory reports about the social and political activism that emerged in Appalachia during the early 1980s. Moreover, progressive commentaries about Appalachian protest movements have uncritically accepted the idea that the region's citizens universally oppose the forces of industry and modernization, ignoring important differences among rural and urban residents, older and younger generations, and citizens of hill, mountain, and valley. Some scholarly works published over the past several decades have even reinforced certain stereotypes about the Appalachian political character; for example, the belief that individuals living in the Appalachian region generally maintain a fatalistic attitude toward political activism and are thus not mobilizable as a social group.[1]

With the exception of several works on the United Mine Workers of America, recent scholarship on Appalachian community protest has severely lagged behind in terms of critically evaluating the problems and prospects of Appalachian grassroots activism. In an attempt to fill the vacuum, this essay assesses the upsurge of community activism that has occurred in the region since the early 1970s. In doing so, I focus attention on the activities of several Appalachian community organizations, particularly those that have been the most successful in challenging the political status quo. Finally, from the vantage point of a sociologist, part-time community organizer, and lifelong native resident, I attempt to summarize each organization's strengths and weaknesses.

I begin the discussion by looking at membership-based community organizations, the most visible and most successful of the Appalachian protest groups.

Membership-based Groups

Save Our Cumberland Mountains (SOCM) and Kentuckians for the Commonwealth (KFTC) are two of the most successful grassroots organizations in the Appalachian region. Founded in 1972, SOCM (pronounced "sock 'em") maintains a due-paying membership of more than 1,500 families, individuals living primarily atop the Cumberland Plateau in east Tennessee. KFTC, the younger of the two organizations, has more than 2,000 members in 90 counties statewide. Both SOCM and KFTC refer to themselves as membership-based community groups, which means they are comprised of a politically active network of due-paying members.

Membership-based groups also employ professional organizers, which further distinguishes them from other community groups in the Appalachian region. SOCM members work on issues ranging from the control of strip-mining and improving water quality to the elimination of hazardous waste dumps. KFTC members work on these and other related issues, although they are primarily known for their work on coal industry reform. SOCM and KFTC have reputations for being model citizens' organizations and are relatively well known both in and outside the Appalachian region.

---

[1] Stephen Foster, *The Past in Another Country: Representation, Historical Consciousness, and Resistance in the Blue Ridge* (Berkeley: University of California Press, 1988) 218–21.

As previously noted, membership-based groups such as KFTC and SOCM are also maintained by a staff of organizers paid to assist members in their various organizing activities. SOCM presently has a staff of six paid organizers whose annual salaries average around $25,000, excluding benefits. All organizing activities, including lobbying efforts, publicity, the filing of lawsuits, and field office maintenance, is paid for by the internal fundraising efforts of members or by annually received foundation grants procured by the staff. During the 1990s, SOCM's annual operating budget exceeded $250,000, of which 40 percent was raised by internal fundraising committees or by SOCM chapters based in local communities.[2]

The SOCM chapter is the primary political unit of the organization. With few exceptions, a SOCM chapter consists of at least twelve active due-paying members who are generally living in the local community. Chapters send representatives to the larger SOCM Board or to various issue-driven steering committees such as the legislative committee, which lobbies state legislators. The SOCM Board and the various committees hold a great deal of power in the SOCM organization and plan much of the group's political activities. If a chapter fails to maintain an active membership over a several-year period, it may lose staff assistance or, in some rare instances, be voted out of the larger organization by SOCM's board of directors. In order to qualify for initial staff assistance, the chapter groups must have been actively working on an issue they have identified themselves in response to some problem originating in their neighborhoods. In theory, the staff organizer is not permitted to direct political strategy or to influence overtly the decision-making process of the local chapter.

KFTC, like SOCM, is also chapter based. KFTC places emphasis on membership control, allowing staff organizers little input during chapter or board meetings. In fact, KFTC staff organizers are reprimanded if they appear in television or newspaper press coverage of the group's activities. This policy was adopted partly because community organizers in the mountains have perennially been accused of manipulating their own constituencies in order to advance their political or organizing agendas. However, in the case of KFTC and SOCM, the adoption of this policy was perhaps less a defensive tactic directed at potential critics than simply good organizing strategy. The organizing staffs of both KFTC and SOCM have been influenced by the writings of longtime grassroots organizer and

---

[2] No author, Save Our Cumberland Mountains Annual Report, LaFollette TN, 1991.

musician Si Kahn, who argues that members must maintain, at all levels, ownership of the organization. Proponents of this style of organizing therefore believe members should fully control the activities of the organizer rather than allow the organizer to control and manipulate the group.

The locally controlled, chapter-based organizational model has been highly successful in the Appalachian region. In terms of organizing accomplishments, both SOCM and KFTC can claim many victories. For example, in 1973 SOCM won a court ruling ordering the state to enforce its Water Quality Law by setting up a division to handle water-quality permits required of mine operators prior to beginning a strip-mine operation. In 1986, SOCM succeeded in stopping plans for a 119,000-acre National Guard training center, saving hundreds of homes and farms and saving taxpayers $250 million in federal expenditures. In 1987, the group won a "lands unsuitable" petition that designated the 25,000-acre Rock Creek Gorge in Bledsoe County, Tennessee, as unsuitable for all surface and underground mining. SOCM has most recently been successful in stopping a proposed medical waste incinerator from being located in Roane County, Tennessee.

In Kentucky, KFTC has also won many battles at the local and state levels, including eliminating the use of the antiquated broad form deed, which legally awarded mineral rights claims to coal companies rather than to local individual landowners. KFTC has been equally successful in changing tax laws in the state to force larger coal companies to pay a more equitable share of county taxes. In 1978, for example, Martin County, Kentucky, received only $92 worth of taxes from the top ten mineral owners whose property was collectively valued at $9.4 million.[3] Though it took several years to accomplish, KFTC was finally able to introduce and pass in 1989 an unmined minerals tax bill in a state legislature that has for a century been dominated by a powerful coal lobby. During the 1990s, both KFTC and SOCM began to fight the dumping of hazardous waste and have been successful in halting a number of toxic waste landfills and incinerators in both urban and rural areas of the state.

KFTC and SOCM are exemplary grassroots organizations fighting for social and environmental change. They effectively involve members in local and state politics and are capable of winning battles once thought unwinnable by even the most seasoned activists in the region. Indeed, it

---

[3] Appalachian Land Ownership Task Force, *Who Owns Appalachia?: Landownership and Its Impact* (Lexington: University of Kentucky Press, 1983) 59–60.

would be difficult to find two more effective grassroots organizations in the entire United States. However, because of their many successes, few activists or scholars in the region have dared to criticize openly groups like KFTC or SOCM. While it is difficult to find fault with much of what these groups do to affect social change, they are certainly not without their political weaknesses or organizing limitations.

One of the problems with membership-based groups in general, I believe, is a blind commitment on the part of the organizers and certain elite members of the group to maintain the growth of the organization, a commitment that often directs or influences the group's entire political agenda. A group that must spend most of its energies on raising funds, recruiting members, or developing leadership skills cannot directly confront the opposition in ways that other "less organized" protest groups can. Also, with larger membership-based groups, the more radical activities of certain individual members are often seen as deterrents to group cohesion, so the board often encourages such members to participate in more socially acceptable political activities such as lobbying, fundraising, or voter registration drives. Participating in these kinds of activities—as opposed to direct-action protest, for example—gives "uncooperative" members a less confrontational way of venting grievances and allows the formal organization to remain in good standing with the political status quo.

Certainly an argument can be made for the superiority of membership-based organizing as currently promoted by KFTC and SOCM. Membership-based groups are highly successful in mobilizing much-needed resources, are largely democratically controlled, and bring a populist sensibility to their organizing that allows them to work within the mainstream political establishment. However, there is a danger that a blind faith in this style of organizing places membership-based groups above constructive criticism. Obviously, the community organizer embracing the membership-based model is correct in stating that long-term social change cannot come about without support from a systemic, organizationally structured movement. But do the reported successes of a single community organization like KFTC or SOCM ensure that economic and social justice has prevailed in the larger community or region? Too often, as Appalachianist Stephen Fisher has noted, the organizing strategy of new populist groups like SOCM and KFTC fails to explore fully the concept "of a 'winnable issue' or to offer criteria for judging the success or failure of a social movement."[4]

How the organizer or organization defines success is a central question that needs to be answered adequately and critically by all membership-based groups. Is passing a bill in the state legislature, for example, a cause for celebration if the law is unenforceable at the local level? Does stopping a low-level hazardous waste incinerator from being located in one community count as a victory if it simply increases the likelihood that the incinerator will be sited in someone else's community? Can success be proclaimed if the opposing community group does not suggest or implement alternative, more ecologically sound waste disposal methods? Ideally, the community group should adopt a perspective that addresses the *entire* social and economic conditions that make the production and disposal of such materials necessary in the first place.

For many Appalachian protest groups, the organizational drive for increased membership and institutional funding has also placed them in a posture of what I call "claiming the victim." I first coined the phrase several years ago to illustrate my concern that organizers of membership-based groups in the Appalachian region were exaggerating the activities of their own organizations while simultaneously downplaying the activities of other protest groups. I found it interesting, for example, that organizers for membership-based groups would sometimes not publicly endorse the activities of other Appalachian community organizations. The other groups to which I refer here are *community*-based protest groups, which, unlike membership-based groups, are generally not supported by large organ-izational structures or run by a paid organizing staff. Like membership-based groups, community-based protest groups in the Appalachian region have numerous organizing strengths and weaknesses.

Community-based Protest Groups

Community-based protest groups in Appalachia are generally locally controlled and therefore largely independent of outside funding agencies for financial support. They are often situated in isolated rural communities and appear to have no formal structure or prescribed political goals other than

---

[4] Stephen Fisher, "A Critique of New Populist Theory," unpublished manuscript, presented at the annual meeting of the American Political Science Association, Atlanta GA, 31 August 31–3 September 1989, 19.

solving an immediate social problem in the neighborhood or community. Some of these protest groups could be classified as "Not in My Back Yard" or NIMBY groups—as they are now popularly called—but most of them have developed a much more critical understanding of the social problem they are politically confronting.

Members of community groups often have little desire to join an already established organization, particularly one that would take their political allegiances outside their immediate community. In most instances, these community groups are most active in their local township, or in some cases in their local municipal district or county. With community-based protest groups, the victims themselves do most of the organizing, though often "outsiders" support the group as consultants or directly aid community protest with their financial support. Community-based groups that have been active in the mountain region include, among others, the Brumley Gap Concerned Citizens in Abingdon, Virginia; the Ivanhoe Civic League in Ivanoehoe, Virginia; the Yellow Creek Concerned Citizens of Middlesboro, Kentucky; the Bumpass Cove Concerned Citizens near Jonesborough, Tennessee; the Guardians of North Chickamauga Creek in Hamilton County, Tennessee; the Crabtree Citizens Against Nuclear Trash in Haywood County, North Carolina; and the Concerned Citizens of Cedar Grove in Walker County, Georgia.

One of the best known and most widely written about community-based groups in the Appalachian region is the Yellow Creek Concerned Citizens (YCCC) of Middlesboro, Kentucky. In 1980 the citizens of the Yellow Creek community formed the organization to protest the pollution of Yellow Creek by the local tannery. For years, residents of the community complained of the creek's odor and frequent fish kills and saw the creek as a dangerous health hazard. Yellow Creek had been polluted since the late nineteenth century, and by the 1970s large stretches of the stream sustained little if any aquatic life. Within a year of its founding, the protest group had more than 400 members.[5]

YCCC activities began with the group challenging the Middlesboro City Council to enforce a sewer use ordinance that would impose restrictions on the waste the tannery was permitted to send to the municipal sewage treatment plant. As environmental sociologist Sherry Cable has noted, "YCCC's most consistent tactic was for members to attend

---

[5] Sherry Cable and Edward Walsh, "Differential Paths to Political Activism," *Social Forces* 66 (June 1988): 951–69.

Middlesboro City Council meetings where two or three men would challenge the mayor to enforce the Sewer Use Ordinance, abide by state and federal water quality laws, and clean up the creek."[6] The meetings often became shouting matches that attracted local media and hundreds of spectators. The mayor persistently ignored the grievances of the YCCC, and their confrontations often ended with the mayor abruptly adjourning the council meeting.

After two years of relatively fruitless organizing, the group decided to file a $31 million class-action suit against the city of Middlesboro. In 1985, YCCC's suit was settled out of court with a consent decree signed by the US Justice Department, the EPA, the state of Kentucky, the city of Middlesboro, YCCC representatives, and the Middlesboro Tanning Company. The legal document established limits for discharges into Yellow Creek and set deadlines for compliance. However, YCCC members had documented numerous decree violations by both the tanning company and the city. At the same time, the EPA did not aggressively enforced compliance of the decree and in 1990 actually drafted and signed a weaker consent decree in response to the city's numerous complaints about discharge limits. In 1995, when the community faced the tannery owners before a jury, courtroom testimony proved devastating to company officials. The jury found the tannery owners guilty of gross negligence and ordered them and the city of Middlesboro to pay the community $11 million to monitor the health effects of the pollution, with another $4 million going directly to the citizens of Middlesboro.[7]

Larry Wilson, a local resident and YCCC's president, has remained an important force of the group. His leadership role and organizing skills have maintained the organization for more than ten years. Wilson also worked for the Highlander Education Center and traveled extensively around the United States, speaking about his organizing experiences with the YCCC. In response to YCCC's political activities, some organizers of membership-based groups like KFTC and SOCM have argued that independent protest groups like the YCCC will not bring about widespread and lasting social

---

[6] Sherry Cable, "From Fussin' to Organizing: Individual and Collective Resistance at Yellow Creek," in *Fighting Back in Appalachia: Traditions of Resistance and Change*, ed. Stephen Fisher (Philadelphia: Temple University Press, 1992).

[7] Valerie Miller, "The Struggle of Yellow Creek," *PLA Notes* 43 (Feburary 2002): 4.

change in a community since they lack formal organizational structure and organize around single local issues.

Proponents of membership-based groups point out that most community groups do not usually remain politically active after having won or lost a particular organizing campaign. A good example would be the Brumley Gap Concerned Citizens Group in Abingdon, Virginia, which politically disbanded after stopping a utilities corporation from damning the New River in the 1970s. Membership-based organizations believe protest groups should never stop fighting for political and social reform, arguing that belonging to a larger social change organization allows members to remain politically active in their communities as new organizing issues arise.

Of course there are several responses to this argument, one being that community-based groups should not be overly condemned for their "short-lived" activism since many of these groups are equally effective in the short run and may later reorganize as newer political challenges confront the community anyway. The YCCC was active in a number of other issues during the 1990s, successfully opposing a municipal incinerator, reporting hazardous waste dumping, and obtaining a "lands unsuitable petition ruling" that bans strip-mining near their community. Another good example is the Crabtree Against Nuclear Trash (CANT) group in western North Carolina who reformed after successfully stopping the DOE's high-level nuclear waste storage facility from being located in the community in 1986. Later, when Haywood County officials announced that a sanitary landfill would be located in the Crabtree community, eighty people were again meeting regularly, planning a strategy to prohibit the radioactive dump.

Moreover, there is no conclusive evidence that membership-based organizations in the region are able to maintain strength and political staying power in individual communities simply because they have more organizational resources and members to mobilize. SOCM's Prentice-Cooper chapter near Chattanooga, Tennessee, and KFTC's Harlan County chapter in east Kentucky are good examples of chapters unable to maintain high levels of political activism within the membership-based organization. SOCM's Prentice-Cooper chapter could not maintain an active membership after their attempt to stop excessive clear-cutting in the 35,000-acre Prentice-Cooper State Forest in Marion County, Tennessee. KFTC's Harlan County chapter, by the organization's own standards, has been a "non-chapter" during much of its existence, despite the fact that the organization claimed it was an active group in annual reports.[8]

Having more financial resources at hand when mobilizing against the opposition is clearly an advantage that membership-based groups share. The Oliver Springs community in Anderson County, Tennessee, one of the newest SOCM chapters, was able afford a half-page ad in the *OakRidger* because of its ties to the SOCM organization. In response to SOCM protest, the Chambers Development Corporation, a prominent Pennsylvania-based landfill conglomerate, was able to purchase, at the cost of $2,000, a full-page ad in the paper announcing its commitment to maintaining a safe and clean landfill at the proposed Oliver Springs dumpsite. After researching the corporation's track record in West Virginia and discovering many environmental violations, the Oliver Springs residents were able to place a counter-ad in the *OakRidger* that summarized Chambers's violation history—at no cost to the local chapter.

As a result, SOCM was able to delay the construction of the landfill while simultaneously challenging the state's decision to grant the company an operating permit. Ultimately, the county government voted not to allow construction at the proposed landfill site, even though the state had issued the company a permit to do so. In response to the county government's decision to sue Chambers for continuing landfill construction, the state chose to revoke the corporation's operating permit—a clear victory for the grassroots organization. Undoubtedly, most organized community groups in the region could not afford the exorbitant advertising expense.

Of course there are many kinds of community-based protest groups, each using different forms of organization and styles of self-government. Some groups are short-lived, while others remain active for much longer periods. There are also community groups that organized around more than a single issue such as a landfill or toxic waste dump. The Ivanhoe Civic League in southwest Virginia, for example, was formed in 1986 to stop the sale of the Ivanhoe Industrial Park, which, according to local residents, was vital to the town's future. Ivanhoe had lost two major industries and more than 1,000 jobs since the late 1960s and by the early 1980s had become one of the poorest towns in the region. In 1987 the Ivanhoe Civic League tried to find new solutions to the town's economic woes and became involved in a variety of community projects through the organizing efforts of Maxine

---

[8] This observation was made by the author as an organizer trainee for the Southern Empowerment Project in 1988.

Waller, the league's president, and Helen Lewis, an author and community educator.[9]

By the early 1990s, the Ivanhoe community has been successful in creating an education center, has published two community history volumes, and has made the Ivanhoe Industrial Park into a tourist park, complete with bike rental, camping and rafting facilities, and a community-owned convenience store. These organizing victories could not have come without great community sacrifice or without the participation of a large number of community members in the process. No single ideological focus directed the community in their efforts; they were simply concerned with making the town a better place to live and sought a variety of ways to accomplish the task.

It is doubtful that the Ivanhoe Civic League will become inactive as a group in the near future or dissolve simply because of its political successes. Through their self-initiated organizing efforts, the citizens of Ivanhoe were able to create a much more viable economic vision for the community. The organizing in Ivanhoe was not only reactive to oppressive social forces; it was also *proactive* in the sense that it sought out newer and more creative solutions to older social problems. As Gene Marshall has argued, community groups that ignore the proactive dimensions of organizing for social change are often unable to empower their community since the status quo against which most of the groups organize never completely relinquishes control of its institutional authority. In many instances, only by rejecting the institutions of the status quo and creating newer, alternative institutions does a community become fully empowered. The counter-institutional emphasis of some community-based groups makes them different from membership-based organizations that often work within already established institutional structures.[10]

In some ways the institutional focus of this kind of community-based organizing is reminiscent of the kind of organizing that originated out of Saul Alinsky's Industrial Areas Foundation in the 1950s and 1960s. Although classic Alinsky organizing claimed to be "community-based," the organizing burden fell primarily on the shoulders of single, professionally trained

---

[9] See, for example, John Gaventa and Helen Lewis, "Rural Area Development: Involvement by the People," *Forum for Applied Research and Public Policy* 4 (1989): 58–62.

[10] Gene Marshall, "Repair of Replacement: An Essay on Ecological Politics," *Realistic Living: A Journal on Ethics and Religion* 8 (June 1988): 3–8.

organizers. In the Appalachian region, community-based organizing is initiated and carried out by the community members themselves, which clearly changes the character and style of community activism. So while the goals and counter-institutional strategies of community-based groups may be similar to those of the Industrial Areas Foundation at a broad theoretical level, the methods and organizational structure of the various community groups are vastly different.

The question of who defines a political issue as well as how the issue is connected to a specific organizing agenda is an important one as additional progressive community organizations emerge in the Appalachian region. While some of the groups focus simply on environmental or land use issues, others are providing a broader political critique of environmental destruction, particularly as this destruction relates to issues of social injustice. A few activists and scholars are beginning to become familiar with many of these emerging groups, although many are largely unaware of their political or organizational agendas. One of these groups is the North American Green Party, which has offered a challenging critique of traditional notions about what constitutes grassroots politics, community organizing, and social and environmental change.

Green Politics

By 1990 there were more than 750 Green Party groups in the United States and Canada, including small active groups in Asheville, North Carolina; Knoxville, Tennessee; and Lexington, Kentucky. In several regions of the country, the Green movement has even become a highly visible political force. In New Haven, Connecticut, for example, the Greens are an official political party with more than fifty registered members. In Vermont, New Hampshire, and Maine, Greens have worked with participants at their local town meetings to stop the federal government from locating high-level nuclear waste dumps in New England. In two college towns, Madison, Wisconsin, and Ann Arbor, Michigan, Green candidates polled as high as 10 percent in local, municipal elections during the early 1990s. In Elkins, West Virginia, hundreds of delegates from Green groups across the country have met to plan organizing strategies for upcoming local and national elections.

According to proponents of the North American Green movement, community- and membership-based groups that allow one, two, or even three "issues" to direct their protest have a narrow focus of what constitutes social change. For Green activists, community organizing is not about selecting or reacting to issues but about building democratic community institutions and actively dismantling undemocratic ones. Community organizing is more than simply winning unrelated political victories for isolated constituencies; it is also about radically and *permanently* changing both political and economic structures to meet the wants and needs of the majority of individuals in a given locale.

Citizens in local communities must be creators—rather than creatures—of social change, argue the Greens. Many members believe that

> grassroots people fall away when they feel the organization is not really theirs; when they are needed only periodically, not as people whose ideas and initiative are valued, but merely as bodies at a demonstration or voters on election day. Such organizing breeds passivity and apathy. It will never create the grassroots strength, substance, and consciousness that we need to make fundamental change in this country, change that will take power from the institutions that now grind on toward extermination, change that will empower people in local communities to construct humanistic, ecological alternatives.[11]

Ultimately the North American Greens believe in the emergence of a community-based environmental and social movement that will link environmental concerns to social issues and to broader public health concerns. The North American Greens' organizing philosophy is also based on the assumption that grassroots activism should first be rooted in the politics of the local community and region before branching out into larger political arenas. The emphasis on participation in local politics echoes the organizing strategies of the People's Appalachian Research Collective (PARC), who, in the early 1970s, advocated the idea of creating a regional confederation of "community unions." PARC members were critical of older forms of labor and community activism and called for the adoption of a radical new approach to social change. Interestingly, the community union idea is based on the principles of anarcho-communalism, an organizing philosophy that continues to inform Green Party politics. In Green organizing, the goal of community unions is to create locally based

---

[11] Green National Clearinghouse Statement, internal document, March 1988, 2.

democratic organizations and decentralized economic institutions. Social theorist Murray Bookchin was a major influence on PARC member proposals and continues to inform the Green Party movement in this country.

Politics for a Green activist is not electoral politics as commonly conceived. The task for a Green is also to change substantially the nature of political institutions so that they directly and democratically represent local interests. They argue that electoral involvement as currently conceived by many community- and membership-based groups is based on a naive assumption that change will occur by simply electing the appropriate leader on election day. The Greens would argue that no matter how critical electoral involvement is to the creation of grassroots democracy, the real task is not simply to get candidates elected to state positions, but to limit the power of the state by electing candidates who will, once in office, actively curtail the state's role in the decision-making process.

To become fully active in local and state politics, however, requires that grassroots leaders and groups involve themselves not only in electoral politics and the electoral process in general, but also in the nuts-and-bolts workings of city, county, and state government. Prior to 1985, most if not all Appalachian protest groups avoided the participation of their members in local or state politics. Running candidates for local office, for example, was seen as less important than organizing independent community organizations or educating individual community activists. As Mike Clark noted, it was a tactical error for institutions like the Highlander Education Center to actively discourage local leaders from running for public office. Yet both politicians *and* political structures must be held accountable by community organizations in the region. Without direct political representation, grassroots organizations will forever be subject to the whims of elite politicians representing nothing more than their own special interests.[12]

Admittedly much of what is the Green movement has occurred in the more progressive and urban areas of the United States. Much of the Green political platform, as originally formulated, will be difficult to transfer to rural areas, particularly if indigenous leadership is unfamiliar with the larger, and perhaps more radical, Green Party agenda. Moreover, the Greens have

---

[12] Mike Clark, "Sowing on the Mountain: Highlander in the Seventies," address prepared for the Myles Horton Memorial Celebration, New Market TN, 5 May 1990.

not aggressively sought out the grassroots, despite their recognizing the importance of the grassroots for the success of the larger movement. Of course, what is lacking in Green politics is a populist element that characterizes almost every Appalachian grassroots organization presently active.

An additional obstacle to Green mobilization is the county seat government that exists throughout the Appalachian region. American Green politics see the township or municipality as the primary arena for affecting social and political change. In theory, unincorporated rural areas in Appalachia would first have to be incorporated into independent, self-governing communities in order to ensure grassroots control of the political process. The practicality or even possibility of community incorporation in the region is a problem future Green advocates must face and overcome.

The transfer of traditional grassroots activism to one that encourages direct involvement in community and state politics will not be easy. Traditionally the left has been suspicious of electoral politics, viewing it as a mechanism for perpetuating the political status quo. "If voting really changed things," states the old anarchist slogan, "it would be illegal." However, as Bob Hall argues in his important book *Environmental Politics*, the shift to an emphasis in grassroots politics is necessary in order for community groups in the region to gain real power and to link organizing issues in a broader and more effective political movement.

Green activists see enormous possibilities in creating locally controlled democratic institutions that collectively can challenge the dominant status quo. The Greens seek to build coalitions with other groups—i.e., feminists, peace activists, and people of color—and have a concrete platform on which to build a future democratic society. Although the Greens have a strong theoretical and ideological base, their politics has not been critically tested in a single community in the region. Using the activities of the YCCC as a case study, we can see that gaining grassroots control of local political institutions is a difficult and uphill battle. In the final analysis, the success of the movement will perhaps depend on whether activists can adapt Green organizing strategies to local situations without alienating themselves from other grassroots groups in the Appalachian region.

Future Problems, Future Prospects

Social and political change in the region will ultimately require new populist strategies like those being adopted by grassroots groups like SOCM and KFTC as well as broader and perhaps more radical political visions such as those being proposed by new left environmental groups like the North American Greens. A coalition built of various Appalachian community-based and membership-based organizations would also improve the odds that individuals and communities could help build the kinds of institutions that would provide sustainable economic development for the region. Community organizations must respond to all levels of political and economic oppression and can no longer afford to ignore the local political institutions and the power these institutions have in maintaining the status quo. If a few communities in a few areas can begin mapping out a more independent, self-reliant course for themselves, they can help others discover how to break the web of dependency that keep so many people—including Appalachian organizers—believing in the present system.

Widespread social reform, as Frances Fox Piven and Richard Cloward have argued, does not occur without major struggle and sacrifice by the people and the radical transformation of all social and political institutions.[13] Issues such as land reform, alternative and safe energy sources, environmentally sound waste disposal, sustainable development, unfair labor practices, and culture conservation should therefore play a major and active role in the political agendas of all Appalachian protest movements. Without the adoption of these and other issues, the political agendas of protest groups in the region will always be dependent on, if not the targets of, institutional forces outside their own. It is for this reason that Appalachian protest groups should build counter political institutions as well as begin altering older, already existing ones.

Despite the popular image of Appalachia as a "third world country" within the borders of the United States, controlled and manipulated by external political forces, some of the oldest and most powerful political institutions in the region are those that have developed internally at the municipal, county, and state levels of government.

If lasting change is to come to the Appalachian region, all political institutions must also be monitored, controlled, and held accountable by grassroots activists and organizations. Community-based organizations have indeed been more successful in influencing local elections, but the latest involvement of community groups in the electoral process has not been entirely successful, since most community groups do not have a substantive

---

[13] Frances Fox Piven and Richard Clower, *Poor People's Movements* (New York: Vintage Books) 1979.

critique of or even an alternative to the representational structure they are fighting at the local polls.

If successful community organizing is indeed possible in the Appalachian region, it must choose to operate within the context of local institutions as they operate at the family, county, and regional levels. Organizers must also learn the critical role that the church, school, and popular culture play in maintaining and creating social networks and political allegiances in the region's rural and urban communities. Though I am aware of many grassroots organizers who understand this fact, many do not go far enough in attempting to learn what those institutions are or how they give meaning to the lives of "ordinary" citizens. I would argue that most of what is southern Appalachian politics and culture is not as anachronistic as folklorists, academics, and many activists might have us believe.

How community organizers and organizations perceive their political agendas and constituencies will be extremely important to the future of Appalachian protest movements. In terms of understanding the future of dissent in the region, one could begin by examining the prominent grassroots groups and critically assessing both their past and present organizing goals and accomplishments. What is equally important for the future of these movements will be the ability of these groups and organizations to form larger coalitions and to work out a more critical analysis of how to radically change the current power structure without defaulting their own ideological belief in bottom-up grassroots resistance and change. At present, the possibility of a broad coalition of such groups seems somewhat remote, however, since many Appalachian citizens' groups maintain very different organizational agendas.

The preoccupation with "issues," and not the people affected by them, often creates an atmosphere of one-dimensional organizing in which a constituency is embraced simply because of their particular attitude toward something like strip-mining, unfair labor practices, or the hazards of toxic landfills. Making a number of issues *connect* in a critical way in order to form allegiances and enable a more critical understanding of how power is held and maintained in a community would bring Appalachian organizing to a much higher dimension—and toward truer success. "Multi-issue organizing" as practiced by organizations in the region will not accomplish this goal if proper connections are not drawn or alliances are not formed, both within and across protest groups and across geographic regions.

Building strong communities cannot be done by simply building strong community organizations, though it is clearly an important first step. Community is also the land and place on which people collectively live, work, and play. Thus to empower members of a community is to ensure that they can experience life to its fullest by creating economic and cultural institutions that neither destroy the environment nor exploit human labor. Community-based organizations must be in it for the long haul, and membership-based groups should realize more creative and radical solutions to the problems confronting Appalachian communities. The Greens should make real efforts to learn the practical lessons of grassroots organizing and apply these lessons to their organizing strategies.

Granted, no single community group or organization can ensure that broader institutional change will occur in the Appalachian region. Fortunately, many of these groups are beginning to realize their weaknesses and are looking beyond their own sometimes narrow organizing strategies. Some membership-based groups are beginning to form broader coalitions and are getting involved in electoral politics at both the county and state levels. Training schools like the Southern Empowerment Project have begun to educate indigenous organizers and to critically address the issue of what constitutes long-term systemic change for the region. In order to keep young leadership in the area, the New South Directory Project is compiling a directory of hundreds of local social justice organizations in the region that are looking to young people for grassroots leadership. In the past several years, Highlander's Stop the Poisoning Schools has been successful in bringing together hundreds of grassroots activists in the region who continue both to challenge and educate public officials about the dangers of toxic wastes. While some groups will undoubtedly continue their older, and perhaps more reformist, organizing strategies—and continue do some good in terms of redistributing power among individuals—the future of the Appalachian region lies in strong, politically active communities.

Chapter 6

Gore in the Balance

Several years have now passed since my friend Steve Smith, founder of the Knoxville-based Center for Global Sustainability, and I stood directly behind Senator Albert Gore, watching as he planted a 3-foot tulip poplar, the state tree of Tennessee, on the University of Tennessee campus lawn. This event was one of the university's many 1990 Earth Day activities and received considerable local media attention, including brief coverage on the local news. Steve and I appeared on television that evening holding a large banner that read in bold green letters: "AL GORE: WE WANT LEADERSHIP NOT SHOWMANSHIP!"

Senator Gore skillfully ignored us, as perhaps only astute politicians can, though he did seem genuinely surprised when an official from the College of Agriculture told him and the audience that University plant biologists had genetically altered the sapling in the laboratory.

This was Monday, 23 April 1990, the day after the "official" Earth Day celebration on campus. It was a dark, gray afternoon and I had just returned from the Knoxville airport, where I had seen Murray Bookchin, a noted author and social ecologist, off to an Earth Day lecture in New Orleans. The spirited though aging Bookchin had spoken to a campus-wide audience the night before, telling us to be wary of mainstream environmentalism. One of the five original speakers at the 1970 University of Michigan Earth Day "teach-in," Bookchin had argued that an environmentalism that only focuses on cosmetic, incremental solutions to environmental problems (e.g., placing recycling bins at local grocery stores) cannot alone solve the environmental crisis. The roots of environmental decay, he forcefully told us, lie within socioeconomic relationships that must also be challenged and substantially altered if we are to fully restore the balance of nature.

I have thought a great deal about Bookchin's Earth Day message, particularly as it relates to the environmental politics and policies of Gore and the like. It is irrefutable that Gore, and others like him in Washington, DC, serve an important political function, introducing and supporting federal legislation that is ostensibly designed to protect the natural environment. In Congress, Gore has been instrumental in creating the Superfund Law that appropriated funds for cleaning up hazardous waste sites throughout the United States. He also helped create the first Interparliamentary Conference on the Global Environment, bringing forty-two nations together in order to draft a multilateral agreement on a range of growing environmental threats to the global environment.

Senator Gore has been politically active on a number of environmental fronts—from holding congressional hearings on the increase of chlorofluorocarbons in the atmosphere to drafting the Global Marshall Plan—but he really hasn't challenged the economic and political status quo responsible for the environmental crisis. Is Gore's voting record on military expenditures, for example—I am thinking here of the nuclear Trident submarine, whose production and maintenance has direct and severe environmental consequences—that of a truly environmentally and socially conscious politician?

While it is difficult for me to answer this question in the affirmative, I must assert that personal and political contradictions are what make this era, the late twentieth century, a postmodern age. At the same time, most environmentalists would agree that Gore's ecological politics are not always based on a selfless, altruistic concern for our rapidly dying planet. Gore is also an astute political strategist, a promoter and seller of self, image—and now books.

Gore's book, *Earth in the Balance* (New York: Houghton Mifflin 1992), is not surprisingly a public relations *tour de force*. On the book's jacket cover we see him seated upon the bare ground, wearing faded blue jeans and a casual, loosely fitted shirt. Inside the cover, Gore pushes all the right buttons, placating to nearly every environmental interest group and addressing, in perfunctory fashion, nearly every ecological concern of recent years. Within the span of more than 400 pages, he touches upon global warming, loss of genetic diversity, deep ecology, Christian stewardship doctrine, air and water pollution, alternative technology, recycling, population growth, garbage disposal, and environmental national security. At times, Gore's awareness of the many ethical positions and trends in the environmental movement is surprising, if not impressive. His sources are current and reputable, as the US senator had convenient access to both the latest government documents and leading scientists in the environmental field.

Only two of the book's fifteen chapters strike me as highly original or at least worthy of special mention or critical attention. Chapter 12, "Dysfunctional Civilization," received considerable attention in early reviews of the book, primarily for what some in the media called Gore's "groundbreaking" analysis of the psychological relationship between human consumption patterns and environmental destruction. Gore maintains that the disharmony in our relationship to the earth stems to a large degree from our unconscious addiction to ecologically destructive consumption patterns. He pushes the addiction metaphor to its logical limit, arguing that we, as addicts of resource consumption, do not allow ourselves to perceive a connection between our own behavior and its destructive ecological consequences. We avoid responsibility for our destructive actions by denying their very existence.

Applying the keen metaphors of addiction, denial, and dysfunctionality to environmental destruction is certainly creative and unique. But in Gore's hands the analysis often descends into diluted pop psychology, which conveniently allows him to ignore other and perhaps more tenable causes for the present environmental crisis. By using the metaphor of the pathological addict, Gore places the responsibility of environmental reform upon innocuous individuals, or even groups of individuals, instead of directly upon social institutions such as American corporations, the ones who have historically been the greatest destroyers and polluters of the natural environment. Numerous studies have shown, for example, that less than one-fourth of all toxic waste is generated by American households, while the remaining three-fourths is produced by corporations such as Eastman-Kodak, General Electric, and Dow Chemical, who also have—through expensive 5th Avenue advertising campaigns—the deft ability to directly control the purchasing patterns of American consumers.

Chapter 15, "A Global Marshall Plan," is the book's last, detailing Gore's "strategic" plan for saving the global environment. This is perhaps the most important chapter in the book, since Gore specifically tells how he plans to translate his own brand of environmentalism into policy programs and political realities. Gore uses the Marshall Plan of the 1940s, which helped rebuild the nations of Western Europe after World War II, as a organizational model for implementing global environmental policy. The primary goals of his Global Marshall Plan are to (1) stabilize world population, (2) develop environmentally appropriate technologies, (3) create a system of economic accounting that assigns appropriate value to the ecological consequences of economic development, (4) negotiate and approve a new generation of international environmental agreements, and (5) establish a cooperative plan for educating the world's citizens about the fragile global environment. The implementation and integration of these five goals, argues Gore, would help developing countries establish a more sustainable and thus less environmentally destructive development course.

On the theoretical surface, Gore's plan is certainly noble and ecologically sound. In most environmental circles, these five policy goals would be highly applauded. Gore's Global Marshall Plan borrows other sustainable development strategies that have been introduced by governments and multilateral agencies. Readers should be aware, however, that advocating sustainable development programs in principle does not commit governments to their full implementation. From its inception in the 1970s, advocates of sustainable development—from the Club of Rome to the World Commission on Environment and Development (the Bruntland Commission)—have made convincing arguments for the political necessity of creating alternative technologies, limiting population growth, and curbing environmentally destructive economic practices. However, few of its proponents—Gore among them—have critically discussed how sustainable development is to be implemented at the local grassroots level.

In fact, there have been many critical responses to the the Brundtland Commission Report, a document that shares, as noted above, many of the same objectives of Gore's Global Marshall Plan. Michael Redclift, in his assessment of the Brundtland Report, notes that while many of the goals of the document are sensible and practical, most are difficult to implement at the local community level. Richard Chambers, of the University of Sussex, agrees but adds that development is sustainable only if the priorities of the globe's poorest populations are put first. He considers the rhetoric of sustainable development as adopted by the Brundtland Commission—and now Gore—as part of a discourse that grossly ignores the primary and more immediate needs of Third World populations.

In Chambers's view, it is presumptuous for the First World to think that those living in abject poverty should give priority to environmental or economic sustainability. By putting emphasis on environmental considerations such as population stability and alternative technology rather than on the more immediate needs of the poor, sustainable development actually restricts the poor's use of natural resources, becoming yet another instrument of First World oppression.

Vandana Shiva, a leading environmental scientist working in India, maintains that sustainable development goals such as Gore's are successful only if ordinary citizens at the local community level are also included in the planning and implementation of the development process. Unfortunately, Gore does not effectively assure his readers that his Global Marshall Plan will include the voices of grassroots citizens in this country or in others. Has he wrongly and naively assumed that his broadly conceived policies will somehow directly influence the environmental, political, and economic realities of local communities?

In the long term, Gore's proposals will do little to change the political and economic status quo, yet at the same time they will create the illusion that he is making great and sweeping changes to global environmental policy.

Chapter 7

Feist or Fiction?:
The Squirrel Dog of the Southern Mountains

The feist, a small, energetic hunting dog, has been an important element of Appalachian culture for more than 100 years. "Go back fifty years and just about everybody in the south has some kind of Feist," says Randy Pannell, co-founder of the World St. Jude Squirrel Dog Championship.[1] Throughout the southern mountains, working dogs like feists have often been the source of family pride and community identity. Good dogs were not only valued for their hunting ability, but also because of their assistance in daily chores or their important role as watchdogs. According to one reputable source, the feist was essential to survival on the Appalachian frontier, serving as family companion, protector, and hunter of "whatever wild game that was available."[2] While it is likely that feists were first used to hunt squirrels and other small game animals, there is some evidence that prior to the turn of the century, the breed was sometimes used for hunting black bears. The dogs were apparently used to "worry" the bear once it was cornered by the much larger bear hounds. In *Go Down Moses*, William

---

[1] Bill Tarrant, "World Squirrel Dog Championship," *Field and Stream* 95 (1990): 120.
[2] Claude Shumate, "The Mountain Feist," *Full Cry*, n.d., n.p.

Faulkner (himself a feist owner) celebrates the bravery of a "fice" dog that is killed by a cornered bear.[3]

Mike Foster, an area supervisor for the Tennessee Wildlife Resources Agency, speculates that the feist originated from the bloodlines of the small mountain cur and terriers that remained isolated in the southern mountains for some years. This is a widely held view among feist owners, who generally believe their dogs share bloodlines with the small terriers of the British Isles, particularly those bred in the last century to hunt rodents and snakes. However, Claude Shumate, who has probably written more about the breed than any other individual, argues convincingly that the modern feist is a descendent of dogs bred by the North American Indians of the late Mississippian era. Shumate also maintains that the small dogs kept by the Indians—dogs such as the short-nosed Indian dog and the small North American Indian dog—are most likely the foundation breeds of the modern feist. He hypothesizes that Indian dogs taken back to Europe in the 1500s "influenced to some degree the development of small dogs in the Old World." According to Shumate, European stock dogs, taken westward across the American frontier by hunters and trappers during the 1600 and 1700s, already carried bloodlines of the various southeastern Indian dogs.[4]

Regardless of whether one accepts Shumate's contention that early dogs brought to the American frontier contained Indian dog bloodlines, there can be little doubt that newly arrived European breeds into America did in fact mix with Native American breeds during the 1600s and 1700s. The intermixing of Indian and European dogs breeds most likely occurred randomly and probably went uncontrolled for more than a century as both dog and human adapted to life on the early American frontier. By the beginning of the twentieth century, we begin to see a more distinct type of feist, a hunting dog probably infused with genes from North American Indian dogs and one that physically resembled British Isle terriers such as the Manchester and fox terrier. These dogs, bred for their alertness, quickness, and ability to use eyes, ears, and nose in the hunt, were invaluable to early mountaineers. They became known for their unsurpassed courage and stamina and were most likely used for hunting a variety of game, including bear, opossum, raccoon, groundhog, and squirrel.

---

[3] William Faulkner, *Go Down Moses* (New York: Random House, 1942) 191–220.

[4] Claude Shumate, "Monthly Column of the American Treeing Feist Association," *Full Cry* (December 1987): 56–57.

Additional but perhaps more anecdotal information about the origin of the breed can be found by doing an etymological study of the word "feist." The *American Dialect Dictionary* says one possible origin of the word is the black dog found in Goethe's *Faust*. In the Faust legend, a small feist-like "poodle-dog" appears to Wagner and Faust outside the city gate and then transforms itself into an hellish beast, the devil incarnate, inside Faust's study.[5] The *American Dialect Dictionary* also gives a number of spellings for feist (feest, faust, fyste, fice, feist, fist) and several definitions of the words. The earliest recorded usage of the word dates to 1890, when in Kentucky the term was "often heard among Negroes and illiterate persons."[6] The *Oxford English Dictionary* maintains that the word "feist" probably originates from the Anglo-Saxon word *fistan*, which literally means to fart or "break wind"—as in a dog that runs as if breaking the wind.[7] Other definitions given in the *American Dialect Dictionary* include a small snarling dog, a small disagreeable dog, and an undersized vicious dog. *Webster's New International Dictionary* defines the feist as "simply a small dog."[8] The earliest mention of feists in Appalachian literature is found in Horace Kephart's *Our Southern Highlanders*, published in 1913. In the book, a North Carolina bear hunter describes the feist as "one o' them little bitty dogs that generally runs on three legs and pretends a whole lot."[9]

The Breed Today

Since the beginning of the twentieth century, feists have been used almost exclusively for hunting small animals such as squirrels, raccoons, and opossums or simply kept as pets. Bill Hartsock, a feist owner from the Virginia coalfields, tells us the dogs are frequently used for hunting groundhogs in the southwest Virginia mountains. During the early 1990s, however, there was a renewed interest in the breed, particularly among squirrel hunters and squirrel dog breeders in the region. In fact, in some areas of the South, the very word "feist" has become synonymous with squirrel hunting. The dogs are renowned for their ability to see, hear, and

---

[5] Goethe, *Faust, Vol. 1* (Baltimore MD: Penguin, 1959) 68–72.
[6] Harold Wentworth, *American Dialect Dictionary* (New York: Crowell, 1944) 213.
[7] *Oxford English Dictionary*, 2nd ed. (Oxford: Clarendon, 1987) 811.
[8] *Webster's New International Dictionary* (Springfield MA: Merriam, 1933) 801.
[9] Horace Kephart, *Our Southern Highlanders* (Knoxville: University of Tennessee Press, 1933) 94.

smell squirrels as well as for their facility for "treeing" them. A "treed" squirrel is one that is kept motionless by the circling and barking dog, thus becoming an easy target for the hunter.

The feist, as a unique or distinct breed, constitutes a curious situation. Even though the American and United Kennel Clubs do not sanction it, many people recognize the dog as a separate breed. Accordingly, a number of feist registries have emerged—for example, the American Treeing Feist Association and the United Squirrel Dog Registry. Moreover, several prominent outdoor writers now consider the contemporary feist dog a purebred, registered breed. However, the issue of just how full-blooded this "purebred" is hasn't been decided and is still a matter of debate.

Although the feist is clearly viewed by some people as a distinct breed, the characteristics that make the dog "a feist" are less than concrete. Feist owner Dale Fowler, who grew up in the mountains of north Georgia, notes that there "seems to be a lot of folks who have their own ideas about what a feist is." Fowler believes, however, that "if you're talking about feists, you're talking about a small dog with black and tan or black and white markings."[10] In terms of specific physical characteristics, feists are generally described as between 10–30 pounds and no more than 18 inches high. Some dog owners said they could be any color, but most agreed with Fowler, saying feists can be a mixture of black, brown, or white. Some of the dogs have their tails "docked" or clipped by their owners, and many have brown spots or "copper pennies" over their eyes. Everyone I interviewed in the region agreed that the dogs' ears are set high on the head and are either straight or tilted forward. Consensus among most owners was that feists should have pointed noses and be shorthaired and well proportioned. Almost all said the breed is aggressive, gritty, alert, and intelligent. One informant said the feist is definitely not a terrier, while a number of others said the dog most likely "has a number of terriers in its background."[11]

Of course many people in the southern mountains still refer to any small, mixed-breed dog as a feist. These individuals, typically non-hunters, perceive the breed in broad, generic terms and have little reason to believe that feist dogs are nothing more than little, mixed-up mongrels. Others,

[10] Morgan Simmons, "Squirrels Are Common Ground for Variety of Dogs," *Knoxville News-Sentinel*, 10 September 1989, C15.
[11] Anonymous, feist owner survey by author, graduate program in Sociology, University of Tennessee at Knoxville, September/December 1990. All owner quotations were taken from this survey.

typically hunters, recognize the breed's impure bloodline but argue that the dogs are similar enough in their physical characteristics and hunting behavior to classify them as a distinct breed. A third group, typically dog breeders and members of organizations like the American Treeing Feist Association, argue that the dog is definitely a separate breed and should be standardized through organized and controlled registries.

In fact, the American Treeing Feist Association (AFTA), the largest of the feist dog registries with more than 600 members nationwide, lists specific characteristics of what constitutes the feist breed. Article IV of AFTA's constitution specifies twelve breed standards, which include the following:

1. Keen to slightly stocky body;
2. Short ears, slightly hung down, flopped straight are all acceptable. Cocked ears are very desirable;
3. Long muzzle, keen;
4. Good strong legs—bench legs are acceptable;
5. Full-length tail; stub tail will not prevent registration;
6. Black, white, tan, red, yellow to lemon, or any variations of foregoing colors;
7. Height: Males, 10" to 18"; Females, 10" to 17";
8. Weight: 30 pounds maximum;
9. Good coat of hair, short; no extremely long- or shaggy-haired dogs;
10. Free gait, hunt with eyes and ears alert;
11. Virtually silent on track;
12. Shall tree squirrel or coon—game must be seen.[12]

The above standards, agreed upon by AFTA's board of directors, do not, as one might suspect, neatly fit everyone's definition of the breed. Some individuals argue that "shaggy" or longhaired dogs should be included in the standard; others say slightly larger or slightly smaller dogs deserve the feist classification. Despite such arguments, the AFTA, using the criteria cited above, has registered more than 600 dogs to date. F. L. Chrisman, the association's president, said any dog not meeting the above criteria will not be registered as a feist. Intimately, through his group's efforts, he sees the breed becoming standardized to the point that "they [the United Kennel

---

[12] American Treeing Feist Association, *Yearbook 1990–1991* (New Market TN: American Treeing Feist Association, 1990) 3–5.

Club] will eventually recognize the feist as a breed." According to Chrisman, the National Kennel Club already registers feists, but in doing so does not adhere to strict breed standards and, in his opinion, does little to help preserve or promote the breed.[13]

In broad terms, the various definitions of the modern feist indicate two things simultaneously: (1) feists are definitely a distinct type of dog and (2) the breed is not yet formalized to the extent that there is not significant variation in people's descriptions of the breed. Admittedly, some of the variation comes from local and regional differences, but other variation is obviously the result of breeders and registries not following a mutually agreed upon standard.

Although I was told a number of times that a feist is just a "little mixed-up dog," everyone interviewed in the study either had specific physical characteristics in mind or could pick out a feist from magazine photographs and therefore had definite ideas on what is or isn't a feist. However, there is certainly enough consistency in the descriptions to say that there is a distinct type of dog called the feist. My own feeling is that the dog is in the process of being formalized as a purebred dog by the various feist interest groups: hunters, field trialers, registry associations, and breeders. It is most likely in an early stage of the process, but I believe there is enough concern and awareness of the breed in the southern region to justify this conclusion.

The Breed's Future

During the very early stages of my research on feists, I assumed the dog was relatively rare and that regional and national registries existed in an effort to preserve the breed. Only a few of the people we interviewed directly addressed the issue of rarity, however. Dale Fowler told us "there are not many around...seems like you never see a lot of these things," but added almost immediately afterward that he personally did not think there was a conservation problem or that the breed should be considered endangered or rare. Apparently the dogs were at one time relatively scarce, but that situation has obviously changed today. Claude Shumate attributes the breed's revival to the lessening of the availability of hunting lands caused by industrial and residential development, which in turn contributed to the resurgence of squirrel hunting, a sport that requires little hunting area. As squirrel hunting grew in popularity in the late 1970s and early 1980s, so did

---

[13] Interview, F. L. Chrisman, 8 September 1990, New Market TN.

the demands for a small, easily handled tree dog like the feist. Claude Shumate adds that feist dogs will continue to be sought after, particularly by older men who can no longer follow the larger, more wide-ranging hound and cur breeds.[14]

As noted earlier, the reemergence of the feist as a popular hunting dog coincides with the emergence of national feist registries. Concerning the issue of whether the existence of feist registries is ultimately a good thing for the breed's future, there is noticeable difference of opinion among dog owners. A few of the people we interviewed locally have notable misgivings about registries. One of the individuals we interviewed, for example, stated that the registries would destroy genetic diversity, while another claimed the registries would create a situation where only registered dogs would be considered pure feists. There is definite disagreement among the dog owners on how official the breed should become. Traditionally, physical difference among dogs has been a prerequisite of the breed, and some respondents felt that registries will minimize regional and local differences that are characteristic of feists. A few others avoided the argument directly and simply stated that as long as there are mountain people hunting small animals, there will be feist dogs, registered or not.

Another misgiving that emerged was stated best by one respondent to our survey who, even though some of his dogs are registered, said "many of the registries simply exist for profit." This feeling was borne out in several local interviews, particularly with owners who do not register their dogs. There is a concern that the registries will accept any application, feist or not, as long as the owner pays the registration fee. The more dogs the register operators can register, goes the argument, the more money they can make—at owner expense. Most of the owners agreed that there are a few honest registries, such as the registry of the American Treeing Feist Association, but also stated that some registries were simply money-making enterprises and thus do not exist for more nobler purposes such as the preservation and proper promotion of the dog breed.

For individuals promoting feist registries, the most common reason given for registering their dogs was to standardize and protect the breed. Others said they register their dogs because it allows the animals to compete in the yearly field trials held by feist registries; each entry must be registered prior to the hunt. One owner who enters dog in trial hunts "strictly for

---

[14] Shumate, "The Mountain Feist," n.p.

pleasure" also said he registered his dogs simply because "they deserve the recognition." Winners of field trials receive awards and trophies as well as the knowledge that their feists are exceptional squirrel dogs.

Certainly the emergence of registries has been a boon to dog traders and sellers and will help promote the breed in the future. However, since the registries started doing business, registering dogs for a small fee, the price of good feist dogs has risen dramatically over the past ten years. A few registered feists now sell for as much as $1,500, and pups readily sell for $150. Ironically, the existence of registries may limit the breeding of feists to those solely belonging to feist registries and associations. According to one feist dog breeder, prior to 1990, buyers did not care if the dog was registered, "and now it's difficult to sell an unregistered dog." It is entirely possible that in the coming years, as interest in the dog continues to rise, feists will be harder to obtain by lower-income individuals who will no longer be able to afford the higher-priced registered dogs. Today, there is a plethora of websites selling registered dogs and puppies, with some animals selling for as much as $2,000.

For many of the owners I interviewed, raising feist dogs was an important income source that contributed directly to family livelihood. One woman told us she raises pups to help cover her husbands' medical costs, while another person told us he yearly sells, for extra income, "a few pups and an occasional trained dog." One of the interviewees told us he regularly places dogs for sale in various hunting dog magazines such as *Full Cry* and the *Squirrel Hunter*. Although people made it known to us that the dogs are potentially worth a lot of money, no one went into detail on how much, in broad terms, the dogs supplemented their own incomes. Squirrels, the ultimate quarry of the dogs, also supplement owner income. Companies such as Strum Hide & Glove in Strum, Wisconsin, readily purchases, for a minimum fee, squirrel tails and hides from hunters.

Everyone I spoke to during the research either has hunted or still hunts squirrels with their feist dogs. However, the dogs seem to be more than simply squirrel-hunting companions. When talking to feist owners, I was aware of their deep personal affection for the dogs. For many of the owners, the dogs are a great source of pride: in some rural communities a dog owner is known for his or her particular feist. Feist enthusiasts often travel great distances to obtain the offspring of a particular animal. For this reason, the dogs are also responsible for creating close friendship bonds with owners extending well beyond the southern mountains.

In preparing this study, I talked to a number of people about an aspect of life that is truly important to them and one they seldom get to express verbally. By illuminating the importance of feist dogs in the lives of rural Appalachians, I hoped to help create a critical understanding of the breed and its importance as a companion and hunting animal. Hopefully the research will also encourage communication between the various interest groups who seek to preserve both feist dogs and the squirrel-hunting tradition that is deeply associated with these animals.

Chapter 8

Roads to Ruins

As one hikes down the Old Settlers Trail, it eventually leaves the main road, following the Little Pigeon River downstream, and feels like the beginning of a wilderness adventure. In wintertime, a musky blanket of moist brown leaves and dark green Christmas ferns covers the trail. Above the trail is a thick canopy of rhododendron, whose leaves often droop downward, indicating sub-freezing temperatures. Far overhead, tall, dark hemlocks wear a frosting of light snow and provide warm shelter for chattering winter wrens and ruby-crowned kinglets. Before leaving behind the noisy creek, a hiker can have the illusion, for a brief moment at least, that this is the nineteenth century and that civilization is hundreds of miles away.

Although most hikers see the trails in the Great Smoky Mountains National Park as an adventure in natural history, the trails are, in truth, a map of *human* history. Traveling the Old Settlers Trail today, for example, a hiker can perhaps see more traces of nineteenth- and early twentieth-century mountain community life than at almost any place in the park. Solitary chimneys and crumbling rock walls are common along this trail as are non-native plants such as daylily, daffodil, privet, boxwood, and lilac that mountain people planted around their homes. Passing through the headwaters of more than a dozen creeks, one gets a good idea of how heavily populated the Smokies were as well as how rural families organized their lives along each watershed.

In fact, most of the park's trails were originally created not with the idea of wilderness exploration; rather, they reflect the history of a people who made use of the natural landscape and its bounty. I drew this conclusion after spending three months investigating more than 800 miles of trails for the Great Smoky Mountains Natural History Association, a nonprofit group. The group's *Hiking Trails of the Smokies*, a hiking guide published in 1994, is based in part on my research. While documenting hundreds of historical sites in the park, I discovered that the trails in the Great Smoky Mountains have a history that mirrors the history of the land itself.

Most scholars studying the park have concluded that the present network of trails through the park was originally the creation of "bear, game, or Indians."[1] The first visitors to the area, individuals like geographer Arnold Guyot, described seeing "bear" trails along nearly every ridge top, especially near grassy balds. It is difficult, however, to document the extent to which the Cherokees used these specific ridge-top trails. Early settlers, including late nineteenth-century observers, noted that what is today highway 441 over Newfound Gap and Indian Gap were major trade routes for the Cherokees. The Cherokees had three major villages in three areas of the park: Oconaluftee, the name of which is a corruption of a Cherokee word meaning "by the river"; Cataloochee, another Cherokee corruption, referring to balsam fir on the ridges that "stand up in ranks"; and Deep Creek, which was once called Kituwah.

In the eighteenth century, a network of trails ran along these watersheds—as they still do—between villages, fields, and areas for fishing and hunting. One of the earliest routes across the mountains was an Indian trail that was later known as the Cataloochee track. The Cataloochee track ran from Cove Creek Gap along what is today the east side of the park and connected the settlements of the Upper French Broad with the Overhill Towns of the Tennessee River.[2]

Although the Cherokee people never lived among the highest peaks of the Smokies, the higher mountaintops played an important role in the spiritual life and mythology of the Cherokees. Clingman's Dome, which today has a road to the top and a wheelchair-accessible lookout tower, was

---

[1] Phil Gersmehl, "A Geographic Approach to a Vegetation Problem: The Case Study of the Southern Appalachian Grassy Balds" (Ph.D. diss., University of Georgia, 1970) 248; William Myer, *Indian Trails of the Southeast* (Nashville: Blue and Gray Press, 1971) 735.

[2] Wilma Dykeman and Jim Stokely, *Highland Homeland: The People of the Great Smokies* (Washington, DC: Department of the Interior, National Park Service, 1978) 10; R. B. Truett, *Trade and Travel Around the Southern Appalachians* (Chapel Hill: University of North Carolina Press, 1935) 5–6.

once *Kuwo-i*, meaning "mulberry place." In a tale recorded by noted ethnologist James Mooney, *Kuwo-i* was one of four mountains beneath which the bears had a council house and danced before going into their winter dens.[3] It is not known whether the Cherokees created trails to these specific religious sites or not, but it seems likely. According to a number of early sources, Indian trails usually led along the higher ground and ridges where the undergrowth wasn't as dense and where there were fewer stream crossings. Trails along the ridge tops also afforded "good opportunity for sighting game and enemies."[4]

Tragically, the major roads across the Blue Ridge to Oconoluftee and Kituwah also brought Revolutionary War general Griffith Rutherford on an extermination campaign in 1776—these villages and their surrounding fields were two of thirty-six destroyed. In 1791, the Cherokees were forced to sign a treaty that ceded Cataloochee and most of the Smokies to North Carolina. The Cherokees regrouped and rebuilt towns on the sites of Oconoluftee and Kituwah, and they were occupied until white settlers forced them out before the Trail of Tears in 1838. In Oconoluftee and Deep Creek, the first white settlers built their homes and planted in the same fields the Indians once cultivated; several of them had actually accompanied Rutherford on his grisly campaign.[5]

As late as 1821, though, there were only two roads into Tennessee, one of which was the Cataloochee track made by the Indians. The first white settlers in the Smokies followed these roads and then settled along the major streams of the Smokies or in the mountain coves, where the soil was the most productive for farming. For this reason, the first settler trails and footpaths were determined largely by the contours of watersheds.[6] However, settlers also built wagon roads to connect their communities to markets in Waynesville, North Carolina, or Maryville, Tennessee. In the mid-1830s, a road was started to connect Cades Cove with North Carolina; a portion of

---

[3] James Mooney, *Myths of the Cherokee*, in *Nineteenth Annual Report of the Bureau of American Ethnology, 1885–86* (Washington, DC: US Government Printing Office, 1900) 526.

[4] R. B. Truett, *Trade and Travel Around the Southern Appalachians Before 1830* (Chapel Hill: University of North Carolina Press, 1935) 6.

[5] William Myer, *Indian Trails of the Southeast*, 39; Mooney, *Myths of the Cherokee*, 49, 205.

[6] Martha Elizabeth Norburn, "The Influence of Physiographic Features of Western North Carolina on the Settlement and Development of the Region" (Ph.D. diss., University of North Carolina Press, 1932) 71.

this unfinished road can be seen from the Bote Mountain Trail in the national park. Another more successful project was the Oconoluftee turnpike, which is now a section of US 441. Not surprisingly, the Cataloochee track and the Oconoluftee turnpike were the two major routes taken by Civil War troops in the area.[7]

By the 1850s, much of the outer rim of what is now the national park was inhabited by white settlers. As communities grew larger, families were forced to move higher up into the more remote valleys and coves. Little Cataloochee, for example, developed when a number of families moved there from Big Cataloochee Valley. By 1910, more than 1,000 people lived in Cataloochee alone. These individuals made their living by a combination of farming and apple orchard cultivation. Because the Cherokees who remained in Big Cove made use of the mountains for hunting and fishing, they frequently encountered whites along the narrow ridge trails. Cherokee women followed the trail over Pin Oak Gap and down Beech Ridge to sell woven baskets for 25 cents.[8]

For almost 100 years, mountain people used the Smokies for grazing hogs and cattle, and this changed both the trail system and the environment. Early on, livestock fell prey to wolves and mountain lions, so in 1812 Tennessee declared a bounty of three dollars per scalp on wolves.[9] With the removal of wolves and other predators, what were once wooded mountaintops would soon become open pastures. In fact, most of the so-called grassy balds of the park were created as a result of the cattle-herding complex that dominated much of the mountaintop landscape by the end of the nineteenth century. Gregory Bald, for example, was named for Russell Gregory, who moved to Cades Cove from Yancey County, North Carolina, in 1835. Although he and his wife Elizabeth Hill owned a farm in the middle of the cove, Gregory bought thousands of acres on the ridge tops specifically for grazing cattle.

The girdling of trees, the deliberate or accidental burning of the woods, and the long-term effects of cattle grazing created most mountain

---

[7] Dykeman and Stokely, *Highland Homeland*, 49.

[8] Donald Davis and Margaret Brown, "Trail History Notebook," unpublished manuscript, Great Smoky Mountains Natural History Association, Sugarlands Visitor Center, Great Smoky Mountains National Park, Gatlinburg, 1992, 27.

[9] Durwood Dunn, *Cades Cove: The Life and Death of a Southern Appalachian Community, 1818–1937* (Knoxville: University of Tennessee Press, 1988) 30.

balds.[10] Likewise, cattle herders first created many of the high-altitude park trails as paths to these balds. The Anthony Creek Trail took Cades Cove residents to Russell Field; the Bote Mountain Trail was a major route to Spence Field. The Sweat Heifer trail, in the Oconaluftee watershed, gets its name from the cattle that used to be chased up and down Sweat Heifer Ridge. As the name implies, the cattle would overheat en route and become lathered with sweat.

Trade routes out of the Smokies, such as Coopers Road and Rich Mountain Road in Cades Cove, allowed residents to take cowpeas, chestnuts, galax, and ginseng to trade in Knoxville for new shoes and clothes. Although there is substantial evidence that mountain communities maintained market connections to the outside world, the evidence is often contradictory. In the Smokies, isolation varied from community to community or even from household to household. Charles Myers, who worked as a mail carrier in Cades Cove until the park took over the land, said, "We never were tied up here and isolated like they might have you think. Why, we used to go to town every day sometimes for weeks."[11]

Although cattle paths and trade routes were responsible for creating much of the national park's trail system, many of the trails were created by the mining and timber industries, which did the most to transform the landscape of the Smokies. In the 1890s, small timber companies that operated in Hazel Creek built splash dams along creek beds, following existing footpaths to float logs downstream. Over the next twenty years, demand for lumber and technology pushed larger companies further away from main rivers and existing paths and roads. Almost all of the trails in Little River, the largest district of the park, were once the bed of narrow gauge railroads built by the Little River Timber Company. The Huskey Gap Trail, one exception, was the route taken by Sugarlands and Gatlinburg residents over the mountain to work for the Little River Timber Company.

On the far east end of the Smokies, the watershed called Big Creek was one of the first to be crisscrossed with logging railroads, and five companies cut over this land by the end of World War I. The Cataloochee Lumber Company alone took 100 million feet of lumber off the area. The Champion Fibre Company, which purchased this land from the Pigeon River Company, built a railroad track with nine switchbacks to reach Mount Sterling and cut the hemlocks and hardwoods in 1911 and 1912; these

---

[10] Gersmehl, "Geographic Approach," 200–50.
[11] Davis and Brown, "Trail History Notebook," 125.

switchbacks would later form the basis of Baxter Creek Trail and Mount
Sterling Ridge Trail.[12]

The heavy loss of timber in the Smokies was due not only to industrial
logging. A deadly Asian fungus called the chestnut blight also dramatically
altered the southern forests and the mountain paths through them. Once the
dominant species in the Appalachian forest, the American chestnut grew as
large as 12 feet in diameter and reached 120 feet in height. By 1915 the
fungus had spread as far south as Henderson County, North Carolina, and
by 1930 most of the chestnut trees in the Smokies were dead or dying. The
loss of this single species had a dramatic effect on black bear, wild turkeys,
white-tailed deer, and tree squirrel populations as well as on the
mountaineers who relied considerably on these animals for food. "The
mountain people," recalled Martin Tipton, "needed those chestnuts. They
ate them themselves, of course, but they depended upon them to feed their
hogs." The sturdy, rot-resistant wood of the chestnut provided mountain
residents framing lumber, furniture, farm fencing, and tannin extract for
leather. "We used to come upon the skeletons of those trees when we'd be
out walking," said Tipton. "Dad said it looked like a third of the mountain
was dying."[13]

Between 1890 and 1925, when mountain people were coping with the
chestnut blight, lumber company railroads, skidders, and skidder-sparked
fires, tourism was becoming yet another obstacle to rural mountain life. In
1920, tourist George Stephens described walking up the Deep Creek Trail
and catching as many as seventy-five trout in a day. In fact, Abrams Creek in
Cades Cove was first stocked with non-native rainbow trout as early as 1908.
According to W. Wayne Oliver, in three years "people came from every
direction to fish. I can remember seeing those fish...tremendous trout.
People dynamited and seined them. Fishermen just flocked in there."[14]

Along the trails created by Indian traders, cattle herders, and
lumbermen came a new generation of Progressive-era preservationists who
saw hiking and outdoor recreation as important to relieving the stress of
modern life. The Smoky Mountain Hiking Club, which was started by
Knoxville residents during the 1920s, described a pastoral Smoky Mountains

---

[12] Donald Davis, "Logging History Facts," unpublished manuscript, Great
Smoky Mountains Natural History Association, Sugarlands Visitor Center, Great
Smoky Mountains National Park, Gatlinburg, 1993, 3.

[13] Davis and Brown, "Trail History Notebook," 122.

[14] Ibid., 54.

in their 1929 *Hiking Guide*: "The only sounds to be heard will be the tinkle of cowbells, the voices of whippoorwills, and the wind in the pines."[15] At the same time, new owners of Henry Ford's Model T formed motor clubs and challenged each other to be the first to drive up the old railroad beds to the top of the mountain. These motor clubs and hiking groups, along with tourist promoters and developers, pushed for the area to be set aside as a national park.

In 1925, the land that would be the park was purchased by North Carolina and Tennessee from 18 lumber companies, and about 1,200 small landowners. Nine communities and more than 5,000 people were removed to create a national park in the Smoky Mountains.[16]

Because the opening of the park in 1930 coincided with Roosevelt's massive spending for the Civilian Conservation Corps, much of the trail system we know today is the result of thousands of work hours provided by young men from all parts of the country. The campgrounds in the park were once lumber camps and then CCC camps, and the trails spun logically out of these camps and up the old rail beds. Railroad ties became bridges, enormous abandoned trees became foot logs, and the stonework done by the CCC and the WPA remain everywhere in the park today.

But the CCC did more than simply smooth routes that already existed. Photographs from park archives show that the crew did extensive alteration to construct the Maddron Bald Trail, for example. About 2,000 feet up from the County Line CCC camp, crews dynamited tons of rock and topsoil in order to create the smooth walking surface taken for granted by hikers today. No less than six trails were designed to go to Mount LeConte, since it was one of the few recognizable "peaks" and guaranteed to be a popular tourist site. Most of these trails were designed by National Park Service engineers, who made sure the routes were wide enough and strong enough for pack horses. "These trails are hand-built, so to speak," one engineer told a newspaper reporter. "No machinery has been used, just picks and shovels." In the superintendent's report, Supt. J. Ross Eakin reported that construction was slow because "50 percent of it required blasting through rock and shale."[17]

---

[15] Ibid., 79.

[16] Margaret Brown, "Power, Privilege, and Tourism: A Revision of the Great Smoky Mountains National Park Story" (Master's thesis, University of Kentucky, Lexington, 1990) 123.

[17] Davis and Brown, "Trail History Notebook," 142.

Records from the Kephart Prong CCC camp in North Carolina show that the site included barracks, officers' quarters, a latrine, a mess hall, an education building, a recreational hall, and woodworking shops. Company 411 improved 6 miles of Highway 107, constructed 22 fish-rearing ponds, 65 miles of horse trails, 14 miles of mountain highway, parking areas for 600 cars, and a water system for Newfound Gap. In just three years, they moved 250,000 cubic yards of dirt and rock, planted 100,000 trees, and reduced fire hazard on 4,000 acres of land. In fact, park records show that Supt. Eakin had so much manpower that it was difficult to keep the CCC boys busy and out of the nearby communities. Thus, he used more than half their time "clearing fire hazard," or removing dead trees left from lumber operations. CCC crews were also supposed to recreate an aesthetic trail as much as possible. According to Bob Brown, who helped build the Bullhead Trail, the man working with dynamite had to be as skilled as a blacksmith to "slip the rock" in order to let it fall gracefully instead of blowing a gaping hole. The young men were then ordered to "moss the stumps" so that the constructed areas would return to a more "natural" appearance.[18]

Throughout the early years of trail creation, the superintendent's goal was more to create a park than a wilderness. "We were more game wardens than anything else in those days," recalled P. Audley Whaley, one of the first park rangers. Whaley, who had grown up in Greenbrier, was one of those charged with burning down the old home sites so that the trails would return to their "natural appearance." He also had to arrest and fine former neighbors for breaking park rules about hunting, fishing, and collecting firewood.[19]

In order to protect an overused resource, the National Park Service has largely reversed its former policy of new trail development and maintenance. Since 1960, the Smokies has become one of the most heavily visited parks in the United States, requiring the National Park Service to place more and more rules on trail use, limit horse travel, and forbid vehicles on what were once footpaths, logging roads, and highways. Today, when the hiker travels along the meandering Old Settlers Trail, he or she can learn that the trail bed was constructed during the 1930s by the Civilian Conservation Corps, who linked the footpaths and road beds of the small farms in adjoining valleys to create the 16-mile trail. Rather than purely a nature walk, the hiker can see the trail as something of a historical tour. Hikers walk, in the

---

[18] Ibid., 65.
[19] Ibid., 46.

first mile, through the center of what was once the Greenbrier community, then down the lane that was called Partonsville, where many families with the surname "Parton" lived.

Lona Mae Parton Tyson, a great-aunt to the famous country singer Dolly Parton, was born in Greenbrier. Tyson and her family shared a general store, a school, a hotel, the Sears Roebuck catalog, the Friendship Missionary Baptist Church, and Greenbrier Primitive Baptist Church. All had small farms with long stone fences to keep animals out of the garden. She and her seven brothers and sisters were charged with repairing and building these stone fences—not to keep farm animals in, but to keep the hogs, cattle, and horses out of the garden.[20] The only visible signs of Tyson and the generations that lived here are few a ghostly chimneys and those stone fences she and her brothers built, historical markers that stand in places more than 5 feet high and sometimes stretch, continuously, for more than 300 yards.

Perhaps Tyson's stone ruins, and many like it, tell the full story of the Great Smokies, a story that is as much about human history as it is natural history. As the national park is allowed to return to its "natural" state, this important lesson will undoubtedly be lost to future generations. When this happens, there will be only hiking trails in the park, and the roads to ruins will be no more.

---

[20] Ibid., 92.

Chapter 9

Shelby Lee Adams's
Appalachian Portraits

It seems that a year cannot pass without the publication of a new picture book about the people of the southern Appalachians. These books, perennially shot in colorless black-and-white, paint a grim and stern portrait of life in the mountains.

Shelby Lee Adams's book *Appalachian Portraits* (Oxford: University of Mississippi Press, 1993) is no exception. A photography instructor at Salem State College in Salem, Massachusetts, Adams has given us another macabre vision of the region and its rural inhabitants. Almost all of his photographs—which are admittedly technically and compositionally striking—border on the grotesque. Adams gives little dignity to his subjects, showing them in stereotypical poses, often with blank, mentally incapacitated facial expressions and from angles that accentuate their peculiarity and marginality. Not surprisingly, the titles of the photographs—the only information Adams offers about the subjects—add more insult to injury: "Hort with Chicken, Spider, Jesus, and Elvis, 1989"; "Bert Sitting in Front of Bed, 1988"; "The Home Funeral, Leatherwood, 1990"; "Leddie with Children, 1990."

Even though Adams claims in the introduction to "love these people" and is from eastern Kentucky himself, one must question the ethics of such a work. Where are the voices of the subjects? Lee Smith's brief introductory narrative, a purely fictionalized account of five mountain families, falls short of providing an adequate context for what must be extraordinary lives. Did

Hort, Leddie, and Bert have any control over the photographs that appear in
the book? Were they, as direct contributors, monetarily compensated by this
nationally recognized photographer?

I am reminded of the young women who sued Ernest Matthew
Micklers for using her image for the cover portrait of *White Trash Cooking*.
She had no idea that her face would one day grace the cover of a national
best-selling book and was certainly justified in demanding her share of
profits from the author. Photographers must know that their images are
commodities to be bought and sold in the media marketplace. As Susan
Sontag has observed, "the very need to photograph everything lies in the
very logic of consumption itself." Mountain people have historically given
up their physical bodies, through countless hours of work and toil, for the
self-interests of others. Is doing the same with their photographic images
any less disturbing?

Certainly there is "truth" to the photography of Shelby Lee Adams; he
knows his subjects, and they him. But without a way to interpret these
images appropriately, purchasers of the book get little more than a gross
caricature of mountain people, and sadly, they will continue to believe that
all who live among the mountains are incestuous, mentally deficient
cripples, with way too much time on their hands.

Chapter 10

Grassroots Movements and Rural Policy in Appalachia

During the 1990s, an increasing number of community groups in industrialized and third-world countries have directed their energies toward a variety of economic, environmental, and related public health concerns. The growing strength and visibility of these citizens' initiatives, voluntary associations, and non-governmental organizations (NGOs) in rural development policy has compelled many social scientists to reconceptualize the relationship of grassroots organizations to the local and national state. The political actions of these emerging grassroots groups, say researchers, demonstrate that ordinary citizens, through organized collective action, are capable of influencing public policy formation at both the state and local levels.

In rural America—and especially in Appalachia—grassroots social movements and non-governmental citizens' organizations have played an important role in shaping state and federal policy. Earlier in the twentieth century, rural-based movements of coalminers and textile workers had a major impact on health, safety, and labor legislation; civil rights activities in the upper South influenced national civil rights policies during the 1950s and 1960s; rural poor people's movements of the 1930s and 1960s contributed to the creation of national social welfare legislation; and farmer's organizations affected federal agricultural policy. More recently, a growing number of community groups have been successful in altering state and federal policy directed at regulating a wide range of environmental and related economic activities, including toxic and hazardous wastes, the strip-mining of coal, water pollution, occupational health, and rural land use. Communities in severe economic crisis have also challenged government policy, especially programs related to social welfare and rural economic development.

On a theoretical level, this emerging grassroots activism challenges conventional wisdom about the ability of local communities to alter substantially and direct public policy. A commonly held assumption among social theorists is that grassroots movements have a relatively insignificant impact on the larger political economy and the structure that maintains it—namely the state. As sociologist Celene Krauss has forcefully asserted, social scientists have generally viewed grassroots protest activities as random or self-interested; that is, as narrow and fleeting responses effecting little long-term social change.[1]

In response to the commonly held view, Krauss argues that to appreciate fully the political possibilities inherent in grassroots movements, one must first view the state as an open political arena. Traditional theoretical models concerning the state, she claims, have conspicuously overlooked the role human agency and popular revolt have played in shaping state political structure and process. Marxist scholars, for example, have persistently argued that grassroots political activity ultimately reproduces the hegemonic ideology of the state within the local community. They see grassroots politics as constrained by a political system that represses, distorts, and even co-opts all attempts by the grassroots to gain long-term political empowerment. Grassroots participation in state politics is therefore a misguided politics, say Marxists, since the ideology of the modern state is also the ideology of the ruling capitalist class.[2] For *neo-*Marxists, the state structure is only slightly more dynamic: capitalists, state bureaucrats, and political leaders align *organizationally* to divide or "disorganize" exploited classes that might, in times of economic crisis, develop a revolutionary or militantly reformist consciousness.[3] In both versions, the state is seen as unified and monolithic, an organizational

[1] Celene Krauss, "Community Struggles and the Shaping of Democratic Consciousness," *Sociological Forum* 4 (Spring 1989): 227–39.

[2] See, for example, James O'Connor, *Accumulation Crisis* (New York: Basil Blackwell, 1984).

[3] Ralph Miliband, "State Power and Class Interests," *New Left Review* 138 (1983): 57–68.

structure that limits, if not eliminates, grassroots participation in the political process.

According to Krauss and others, pluralist notions about state structure and process are equally problematic for understanding how the grassroots might become progressive agents in state policy formation. Both pluralists and neo-pluralist proponents of liberal democracy have historically assumed that the political system is equally open to all organized groups. Pluralists insist that the state, as a neutral mediator of conflicting interests, willfully and adequately responds to all community grievances. Policy decisions and their implementation are simply a function of shifting coalitions of organized economic, political, and social groups. Nor do pluralists accept the Marxian critique that modern liberal democracies privilege capitalist interests over all others. For pluralist theorists, government policy promotes the general welfare because public policy results from a balanced "interaction of diverse and contending sectoral interests in the larger society."[4]

From my vantage point, pluralists have been overly optimistic about the democratic promises of the modern liberal state. In general, pluralist theories have ignored the hidden faces of power that prevent participation of the relatively powerless in society from acting on their own affairs. Admittedly, the pluralist model of the state theoretically allows—via interest-group politics—grassroots participation in the formation of government policy. At the same time, conventional pluralist political theory relies on a conception of interest-group political participation that ignores both the realities of the powerless as well as the ability of the powerful to mobilize resources against the rural poor. In political reality, grassroots struggles are often centered on the inability of the state to mediate conflicting interests, especially interests related to economic growth and environmental protection. The pluralist conception of the state grossly underestimates the state's functional autonomy, which it often uses to legitimize its own authority and to delegitimize the wishes of local communities.

While it is not my intention here to develop an all-inclusive "theory of the state," one that will complement the following discussion of Appalachian grassroots movements and rural policy formation in general, I do think existing theories of state process and structure have underestimated the

---

[4] Ted Gurr and Desmond King, *The State and the City* (Chicago: University of Chicago Press, 1987) 7.

political strengths of grassroots citizens' movements. In agreement with Krauss, I see theoretical weaknesses in both Marxist and pluralist theories of the state, particularly as they have been applied to local citizens' protest movements. Ultimately the key to understanding the possibilities for grassroots participation in rural policy formation lies not in a deeper understanding of theories about the state, but in a greater understanding of the dialectical social relations and organizational processes that influence local, national, and even international politics.

Unfortunately, American history is replete with examples of national policies and development agendas that have exploited and in some instances even destroyed rural communities for the "greater good" of the state. Two attempts to shape rural development in Appalachia include programs adopted and implemented by the Tennessee Valley Authority (TVA) and the Appalachian Regional Commission (ARC)—historically two of North America's largest development agencies. Although leaders of both government agencies have historically claimed to have included the grassroots in their decision-making processes, a closer look at the development programs of TVA and the ARC reveals that neither adopted a truly grassroots approach.

TVA and ARC Federalism

The TVA and the ARC have similar histories in that both agencies were initially designed to generate economic stability and growth in the Appalachian region. Of course, both agencies embraced the concept of *regional* development, an idea with origins in the writings of Frederick Jackson Turner, Lewis Mumford, Howard Odum, and several others, including a central statement issued by the US Natural Resources Committee published in 1935. Public Affairs analyst Ann Markusen has labeled the regional development approach of federal institutions like the TVA and ARC "organic regionalism," which, as she rightly points out, "culminated in the 1930s in the advocacy of individually tailored regional plans based on the assumed dominance of natural factors in differentiating regions, reinforced by evolved cultures."[5] Both agencies were influenced by the rhetoric found in New Deal programs of the 1930s and the War on

---

[5] Ann R. Markusen, *Regions: The Economies and Politics of Territory* (Totowa NJ: Rowman and Littlefield, 1987) 252.

Poverty programs of the 1960s that called for increased citizen participation in policy-making processes.

Established in 1933, TVA, the older of the two agencies, clearly saw its development mission within the organic regionalist framework first outlined by Turner, Odum, and the other proponents of organic regionalism. An important component of TVA's regional development, and one most directly germane to our discussion here (though we will return to broader regional development concerns momentarily), was their desire to decentralize the decision-making process of federal government. TVA's two headquarters, for example, were located in the heart of the Tennessee Valley instead of in Washington, DC, and the administration itself was to be a decentralized one in order to ensure grassroots participation. In fact, codified early in the agency's history was a "grassroots doctrine" that would provide accountability and increase responsiveness to the local needs of the rural population.[6]

Despite organizational claims to the contrary, grassroots participation has historically been considerably lacking, if not entirely absent, in most TVA development programs. Throughout its sixty-year history, TVA has been plagued by an inability to include fully the grassroots in policy formation. Almost every TVA program surveyed, including the agency's reservoir resettlement agriculture and electrification programs, failed on this score. Victor Hobday, in his study of TVA municipal power boards, concluded that local municipalities in the valley had comparably little influence upon power board policy. He found that most TVA policies were made by engineers not subject to disinterested review and were thus seldom overruled by the TVA board.[7] Historians Michael McDonald and John Muldowny, in their well-known book *TVA and the Dispossessed*, documented a host of problems with TVA's reservoir relocation and resettlement program in the Norris Basin of east Tennessee. In reviewing their study, it is clear that grassroots interests were not met during the land acquisition phases of that operation and that TVA had not dealt fairly with the local

---

[6] See, for example, David Lilienthal, *TVA: Democracy on the March* (New York: Harper & Brothers, 1944) 5–25, 150–66.

[7] Victor C. Hobday, *Sparks at the Grassroots: Municipal Distribution of TVA Electricity in Tennessee* (Knoxville: University of Tennessee Press, 1969).

residents in procuring homes and communities for the Norris Basin flood plain.[8]

Perhaps the most serious charge against TVA's so-called grassroots doctrine concerns its agriculture and rural development programs. Norman Wengert, in *Valley of Tomorrow*, criticized TVA for its excessive reliance on land-grant colleges and their extension departments for the operational aspects of its rural development activities of the 1930s and 1940s.[9] In an even earlier study, sociologist Philip Selznick proposed that because of its "co-optive" relationship with land-grant universities, TVA agriculture programs were mostly conservative and class-based, assisting only the most prosperous farmers in the valley.[10] And in a later survey, Handy Williamson found that TVA largely omitted black agricultural schools from its rural development programs, thus ignoring an entire population of disadvantaged farmers.[11] Without question, TVA's organizational bias toward wealthier farmers and the agricultural establishment defies the notion that TVA's rural development programs were developed and controlled by the grassroots.

Selznick, in perhaps the first critical analysis of TVA's so-called "grassroots doctrine," argued that organizational demands, internal disputes, and inequities among existing local institutions prohibited TVA from guaranteeing democratic and grassroots control of the agency. Despite progressive tendencies, TVA directors, like most defenders of modern planning, had, by the 1940s, developed an unwavering faith in solving economic and social ills with more advanced technology, thus increasingly putting the burden of proof on agency experts who saw grassroots input as irrelevant at best and disruptive at worst. Moreover, the agency's technological proficiency in power production allowed it to continue its "growth spiral" policy of increasing energy demand and consumption so that, by the 1960s, TVA had "turned much of both the Tennessee Valley and the adjacent coal-bearing areas of Appalachia into a national energy

[8] Michael McDonald and John Muldowny, *TVA and the Dispossessed* (Knoxville: University of Tennessee Press, 1982).

[9] Norman Wengart, *Valley of Tomorrow: The TVA and Agriculture* (Knoxville: University of Tennessee, Bureau of Public Administration, 1952).

[10] Philip Selznick, *TVA and the Grassroots* (Berkeley: University of Berkeley Press, 1984).

[11] Handy Williamson, *The Tennessee Valley Authority and Rural Development, 1979 Summer Policy Study: The Role of TVA Programs in Regional Development* (Knoxville: TVA Office of Planning and Budget, March 1981).

reservation in which every other [development] consideration was subordinate to large-scale power production."[12]

In the 1950s, in order to keep up with increasing power demands, TVA built ten coal-fired generating plants that required the use of strip-mined coal. By 1968, TVA coal purchases amounted to 5.5 percent of the total coal mined in the United States, making the TVA, as it remains today, the single largest user of strip-mined coal. Much of the coal was purchased by the agency in order to meet the energy demands of the atomic bomb complexes and growing defense industry in the Tennessee Valley region. In 1981 alone, the Department of Defense awarded fourteen Kentucky coal operators a total of thirty-six contracts worth approximately $15 billion, or 15 percent of DOD's total coal purchases. A historical review of TVA energy policy over the past fifty years suggests that it has been dictated to a great extent by the demands of the defense industry, whose policies, in turn, had direct effects on the development of both the Tennessee Valley and the surrounding mountain region.[13]

In addition to the increased destruction of rural land and communities caused by strip-mining, the burning of coal in the generating plants vastly increased sulfur dioxide emissions, a major contributor to acid rain and other environmental problems. By 1974, TVA accounted for 52 percent of all utility-produced SO2 emissions in the Environmental Protection Agency's Region IV and 12 percent of total utility-produced emissions in the United States. Although able to install high-tech scrubbers to reduce SO2 emissions in these plants and continue their use within EPA guidelines, the TVA quickly turned its attention to nuclear power, which brought new and even more challenging problems for grassroots participation in agency policy formation.[14]

The 1960s saw not only increased coal production in many parts of the Appalachian region, but also increased hardship among local residents, particularly in areas that were most directly affected by TVA's coal-purchasing policies. In many communities, acid runoff from abandoned coal mines contaminated water supplies, and in others, extensive flooding

---

[12] David Whisnant, *Modernizing the Mountaineer: People, Power, and Planning in Appalachia* (Boone NC: Appalachian Consortium Press, 1980) 63.

[13] Tom Schlesinger, John Gaventa, and Juliet Merrifield, *Our Own Worst Enemy: The Impact of Military Production on the Upper South* (New Market: Highlander Research and Education Center, 1983) 99.

[14] Whisnant, *Modernizing the Mountaineer*, 51.

resulted from erosion caused by the strip-mining process itself. Automation in conventional mining practices increased unemployment rates in many Tennessee Valley counties. US senator Estes Kefauver, for example, described Grundy, Sequatchie, and Marion counties in southeast Tennessee as being in a "critical economic depression." High unemployment rates, the closing of factories, regional out-migration, and escalating environmental destruction made the area ripe for a new federal program designed to address the social and economic ills of the larger Appalachian region.

A variety of legislative federal aid proposals were adopted by the government during the early 1960s, most notably the Area Redevelopment Act of 1961. This act created the Area Redevelopment Administration (ARA), a federal agency responsible for channeling more than $500 million in grants and loans to state and local governments. The ARA, however, became more effective at developing tourism than at reviving depressed economies in the Appalachian region, and it was phased out after only nine months of operation. The phasing out of the ARA opened the door for the creation of a new federal agency that would soon become the largest rural economic development agency in the history of the United States—the Appalachian Regional Commission, whose aggregate expenditures would soon exceed $15 billion.[15]

The Appalachian Regional Commission (ARC), another highly understudied agency of rural development, was first established by the Appalachian Regional Development Act of 1965. Like TVA, the ARC in the beginning used the language of decentralization to legitimate its regional and local policy formation. The ARC was initially given $5 billion by Congress to induce internal development, increase income levels, teach work skills, and generally uplift the entire Appalachian region. Title I of the act established the ARC as a joint federal-state agency, which meant the expenditures of federal money relied primarily upon state plans and authority. The goal of the act's "new federalism" was to provide states with an enlarged role in project implementation so that a more coherent rural development program in the larger region would follow.[16]

Inherent in the ARC's federalist approach was an assumption that the new federal-state body would be responsive and accountable to all people in

---

    [15] John Gaventa and Helen Lewis, "Rural Area Development: Involvement by the People," *Forum for Applied Research and Public Policy* 4 (Fall 1989): 58.

    [16] James Sundquist, *Making Federalism Work* (Washington, DC: Brookings Institution, 1969).

the region. However, the ARC neither located its permanent office in the region nor appointed native residents to important staff positions. Historian David Whisnant notes that by 1970, almost no natives of the region remained on the ARC staff at its Washington, DC, headquarters. Commission structure consisted of a federal co-chairman and the governors of the thirteen states. The organizational design of the commission, argued many ARC critics, did not ensure grassroots representation or local accountability. The ARC's "top-down" hierarchical structure, it was argued, ensured that the extra-local interests of the regional authority would be given priority over the more immediate concerns of the local community.

In actual practice, the ARC has followed a development strategy similar to that embraced by nearly all modern development agencies. Like TVA, the ARC adopted a "bricks and mortar" or infrastructure approach to solving basic social problems, ignoring existing institutional and structural forces at work in the regional political economy. Social problems related to increased environmental destruction caused by strip-mining, widespread absentee corporate ownership of land, the inability of local governments to collect taxes on corporate-owned mineral resources, and the obvious lack of essential human services were downplayed or even ignored by the agency. Instead of working directly on poverty or unemployment in rural communities, the ARC chose to stimulate economic development by creating various regional "growth centers." High unemployment in remoter rural areas could be solved, said the agency, by simply building a network of major highways linking rural areas to urban growth centers. Instead of working on increasing the minimum wage or extending collective bargaining laws for area workers, the commission devoted its energies to attracting additional low-wage industries to the area.

While both TVA and the ARC claimed to operate in a decentralized and participatory fashion, each agency ended up responding more to local economic and political elites than to the needs of local communities. True, TVA and the ARC did sometimes listen to the concerns of the grassroots, but they seldom acted or created federal policy in their behalf. It is clear from the history of the two agencies that regionalism and decentralization cannot be equated with participatory or truly grassroots economic development. In fact, in most cases, the agencies simply served to strengthen the role of local elites while using the rhetoric of participation to legitimate their own "top-down" policy agendas.

While both TVA and the ARC have received enormous budget cuts in recent years, both agencies continue to operate within a regionalist/federalist development paradigm. Minor structural changes have been made in both organizations over the years to better accommodate local responses to their government programs, but neither institution appeals directly to the grassroots for policy direction. Unfortunately, poverty, hunger, high energy costs, environmental destruction, high unemployment, and unfair labor practices persist throughout the Appalachian region. Despite twenty-five years of intense economic development activity by TVA and ARC, almost two-thirds of the counties in Appalachia have declined economically relative to the rest of the nation. According to employment statistics, as late as 1985 four-fifths of the region's counties had an official unemployment rate higher than the national rate of 6.7 percent; eighty-five counties had double the national rate; and twenty-eight had triple the national rate, equaling an official unemployment rate of more than 20 percent.[17] These figures alone should at least partly demonstrate the inability of federal development agencies to promote balanced and sustainable growth in a region historically plagued by unequal distribution of wealth and power, both within rural areas and between urban growth centers and local rural communities.

To this point, my analysis has focused on the kinds of constraints the grassroots in Appalachia have faced as agents and benefactors of federal and state policy and development. The organizational and ideological structure of federal agencies such as TVA and the ARC have largely restricted grassroots participation in policy formation, often to the point of creating newer and even more complex social problems. In response to those policies and the government structure that creates them, the grassroots has responded with direct and sometimes even violent community protest. However, in recent years, grassroots community activism has been directed at politically challenging not only what the grassroots sees as undemocratic state policy, but also toward the creation of new and arguably more participatory forms of state and local government.

As in developing countries, the failure of government agencies to bring about substantial or equitable change has led to an increase in the number of non-governmental organizations in Appalachia attempting to influence the policy formation processes of the state. During the 1970s, these were seen in

---

[17] Donald Davis, "Homegrown Activism Takes Root in Appalachia," *Utne Reader* (May/June 1989): 26.

the form of regional coalitions such as the Appalachian Alliance or, at the national level, citizens' organizations such as the Rural Coalition. In the 1980s, partly in response to the Reagan administration's shifting of many government programs to the states, members of these organizations began to devote more and more attention to influencing local and state policy. Today, these organizations represent a grassroots movement that attempts to link environmental issues with poverty and rural economic development concerns.

The Grassroots Response

Save Our Cumberland Mountains (SOCM) and Kentuckians for the Commonwealth (KFTC) are among the most successful grassroots organizations in the Appalachian region, both gaining national recognition for their organizing efforts. Founded in 1972, SOCM maintains a membership of more than several thousand individuals, most of whom reside atop the Cumberland Plateau of east Tennessee. KFTC, the younger of the two groups, has more than 2,500 members in 90 counties statewide but focuses much of its organizing activities in the Appalachian counties of eastern Kentucky. Both SOCM and KFTC are "membership-based" grassroots groups, which means they are comprised of a local network of due-paying members. SOCM and KFTC also employ a staff of paid organizers, a fact that distinguishes them from other community groups in the Appalachian region.

Simply stated, SOCM's mission is to assist Tennessee residents in protecting, defending, and improving the quality of life in their home communities. SOCM members thus work on a broad range of environmental issues, such as controlling strip-mining, improving water quality, and stopping forest clear-cutting. Founded in 1981, KFTC has evolved into a group that also works on a variety of community issues, though like SOCM it has had the greatest success in coal industry reform.

The SOCM organization is comprised of local chapters, entities organized by geographic area. Chapters nearly always refer to themselves using county names—for example, the Cumberland County Chapter of East Tennessee. Chapters can be formed when an already existing community group formally applies to SOCM to become a chapter or when an unorganized group takes on a politically charged issue and looks to SOCM for assistance. Official chapters have a facilitator or chairperson who is also responsible for appointing members to various subcommittees that comprise the larger SOCM organization. Although the staff is discouraged from directly influencing the decision-making processes of the group, SOCM's board of directors works closely with the executive director, who holds a paid position.

In terms of organizing accomplishments, both SOCM and KFTC have been highly successful. In 1973, only a year after SOCM was formed, the group's members succeeded in raising the severance tax on the coal industry from 10 cents per ton to 20 cents per ton. In 1986,after officially becoming a "multi-issue organization," SOCM was able to convince Governor Lamar Alexander to veto plans for a high-level radioactive waste storage facility in the Oak Ridge, Tennessee, area. During the 1990s, the group was able to convince state officials to monitor better the impact of forest clear-cutting on both private and public lands. And in 2000, SOCM won a ten-year battle to protect Fall Creek Falls State Park from acid mine drainage after the Department of Interior's Office of Surface Mining upheld the group's "Land Unsuitable for Mining" petition. In fact, Secretary of the Interior Bruce Babbitt made the public announcement at the state park, further legitimizing the hard work of the SOCM organization.

In Kentucky, KFTC has had similar successes, including changing the state constitution in order to stop the use of the Broad-form Deed, a document that legally awarded all mineral rights to coal companies. Under Kentucky law, companies with broad-form deeds "could legally strip-mine without permission to within 300 feet of the surface-property owner's house, and the surface owner's rights were subservient to the mineral owner's."[18] Working with state legislators, in 1984 KFTC members helped pass a law forbidding the strip-mining of private land without surface owner consent. This law had little immediate effect, however, as the state continued to issue strip-mine permits to coal companies holding broad-form deeds. KFTC then sued the state, which contended that the new law was unconstitutional. In mid-1987 the Kentucky Supreme Court overturned the law, again giving coal companies the legal right to destroy indiscriminately the property of surface owners.[19]

---

[18] Kristan Szakos, "People Power: Working for the Future in the East Kentucky Coalfields," in John Gaventa, Barbara Ellen Smith, Alex Willingham, eds., *Communities in Economic Crisis: Appalachia and the South* (Philadelphia: Temple University Press, 1990) 34.

[19] Maynard Tetreault, "Broad Form Deeds in Kentucky: A Chronology," *Balancing the Scales*, 20 October 1988, 2–3.

In response to the state's actions, KFTC members helped to introduce and subsequently promote a state constitutional amendment—amendment 2—that would limit coal extraction under the type of mining in existence at the time broad-form deeds were first signed. As Catholic priest Maynard Tetreault has found, strip-mining was essentially nonexistent prior to 1945, as underground mining was the most common method of coal extraction in the region at the time broad-form deeds were signed by landowners. KFTC's constitutional amendment, if passed, would have provided landowners with the same protection found in the law of 1984. Although the bill quickly passed in the General Assembly, it required a majority of the popular vote in order to become state law. Because of this fact, KFTC had to launch an aggressive grassroots campaign in order to convince both coal interests and the general population living outside rural eastern Kentucky that broad-form deed practices should be abolished. After producing a series of television and radio advertisements, KFTC members set up information booths at county fairs and festivals and held bake sales at local supermarkets to raise additional funds and increase issue awareness. In the 1988 November election, amendment 2 received 82 percent of the popular vote, winning in all of Kentucky's 120 counties, despite a $500,000 media campaign by the coal industry to defeat the amendment's passage.[20]

In the same year, KFTC was equally successful in changing state tax laws to force larger coal companies to pay a more equitable share of local county taxes. In 1978, for example, Martin County, Kentucky, one of the poorest counties in the US, received only $76 worth of taxes from the top mineral owner Pocahontas Kentucky, whose property was collectively valued at $7.6 million.[21] Although the Appalachian Regional Commission saw untaxed minerals as a "non-issue" in 1988, KFTC was able to introduce and pass an unmined minerals tax bill in a legislature that had for a century been dominated by a powerful coal lobby. The passage of the bill allowed local governments and school districts to tax the mineral wealth of absentee

[20] "It's Time for a Change in Kentucky, Say KFTC Members Working for Passage of Broad-form Deed Amendment," *Balancing the Scales*, 20 October 1988, 1; "Eighty-two Percent of Kentucky Voters Say YES to Broad form Deed Amendment," *Balancing the Scales*, 17 November 1988, 1, 5.

[21] Appalachian Land Ownership Task Force, *Who Owns Appalachia?: Land Ownership and Its Impact* (Lexington: University Press of Kentucky, 1983) 49.

coal corporations as property tax in order to receive badly needed revenues for their nearly bankrupt educational system.[22]

During the 1990s, both KFTC and SOCM also began to fight the dumping of hazardous waste in rural and urban areas and were successful in halting the placement of a number of toxic landfills and incinerators in their respective states. In 1990, SOCM was able to delay and eventually stop the construction of a proposed landfill in the Oliver Springs community after group members challenged the state's permitting process. In 2001, KFTC was successful in saving a historic mountain pass in eastern Kentucky after Columbia Natural Resources proposed building a 26-mile natural gas pipeline through Letcher and Knott counties.

Believing in the power of ordinary citizens working together to challenge injustices, both KFTC and SOCM have obviously improved the quality of life for those living in the mountain region. Many Appalachian communities remain unorganized, however, and do not have the necessary resources or political power to influence state or local governments. Throughout rural Appalachia, political institutions remain an obstacle to many grassroots efforts, especially for communities trying to influence the direction of economic development. Unfortunately, economic development is most often controlled by enterprising local elites who indiscriminately recruit industry to rural areas in order to further their individual self-interests. Moreover, in the current climate of global competitiveness, industry recruiters must increasingly look to foreign sources of capital, making the likelihood of their success relatively low. In fact, the general failure of the "chasing smokestacks" approach to economic development has led to a number of individuals in the Appalachian region to call for "development from within"; that is, the promotion of development projects that would help foster local economic growth. The idea is to link economic development with grassroots participation and to build upon local knowledge and culture as opposed to embracing technical knowledge and outside expertise. One Appalachian community embracing this alternative economic model is Ivanhoe, Virginia.[23]

---

[22] Szakos, "People Power," 31–32.

[23] Stephen Fisher,"National Economic Renewal Programs and their Implications for Appalachia and the South," in John Gaventa, Barbara Smith, and Alex Willingham, eds., *Communities in Economic Crisis: Appalachian and the South* (Philadelphia: Temple University Press, 1989) 263–78.

The town of Ivanhoe is located on the border of Wythe and Carroll counties, two of southwest Virginia's poorest rural counties. For nearly a century, as Noah Adams has reminded us in his book *Far Appalachia*, Ivanhoe was a prosperous mining center, rich in iron, lead, zinc, and manganese deposits. Both National Carbide and the New Jersey Zinc Company were located in Ivanhoe during its boom days of the 1940s. At that time, the town's population exceeded 4,000 residents, and the community supported a railroad, school, hotel, theater, and restaurant. The town lost its high school in 1953 and its elementary school several years later. In 1966, National Carbide closed, leaving 450 residents without jobs. New Jersey Zinc closed in 1981, at which time the firm employed more than 350 people. Additional plant closings in the surrounding area left the town economically devastated by the mid-1980s. Further out-migration reduced the population to 1,300, and the town no longer has a school, theater, railroad, or store. Employment opportunities became limited for Ivanhoe residents, and those who did find work commuted an average of 63 miles often to low-paying jobs.[24]

In 1986, local citizens formed the Ivanhoe Civic League in order to stop the Wythe and Carroll county governments from selling an abandoned industrial park located in the township. The industrial park, as local residents explain it, "had been left to the local industrial development authorities twenty years earlier, when National Carbide, long the town's major employer, closed down its operation. The announcement that the property was for sale was the signal that local economic development officials were giving up all hope of locating another industry for the community." In response, the civic league started a grassroots initiative to stop the county government from selling the industrial park and to recruit outside industry themselves. Their efforts made national news, including an emotional "Hands Across Ivanhoe" event in which 3,000 people paid three dollars to hold hands in support of their community.[25]

In the same year, local industrial development authorities agreed not to sell the park for two years in order to give the league time to recruit new

---

[24] Noah Adams, *Far Appalachia: Following the New River North* (New York: Delacourte Press, 2001); Donald P. Baker, "Virginia Town Staves Off Disaster," *Washington Post*, 12 February 1984, B7.

[25] Mary Hinsdale, Helen Lewis, and Maxine Waller, *It Comes from the People: Community Development and Local Theology* (Philadelphia: Temple University Press, 1990) 7–23.

industry to the park. As the league began a vigorous campaign to bring jobs to the community, county developers steered potentially interested industries away from Ivanhoe to newer growth areas along the county's main interstates. After several failed attempts at securing new industries to the park, the citizens began exploring other alternatives, focusing instead on smaller development projects. During the first summer, league members and community volunteers cleaned up land along the New River, where the park is located. The civic league named the land Jubilee Park and began a campaign to secure it for a permanent recreation park that would be community-owned and operated. The park would have camping facilities, bike and raft rentals, and a convenience store providing both jobs and recreation for the community. The league hoped to use income from the recreation project to finance further economic development.[26]

Local authorities resisted Ivanhoe's efforts, refusing to count Jubilee Park as "industry." Schooled in traditional economic development approaches, the authorities would not allow the civic league to lease or buy the land. During public hearings, local authorities were often condescending to residents, giving development experts and authorities priority in the decision-making process. As a result of their oppositional encounters with local government, the league began focusing on other community development programs based on their own needs and resources. They organized a senior citizens and youth recreation program and began literacy education classes. The league renovated the town's old company store and created a community-controlled education center where college extension classes could be held. Participants in the extension classes later began researching the town's history and published a well-documented, two-volume community history of Ivanhoe and the surrounding area. All of these organizing activities utilized the local knowledge of the residents and helped maintain their cultural heritage and identity. In sum, the civic league worked toward creating a new model of community development, one that is self-sufficient, locally based, and grassroots controlled.

Rural Policy: Limitations and Possibilities

Grassroots initiatives like those undertaken by SOCM, KFTC, and the Ivanhoe Civic League clearly question the logic of conventional planning and development models. Traditional rural planning and development

---

[26] Ibid., 23–61.

emphasizes the necessity of infrastructure that engages the state in the physical construction of dams, roads, and sewage systems or employs itself in the often indiscriminate recruitment of industry. As I have consistently argued, infrastructure development models such as those promoted by TVA, ARC, and other development agencies neither actively engage the grassroots in policy formation nor provide long-term solutions to rural poverty and underdevelopment. When managed by community or state elites, industrial development is little more than the practice of writing off a company's relocation expenditures in exchange for the promise of new jobs or increased tax revenues. However, as many studies of rural industrial recruitment have shown, this development strategy does not always ensure quality jobs for local residents or substantially increased tax revenues for local governments. Ivanhoe residents were able to go beyond the goals of industrial development, providing workable alternatives to the traditional development model while simultaneously preserving local knowledge and culture.

Appalachian citizens' groups like KFTC, SOCM, and the Ivanhoe Civic League and voluntary citizens' initiatives are effectively altering state policy and structure, creating the necessary preconditions for larger societal change. By participating in the formation of government policy, grassroots movements are altering the political process while simultaneously holding the modern state to its democratic promise. Obviously, the actual political role of grassroots movements in a rural region depends ultimately on the form and function of the state in that area. However, as we have seen, the state is seldom so monolithic or functionally hegemonic that an organized and active citizenry cannot alter its planning agendas. KFTC, in drafting and passing state legislation, was able to change mining policies that had existed in the state for more than a century. SOCM, in actively demonstrating against a proposed landfill, convinced local government to stop the construction of the landfill while simultaneously challenging the state's permitting process. These movement activities are thus not merely isolated instances or random, self-interested actions, illustrating the contribution grassroots organizations can offer in the development of future rural policy.

The potential for grassroots participation in government policy should not be underestimated. However, a variety of political constraints and economic pressures will continue to exert influence over rural populations, restricting their full inclusion in the decision-making processes of development policy. In Appalachia and around the globe, major social and economic changes are taking place as more and more local and regional markets are incorporated into the international global economy.

In many rural areas, particularly in the United States and other developed countries, deindustrialization threatens to destroy many rural communities dependent on industrial manufacturing. Major technological advances in genetic engineering also threaten to destroy indigenous agriculture practices as well as alter agricultural production cycles in the first world. In many rural communities, especially those having a history of gross power inequities, rural groups still face the basic obstacles of violence, intimidation, and lack of resources when they attempt to organize. All of these factors call for an enhanced awareness of the social and economic problems confronting rural areas and a better appreciation for the political complexities rural people must face when confronting state policy.

The limitations and challenges facing the new citizens' movements in rural areas are indeed numerous. The first is the difficulty of local efforts to address fully underlying problems that are regional, national, and international in scope. For this reason, grassroots movements need to develop organizations that will work across sectoral lines and geographic boundaries. Evidence indicates this is an organizational possibility; in the GATT negotiations, local farmers from central and eastern Kentucky joined thousands of other farmers in Brussels to protest proposed GATT policy. At free-trade hearings in Atlanta, rural workers from Tennessee testified about how their poverty was directly affected by the rise of the Maquiladora industries in northern Mexico. In many rural community organizations, there is a growing awareness of the international scope of "local" problems.

A second limitation faced by grassroots movements is whether the actions at the local level represent victories that ultimately challenge the underlying structures of power and inequality. There is a tendency in community organizing to focus on "winnable issues" as a vehicle for building the organization's grassroots base and level of participation. For example, do the reported successes of a single community organization like KFTC or SOCM ensure that economic and social justice has prevailed across the region? Is passing a bill in the state legislature a cause for celebration if the law is unenforceable at the local level? To focus only on what is winnable also forces many grassroots groups to ignore what is both possible and necessary to promote widespread systemic change. The key question to ask these organizations is how their immediate actions will help build a broader social vision for all rural areas.

A third challenge of rural citizens' movements in the region is simply organizational survival. Although I have focused on several success stories, many other citizens' organizations have failed both politically and organizationally. Failures at the grassroots level in the 1980s are directly related to changes in policy and rhetoric at the national level. The decline of Keynesianism during the 1980s produced a sharp decline in the levels of funding for "self-help" and other citizen participation initiatives. Perhaps more importantly, the national conservatism of the 1980s led to a retreat from the rhetoric and ideology of support for citizen participation in public policy, a decline in support for citizen advocacy, and a greater emphasis by governments and funding agencies on approaching rural problems through technical and intermediary strategies or organizations.

Moreover, federal spending policies have themselves shifted from an emphasis on developing rural communities to ones favoring larger metropolitan areas. Rural sociologists Cornelia and Jan Flora, who have analyzed shifts in federal spending, report that during the 1980s per capita federal domestic and military spending rose substantially more rapidly in metropolitan areas than in non-metropolitan areas. Farm program payments to the largest non-family type farms have also grown substantially, and discretionary non-military spending, while declining only modestly in metropolitan areas, has decreased precipitously in non-metropolitan areas. These and other anti-rural policies of the federal government—e.g., tax laws favoring capital-intensive urban and suburban development—severely limit the political and economic options of rural communities undergoing financial hardship.[27]

The decline in a national rhetoric that legitimizes grassroots social action has perhaps contributed inattention to problems of power and reprisal rural citizens face when they do organize. Citizens who speak out against a community's major employer or industry might suffer physical reprisals, ranging from beatings to house burnings. Violation of the free speech and civil rights of rural activists, often thought to be an issue only of the prior labor or civil rights movements, continues to persist. With the increased mobility of capital and the related decline of rural economies, economic blackmail often serves to silence political dissent. The threat of plant closings in the face of citizen or worker demands and the promise of jobs in response to community concessions or silence are effective tools of

---

[27] Cornelia Flora and Jan Flora, "Rural Area Development: The Impact of Change," *Forum for Applied Research and Public Policy* (Fall 1989): 50–52.

power against those who might otherwise challenge the status quo in rural Appalachia.

Perhaps a less obvious constraint on grassroots participation in rural policy is the university, as there is an enormous knowledge gap between what appears in the academic literature and what occurs in the daily lives and struggles of rural people. I am struck, for instance, by the lack of significant critical studies on the impact of the state on the everyday life of the rural poor, especially in non-farm areas.

To the extent that most scholars fail to analyze critically the impact of the state and corporate capital on rural people in Appalachia and elsewhere, and to the extent that the successful actions of grassroots groups continue to be invisible in the academic disciplines, then universities are also part of the bias against grassroots mobilization. The simple recognition of grassroots movements by researchers would help grassroots organizations in the region gain the political legitimacy they need to become important players in policy formation. Scholarly investigations and documentation of grassroots activities could therefore assist community organizations in their battle of legitimacy with politicians, the state, and research institutions, as well as provide important knowledge about the growth and development of Appalachian social movements.

Chapter 11

Before Albion's Seed

Scholars studying Appalachia largely ignore the 300 years of human history that preceded the eighteenth-century frontier. Most who have written about the settlement of the southern mountains have not recognized the important contributions the Mississippians, Cherokees, and even Spanish made to the history of the region. While specific European skills and Old World land-use practices were certainly important to the settlement and social development of the region, Europeans settled lands that already had a long history of human habitation. The Appalachian environment created new and difficult challenges for the settlers. In the southern mountains, culture evolved in relationship to both social and environmental influences.

Major Periods of Cultural Change

The process of culture formation and change is a complex phenomenon. In the southern Appalachians, we find no fewer than three major periods of cultural change prior to 1820. The Spanish started the process during the sixteenth century, introducing important new crops and initiating trade in furs and other goods. The Spanish also brought deadly microbes into the region, destroying a large percentage of the native Mississippian population. The social chaos that resulted forced native peoples to migrate both to and from the area, weakening traditional cultural traditions and practices. Within a century, pre-Columbian Mississippian life had all but vanished from the Appalachian South.[1]

---

[1] Marvin Smith, *Archaeology of Aboriginal Culture Change in the Interior Southeast: Depopulation During the Early Historic Period* (Gainesville: University of Florida Press,

The second period of social and environmental change occurred after the English and French initiated trade with the Cherokees during the early part of the eighteenth century. Initially the Cherokees saw the fur trade as beneficial to their people, and participation in it was not necessarily discouraged. As game became scarce, the Cherokees became more and more dependent on English goods for their sustenance. Debts were often paid in large tracts of land, which further decreased their access to wild game.

Fur traders became the first Europeans to live actively among the Cherokees, and their presence in the region had a profound influence on the lives of the natives. Fur traders married Cherokee women and introduced cattle and hogs into the surrounding countryside. When the French encouraged Cherokee warriors to fight against the British in the 1760s, English armies retaliated by destroying Cherokee dwellings and grain supplies. As a result of these losses, natives found it harder to maintain their traditional cultural practices.[2]

White settlement of the region represents the third and final era of cultural (as well as ecological) change in the southern mountains for this period. As early as 1745, Europeans cleared and settled land in what is today southwest Virginia. However, Cherokee control of the mountains made it difficult for settlers to push deeper into the area until after the Revolutionary War. The first settlers to the region were mostly of English, Scots-Irish, or German extraction, and they brought a variety of European grasses, plants, and livestock with them. Many introduced plants, particularly weeds and grasses, flourished in the rich soils of the mountain river valleys, overtaking some indigenous species. As timber was cut for fences, dwellings, and pasture, more and more openings appeared in the mountain forest. By 1820 only the most remote mountain coves and ridge tops had not been settled by whites.

Because Cherokees continued to occupy the region throughout the frontier period, Native American influence on mountain culture remained significant. When many Old World crops proved unproductive in mountain soils, settlers began cultivating native Cherokee varieties. Corn, pumpkins,

---

1987); Charles Hudson and Carman Chaves, eds., *The Forgotten Centuries: Indians and Europeans in the American South* (Athens: University of Georgia Press, 1994).

   [2] Mary Rothrock, "Carolina Traders Among the Overhill Cherokee, 1690–1760," *East Tennessee Historical Society's Publications* 1 (1929): 3–18; Thomas Hatley, *The Dividing Paths: Cherokee and South Carolinians through the Year of Revolution* (New York: Oxford University Press, 1993) 230–35.

squash, gourds, beans, and melons became popular among the white settlers, as did Cherokee preservation methods. Hunting and fishing techniques were also routinely borrowed from the natives. Pioneer women adopted Cherokee use of medicinal herbs and soon were making home remedies in a similar manner. Likewise, Cherokee women learned how to milk dairy cows, tend poultry flocks, and spin and weave European fabrics. Since some of the invading plants (such as upland cresses) brought by the settlers also became popular with Cherokees, and since some native crops were critical to settlers, it is clear that cultural change after European contact went both ways.

The three seemingly distinct historical periods did not occur in isolation of each other. Peaches, watermelons, and sweet potatoes, all Spanish-introduced crops of the seventeenth century, became central to the diets of the Cherokees and later became important to the first European settlers. The building of weir-dam fish traps, a common subsistence practice of the Mississippians, was taken up by the Cherokees and later the first pioneer settlers. In fact, the early Cherokees inherited a considerable amount of material culture from the Mississippians, including wattle and daub building construction and the making of cane mats and baskets. Cherokees preferred sites formerly inhabited by the Mississippian Indians, and settlers regularly sought out lands farmed by the Cherokees.[3]

Settlement Patterns

Rivers played an important role in the early settlement history of the region. The Mississippians, Cherokees, and eighteenth-century white settlers all chose to live along rivers, largely because the alluvial soils of river bottoms were easy to cultivate and adjacent canebrakes provided winter fodder for cattle and hogs. Rivers provided transportation networks for canoes and keelboats and water power for grist- and sawmills. Site selection obviously changed from century to century, since each social group preferred some locations to others. During the sixteenth century, Mississippians preferred to settle along the largest rivers of the region, so the majority of villages were found either in the Ridge and Valley or Blue

[3] Gary Goodwin, *Cherokees in Transition: A Study of Changing Culture and Environment Prior to 1775* (Chicago: University of Chicago, Department of Geography, 1977); Donald E. Davis, "Where There Be Mountains: Environmental and Cultural Change in the Appalachian South, 1500–1800," Ph.D. diss., University of Tennessee, Knoxville, 1993.

Ridge provinces of southern Appalachia. Archaeologist Roy Dickens, for example, recorded the existence of more than 300 Mississippian sites in the Blue Ridge province of western North Carolina, all along sizable mountain streams. On the Cumberland Plateau, Mississippian occupation was somewhat less prevalent, although sizable villages were certainly present along the Cumberland and Kanawha rivers. The largest Mississippian townships, however, were those located in east Tennessee and north Georgia, in the southern end of the mountain region. Here the soils of the Ridge and Valley were suited for corn and bean production, and the proximity to the slower-moving rivers provided convenient access to fish, mussels, and waterfowl. Because the Mississippian settlement pattern was generally organized around a large central chiefdom, distances between villages were often large.[4]

The Spanish displacement of the Mississippians through warfare and the spread of disease no doubt greatly altered the social organization and settlement pattern of the region. The Cherokees, who moved into the area, occupied former Mississippian village sites and established new ones as well. Cherokee social organization was less centralized and the group's numerous villages much smaller. The Cherokees spread out linearly along rivers, generally in close proximity to one another and often on the same river, stream, or watershed. As populations increased during the seventeenth century, the Cherokees occupied more and more river systems. On the Tuckaseegee River in western North Carolina, for example, five Cherokee towns existed along a single 30-mile stretch of the river. Cherokees also burned the woods, leaving numerous clearings and adjoining canebrakes that provided important browse for livestock.[5]

The fur traders and first frontier settlers gravitated toward Cherokee villages, which were nearly always found along level river bottoms where the soil was most productive. Because bottomlands of the largest rivers were the first areas occupied, smaller streams became the preferred destination of later arrivals. Gristmills, used to grind grain into meal and flour, were erected along these creeks and rivers and served as important centers of

---

[4] Roy Dickens, "Mississippian Settlement Patterns in the Appalachian Summit Area: The Pisgah and Qualla Phases," in Bruce D. Smith, ed., *Mississippian Settlement Patterns* (New York: Academic Press, 1978) 115–39.

[5] Bard Alan Bays, "The Historical Geography of Cattle Herding Among the Cherokee Indians, 1761–1861" (Master's thesis, University of Tennessee, Knoxville, 1991).

commercial activity. Those who could not find or afford land along streams built homesteads near small springs or, as a last resort, settled away from water on hillsides and ridge tops. The major role the Ridge and Valley and Blue Ridge played in the early settlement history of Appalachia can be partly explained by the fact that the largest rivers are found in these two subregions.

The Role of External Forces

Prior to the sixteenth century, the Appalachian South remained largely outside the world economic system. From the sixteenth century on, population pressures, warfare, land scarcity, and external economic relations have all had a major impact on the settlement of the region. The desire for gold and silver brought the Spanish to the area, the fur trade brought the fur trader, and many European settlers came seeking refuge from servile living conditions in the Old World. Soon the native population felt the effects of an expanding global economy. By the early seventeenth century, the natives were trading in furs, albeit largely through middlemen to the south; some Old World crops from Europe and Africa had been introduced into the mountains; and thousands of natives had perished from introduced diseases. As the Mississippian case demonstrates, world commerce and trade profoundly affected the culture and ecology of the region as early as the seventeenth century.

During the eighteenth century, the Cherokees were drawn even deeper into world economic relations. By the early 1700s, Charleston had become an important center of trade, exporting skins, ginseng, and other commodities from the region to the European continent. Initially, Cherokee participation in the fur trade changed the people's lives relatively little. Hunting deer had long been part of their traditional culture, and the killing of surplus animals did not immediately bring significant changes to their lives. The Cherokees bartered furs for weapons, tools, and other Europeans goods, and they largely controlled the rate of exchange. In the 1720s, as competition for furs increased, traders made permanent settlements in the area, enticing the Cherokees into acquiring more skins by offering them durable fabrics, colorful glass beads, and alcohol. Because of their close proximity to Charleston, Cherokees living in the southern Blue Ridge were the first to engage in the trade networks and to experience the resulting ecological changes.

As their participation in the fur trade increased, Cherokees began to lose skills such as the making of bows and arrows and the crafting of stone celts and arrowheads; they became increasingly dependent on European weapons and ammunition (which could only be obtained by killing more deer). As deer became harder to find locally, the Cherokee people had to make longer excursions into the upland forests in order to supply their villages with meat and skins. In 1760, after relations between the Cherokees and the English—the primary purchaser of southern Appalachian furs—became strained, the two groups engaged in warfare. The British were largely successful in defeating the Cherokees, destroying their most valuable orchards, granaries, and croplands. The British victory ensured the acquisition of thousands of acres of prime Cherokee hunting land, leaving the native population even more dependent on Europeans for their sustenance.[6]

Extraction of natural resources for European markets did not by any means cease with white settlement. Fur trappers and long hunters (frontiersmen who traveled long distances to hunt game) in direct competition with the Cherokees, traded elk, buffalo, deer, and beaver skins to exporters from Charleston, Augusta, and Savannah. Frontier settlers also collected and sold ginseng, which was shipped to France and then China. Because overland travel across the mountain region was often difficult, river settlements became important outposts for commercial trade. On the Cumberland Plateau, products were regularly sent down the Cumberland River to shipping ports as far away as New Orleans. From there, goods from the southern mountains might find their way to the Caribbean, Spain, England, France, or even Asia.[7]

Process of Cultural Change

While external economic forces were powerful in shaping the subsistence culture of the Appalachian region, they do not tell us everything about the process of cultural change. Despite devastating military defeats, the Cherokees retained agency in governing their affairs. For the Cherokees, cultural change involved both proactive and reactive responses to outside

[6] Samuel Cole Williams, *Lieutenant Henry Timberlake's Memoirs, 1756–1765* (Johnson City TN: Watauga Press, 1927); Samuel Cole Williams, *Early Travels in the Tennessee Country, 1540–1800* (Johnson City TN: Watauga Press, 1928).

[7] John Otto, *The Southern Frontiers, 1607–1860: The Agricultural Evolution of the Colonial and Antebellum South* (New York: Greenwood Press, 1989).

forces. When Cherokees briefly became political allies of the French in the early 1760s, they were partially directing the course of world trade. Cherokee factions always resented European presence in the region. One example is Chief Dragging Canoe, who fought to his death to save his homeland from white settlement. Cherokee women—devoted agriculturalists, basket makers, and weavers of native fabrics—maintain many of these cultural traditions even today. Appalachia was, in many ways, a "middle ground," a place historian Richard White has described as "between cultures, peoples, and in between empires...the area between the historical foreground of European invasion and occupation and the background of Indian defeat and retreat."[8]

From my own perspective, cultural change in Appalachia was a syncretic process. No single culture group avoided absorbing aspects of the other. The Spanish armies of De Soto and Pardo survived excursions into the Appalachian backcountry by eating Indian corn, a New World crop that quickly became the agricultural mainstay of the Iberian Peninsula. The Cherokees eventually adopted the practice of raising cattle, and the white Europeans borrowed a great number of subsistence techniques from the Cherokees. Unlike the one-dimensional acculturation theories of David Hackett Fischer[9] and others, cultural syncretism suggests that all culture groups, not only subordinate ones, share in the process of cultural change.

Proponents of syncretism focus attention almost entirely on social relationships; that is, on the cultural dynamics that occur between two or more groups. But often the physical environment remains the fulcrum upon which cultural identity rests. As powerful as they may be, members of colonizing groups generally find themselves strangers in a strange land. Having little knowledge of their new surroundings, they rely heavily on the ecological knowledge of native peoples, which, in turn, changes the nature of the relationship between the two groups. In helping to maintain the local economy of the native population, the environment, as long as it remains unchanged, provides cultural stability. Dependency on other groups increases only when access to environmental resources is severely restricted or denied. Ecological forces are equally important to the cultural change

[8] Richard White, *Middle Ground: Indians, Empires, and Republics in the Great Lakes Region, 1650–1815* (New York: Cambridge University Press, 1991) x.
[9] David Hackett Fischer, *Albion's Seed: Four British Folkways in America* (New York: Oxford University Press, 1990).

equation. In the southern mountains culture did not arise in a social vacuum; it was the product of both human history and natural history.

Before European contact, the living landscape of the region was less a resource to be consumed than a matrix for sustaining individual and community life. Prior to the fur trade, frontier settlement, and nineteenth-century industrialization, the Appalachian environment was something to which one adapted, not something one radically changed to fit one's own image. Pre-contact Mississippians and Cherokees found ways of changing the local landscape, but their subsistence methods did not, in the long view, vastly alter the ecology of the region. This is not to say they didn't have an impact on the environment but that, more accurately, the impact differed from that of the Europeans. Human beings have been altering the environment in the southern mountains for the last 10,000 years. It is the *magnitude* of the interaction that ultimately affects the degree and rate of environmental change.

In the final analysis, culture must be viewed as a product of both social and environmental forces. By emphasizing the environment in our cultural investigation, a more complex story of social evolution and environmental change is told. Culture is never simply the outcome of social *and* environmental forces: it is, more accurately, the product of complex interactions between the two. When humans and the environment came together in the southern mountains, each influenced the other.

Chapter 12

The Forest for the Trees

During the 1990s, for the first time in its history, the United States Forest Service assessed the entire southern Appalachians in order to determine how these federal lands should be ultimately managed. Completed after the turn of the twenty-first century, their assessment was intended to produce a series of farsighted management plans for the entire region. This was the stated hope, but those who have been involved in grassroots environmental groups remain skeptical. Efforts at public participation and input into the process at this juncture seem like formalities. In the interim, timber harvesting on national forest land continues, and if newly proposed federal legislation is passed, it will actually increase in the near future.

Excessive timber harvesting, clear-cutting, and road building have taken their toll on public lands in the southern Appalachian region, an area comprising more than 2.6 million acres in five states. Native biological diversity has also suffered considerably, forcing local residents and community groups to begin challenging US Forest Service activities in the region's six national forests. More than a dozen organized groups are active in the mountain region, including the Western North Carolina Alliance, an 800-member organization based in Asheville, North Carolina. In fact, the Southern Appalachian Forest Coalition, a consortium of member groups that includes the Southern Environmental Law Center, Georgia Forestwatch, and the Bankhead Monitor of northern Alabama, was formed during the late 1990s to help coordinate the groups' activities within the larger Appalachian region.

The rise in local opposition to timber harvesting on federal lands is understandable for a variety of reasons, several of which are not directly related to current USFS timber management practices. As more private land is lost to commercial development, residents increasingly look to national forest land for outdoor and recreational use. In Georgia, for example, an estimated 300,000 acres is annually lost to development. In addition, environmental protests in northwestern U.S. have caused many private timber companies to look to the southeast as a new untapped resource. The population of the Appalachian region has also increased dramatically, in part due to a growing number of retirees who have moved to the area. These and other newcomers see timber harvesting of any kind as detrimental to the scenic beauty of the surrounding community, decreasing property values and ultimately jeopardizing, they believe, their quality of life.

In most communities in southern Appalachia, however, opposition to US Forest Service timber management practices centers on four basic issues: clear-cutting, the increase in pine species, excessive road building, and biodiversity. All of these concerns are somewhat interrelated, as discussed below. Data is drawn largely from US Forest Service documents, case studies of several of the opposing group's activities, internally generated newsletters and publications, and the author's own field experience as an organizer for the Armuchee Alliance, a citizen's group challenging USFS practices in the Chattahoochee National Forest of northwest Georgia.

Clear-cutting

Clear-cutting remains one of the most highly charged environmental concerns in the southern Appalachians. Like elsewhere in the US, public sentiment has consistently run high against clear-cutting large tracts of forests, despite persistent claims by the US Forest Service that the practice enhances wildlife habitat and species diversity. Many grassroots environmental groups in the region have been successful in curtailing both the number and size of clear-cuts on public lands, especially the Western North Carolina Alliance, whose work inspired the provocative Appalshop documentary *Ready for Harvest* (1994).

One of the main objectives to clear-cutting in the region, besides obvious unsightly effects on the mountain environment, is increased erosion caused by the subsequent loss of topsoil or duff material. After an area is cut, heavy rains literally wash tons of soil and debris into nearby streambeds. The increased siltation severely damages sensitive riparian environments, destroying trout and other game fish habitat. Proposed timber cuts on John's Mountain in northwest Georgia, for example, by the US Forest Service's own estimates, would produce 38 tons of siltation, most of which would likely end up in nearby East Armuchee Creek. Because of the potential hazard of these cuts to the stream, the Armuchee Alliance formally appealed the timber sale, largely on the grounds that soil erosion would destroy habitat for the native Coosa bass, a threatened species, and several federally endangered freshwater mussels. In response to the Armuchee Alliance's appeal, the US Forest Service formally withdrew the sale until further biological evaluations could be done at the site in order to determine the long-term effects of the timber harvest on these unique aquatic species. Several protected freshwater mussels were discovered as a result of the biological evaluations, which further limited the size of the timber sale.

Because of efforts like those of the Armuchee Alliance and other grassroots environmental groups in the region, the US Forest Service has started phasing out large clear-cuts as a method of timber harvest. In most Forest Service ranger districts in the southern Appalachians, clear-cuts are becoming the exception rather than the rule. In addition, the size of a single clear-cut may no longer exceed 40 contiguous acres, and protective buffer zones are now left between harvested stands. In place of clear-cuts, the federal agency now employs shelter-wood and seed-tree cuts, harvesting methods less environmentally destructive but still problematic for mountain ecosystems.

In fact, many opposing groups argue that shelter-wood and seed-tree cuts are simply clear-cuts by another name. Although more trees are left per acre, many of the remaining trees die from increased exposure to sunlight or succumb to root damage caused by heavy logging machinery. In other instances, herbicides are injected directly into the remaining seed trees in order to allow shade-intolerant seedlings to grow. The Appalachian Forest Organizing Project, a recently emerged coalition of grassroots citizens' groups in the region, believes the evidence against shelter-wood cutting is strong enough to demand the termination of the harvesting method in three of the region's six national forests.

Never a Lonesome Pine

As presently implemented by the US Forest Service, clear-cutting, shelter-wood cuts, and seed-tree cuts all favor the regeneration of successional species such as loblolly, shortleaf, and white pine—shade-intolerant trees that need sun exposure to grow. In many areas where full-scale commercial logging operations devastated the region at the turn of the nineteenth century, the number of pine stands has increased considerably. In the 1990s, as these second-growth stands were cut once again, pines returned in even greater numbers, further reducing the number of hardwood species and thus the native diversity of the Appalachian forests.

Because pine is a far more merchantable timber with a variety of commercial uses, most Forest Service management practices are biased toward pine regeneration. In the majority of seed-tree cuts and clear-cuts, loblolly or shortleaf pine species are manually replanted in 8-to-12-foot intervals. The area is often then treated with chemical fertilizers, since loss of duff and topsoil reduces nitrogen levels in the remaining soil base. Southern pines grow rapidly, however, surviving in drier, lower-quality soils. In fifteen years, the trees can be harvested for pulpwood; in thirty years, they are merchantable saw timber.

Since most hardwoods do not tolerate a great deal of direct sunlight, they have much more difficulty growing in cut areas. Hardwoods do, however, grow on logging sites from sprouts that spontaneously generate from remaining stumps. When this occurs, the stumps are either sprayed with herbicides to "release" the pines, thus killing hardwoods, or they simply grow unattended, scattered among the pine seedlings. Groups like the Chattooga River Watershed Coalition in northeast Georgia contend that stump-regenerated hardwoods are inferior, slow-growing specimens with bent or multiple trunks. The "trees" seldom grow to maximum heights and are often too irregular to be used by local sawmills.

Pine regeneration also reduces mast production—acorns and hickory nuts that provide valuable food for game animals such as deer, turkey, and squirrels. This fact has created, in some of the local groups, an unlikely coalition between hunters and environmentalists. Both oppose pine mono-cropping on the grounds that game animal populations will suffer. While timber harvests do produce important browse materials like grasses and soft mast in the short term, high mast production appears more vital to the long-term health of most game species. White-tailed deer, for example, reach their optimum size and weight in areas that have a continuous supply of acorns, possible only in areas where a variety of oak species exist.

The emphasis on pine timber management in southern Appalachian national forests is a surprisingly recent phenomenon, arising during the 1960s as large pulp and paper interests began moving to the region. Their goal was simple: turn a largely oak-hickory forest into a more easily managed corn-row pine plantation. Data on private timberlands in the southern Appalachians reveals that the industrial firms have successfully achieved their goal. The primary forest type is the loblolly/shortleaf forest, comprising more than 85 percent of all private timberlands in the region.

Because of demand from private timber companies, the trend toward pine regeneration has not slowed in southern Appalachian national forests. Aggregate data shows that 242,654 acres, or 11 percent of the region's national forest timberland, was in pine stands, and an additional 19.4 percent, or 433,177 acres, was in oak-pine stands at the turn of the twenty-first century. In individual ranger districts, however, large tracts of oak-hickory and oak-pine stands are being transformed into pure pine plantations. Within the 6,000-acre Johns Mountain Scenic Recreation in the Chattahoochee National Forest area in northwest Georgia, for example, more than 3,000 acres are already pure pine forests.

Timber Highways

Issues involving roads and road building are among the most controversial surrounding the management of our national forests. In order to harvest what would otherwise be inaccessible timber, the US Forest Service annually builds hundreds of miles of roadbed to logging sites. Not only are native wildflower stands and archaeological sites destroyed by the construction of these roads, but high road densities can also eliminate entire forest tracts from being considered wilderness areas, the only management designation that permanently restricts all logging practices.

Roads are also significant source of soil erosion, especially in the southern Appalachians where the terrain is steep and rainfall often excessive. At one proposed timber sale in the Armuchee Ranger District in northwest Georgia, siltation loads from road construction and subsequent timber harvests were estimated to reach more than 95 tons. Despite proposed mitigation measures, soil erosion from timbering operations nearly always has a major impact on surrounding riparian environments. In their formal appeal of the Dunaway Gap timber sale, members of the Armuchee Alliance noted that a single road crossing over East Armuchee Creek, a potential put-and-take trout stream, would destroy habitat for several threatened freshwater mussels endemic to the area, including the upland combshell, southern acornshell, and Coosa moccasinshell.

Roads cause major forest fragmentation, slicing up contiguous interior forest and creating more forest edge habitats. Roads also bring motorized vehicles, cause air and noise pollution, and squeeze native plant and animal species into increasingly smaller areas. Environmental groups like the Wilderness Society argue that road construction in southern Appalachian forests has caused the greatest environmental damage of any single US Forest Service activity. Believing that logging should be limited to existing roaded public lands, the Wilderness Society has asked for a moratorium on all new permanent road construction in the southern Appalachians.

Aside from destroying biological diversity and ruining scenic values in the region, roads are economically expensive to build and maintain. Under what is called internally a "purchaser credits" program, the building of US Forest Service roads is actually subsidized by US taxpayers. In essence, when a logging company purchases timber, the Forest Service deducts the price of road construction from the overall price of the timber. According to Forest Service spokespeople, this accounting process allows roads to be counted as a benefit rather than a loss because the road is used later after the timber has been harvested. On paper at least, the Forest Service gives the impression that they are making money selling timber when they are, in many instances, losing money. According to an important GAO report, the Chattahoochee-Oconee National Forest lost more than $1.1 million in 1994 from its timber sales program, due largely to excessive road construction.[1]

Biodiversity Loss

The national forests and national parks of the southern Appalachians are home to more than 80 percent of the vertebrates and plants native to the South. They support 61 globally rare vertebrates, 18 of which are listed by the US Fish and Wildlife Service as endangered or threatened, and 149 globally rare plants, 22 of which are federally listed. Without question, few regions in the North American temperate zone contain such biologically diverse flora and fauna as do the southern Appalachians. By some estimates, more than 100 tree species, 500 vertebrate species, and 2,000 higher plant species are native to the Blue Ridge Mountains alone.

---

[1] General Accounting Office, Forest Service, distribution of timber sales receipts, fiscal years 1992–1994, fact sheet for the Subcommittee on Interior and Related Agencies (Washington, DC: US Government Printing Office, September 1995) 1–6.

Managing forests for timber production and not for the health of the entire ecosystem is threatening the diversity of southern Appalachian forests. To preserve biodiversity, the Forest Service should focus more attention on protecting "old-growth" timber stands; that is, groups of trees that are 100-plus years old. Old-growth protection is critical not only because the resource is scarce, but also because of the biotic complexity often prevalent in these aging forest communities. The deep shade of 100-year-old tree stands produces rich moist soils, prime habitat for endemic lilies and orchids and for numerous rare salamander species. Presently, only 1.5 million acres of old-growth and potential old-growth timber stands exist across the entire southern Appalachians, less than 3 percent of the entire forest.

By managing timber using planned eighty-year rotations, southern Appalachian forests will never attain the biological complexity that develops with stand maturity. As a result, important animal species will suffer, including neo-tropical migrant songbirds and small mammal populations. By converting more and more mature forests into wide-open clearings, logging companies and the National Forest Service put black bear populations at risk, since this species requires maximum levels of forest isolation as well as large hardwoods for den trees. Cool, shady stream environments also protect freshwater mussels, rare fish, and numerous amphibian species found only in the southern Appalachians. Excessive emphasis on timber production will ultimately destroy these habitats, making the survival of native mountain ecosystems increasingly unlikely.

Despite the Forest Service's past emphasis on clear-cutting, road building, and pine plantation timber management, national forests and other public lands still offer the best option for protecting large blocks of wild lands in the southern Appalachians. Due to the increasing loss of forested acres on private timberlands, public lands provide the only viable habitat for many rare plants and mammals in the region. The US Forest Service should therefore consider the cumulative ecological effects of current timber management plans, reforming any silvicultural practice that does not ensure the long-term health of the forest. If managed solely for commercial tree production, southern Appalachia's national forests will become a biological desert, void not only of native plant and animal species, but of human beings as well.

Chapter 13

Living on the Land: Blue Ridge Life and Culture

Often celebrated for its unique natural history, the Blue Ridge Mountains are home to an equally unique cultural history. For more than 500 years, humans have lived in permanent settlements among the peaks and valleys of the physiographic province. The first peoples to inhabit the southern mountains in permanent settlements were the Mississippians. From AD 900 to 1200, Mississippian civilization in southern Appalachia developed into a network of state-like chiefdoms that reigned over the entire southern mountain region. What anthropologists generally call the Late Mississippian period began around AD 1200 with the introduction of eastern flint corn and the common pole bean into Mississippian agriculture.

At the time of first Spanish contact in 1540, the largest populations of Mississippians were found along slower-moving streams that drained the southern-most river valleys of the region. The Coosa township, a major Mississippian village located on the Coosawatee River near Carters, Georgia, probably maintained a population of 4,000 residents at its peak. Most Mississippian settlements in the mountain region were smaller, containing between 500 and 1,000 individuals.

Despite the fact that the native peoples of the region had a great deal in common, archaeologists tell us that Mississippians living in the Blue Ridge Mountains were not altogether culturally homogenous. Mississippians living in northeast Georgia and western North Carolina exhibited a culture known as Pisgah, whereas those living along the western edges of the Blue Ridge in

Tennessee are known as Mouse Creek and Lamar peoples. According to archaeologists, what distinguishes these culture groups from one another is largely the type of pottery made by each group. There is also some evidence that the groups spoke different languages and varied in their degree of social organization.

All Mississippians inhabiting the Blue Ridge made their settlements along the floodplains of meander-belt river bottoms. They established villages at these sites not only because of the availability of easily tilled alluvial soils, but also because of the sites' proximity to a large range of plant and animal life. Immersed within the floodplain ecosystem, Mississippians were able to utilize a variety of protein-rich fish and waterfowl species. The proximity to water also provided the Mississippians a route for their dugout canoes, which they used to transport food and other goods to distant villages upstream and downstream.

The environment of the floodplain river bottom also gave the Mississippians access to one of their most significant natural resources: river cane. The people used river cane, a bamboo-like reed that once grew abundantly in the Blue Ridge Mountains, for tools, arrow shafts, basketry, and dwelling construction. Throughout the mountains, Mississippian craftsmen constructed circular or rectangular dwellings by first placing small saplings firmly into the ground several inches apart. They then stabilized the framework by weaving additional saplings horizontally across the structure. Finally, they covered the walls with a thick cane lathing and a coating of tempered clay made with mud and crushed freshwater clamshells.

Perhaps most unique to Mississippian village sites were the large earthen platform mounds that were centrally located above the town's main plaza. The Estatoe Mound, located in Stephens County along the Chattooga River, is an example of a Mississippian platform mound. The Mississippians directed their public activity toward the structure built atop these mounds, a sacred temple that also served as the residence of the principle ruler. Because the sun played such an important role in the religious beliefs of the Mississippians, almost all temple mounds and the structures atop them had an eastward orientation toward the rising sun.

Not only did the environment of the Blue Ridge Mountains help shape the Mississippians' religious beliefs and practices, but the mountain ecosystem also influenced their daily activities. Archaeological and historical evidence has given us new and important insight concerning the use of the local environment by these fascinating native peoples.

Of course, the Mississippians were not the first native group to play a role in shaping the landscape of the Blue Ridge. Paleoecological evidence confirms human disturbance in the region over the last 12,000 years. The Mississippians did, however, intensify the rate of change. As villages increased in size and social complexity, additional clearing of land for settlement and cultivation became necessary in order to keep pace with the demands of a growing population. It is also likely that the Mississippians used fire to control the growth of underbrush around villages, a land-use practice that provided additional habitat for white-tailed deer, wild turkey, ruffed grouse, and bobwhite quail. However, burning the woods would have been restricted to riparian areas along river bottoms and would have not been regularly used in the surrounding uplands.

In addition to hunting large and small mammals in the near and distant forest, Mississippians fished the local streams and rivers. Freshwater fish, mussels, turtles, and migratory waterfowl were important to their subsistence base. They caught fish using a variety of ingeniously designed traps, the largest and most productive being the V-shaped weir dam built across streams and rivers. The size and shape of the dam forced moving fish downstream toward the narrow end of the weir, where strategically placed cane traps kept the fish from moving back upstream.

The American freshwater eel, a native fish that may weigh as much as 7 pounds and grow to 40 inches in length, was no doubt a frequent find in the fish traps of the Mississippians. Before the construction of hydroelectric dams, few obstacles blocked the migratory route of this species to saltwater spawning grounds. Prior to the twentieth century, American eels were fairly common as far upstream as the Chattooga and Tugaloo rivers.

The Mississippians also made use of abundant freshwater mussels. They preferred unios or quahogs, large mollusks that commonly reach 6 inches in length. These mussels were a readily available source of protein and were also the source of an important prestige good—the pearl. The Mississippians carved the opulent "mother-of-pearl" shell of the freshwater mussel into decorative gorgets, ear and body ornaments, and cylindrical beads for necklaces.

As important as shellfish and other specific animals were to the maintenance of the Mississippians' life and culture, the people utilized the entire range of available plant and animal life. The fish of the mountain rivers, the flora and fauna of the river-bottom terrain, and the birds had important roles in the Mississippians' daily subsistence activities. Of course, nature refused to give up her gifts all at once, so the Mississippians chose to organize their lives according to her seasonal rhythms. For example, early spring was the time for preparing garden plots and larger outfields. In late spring, the people gathered large numbers of wild mulberries and strawberries. Midsummer signaled the ripening of huckleberries and blueberries and the ceremonial harvest of green corn, beans, squash, and the seeds of the semi-domesticated sunflower, sumpweed, and chenopodium. Early fall was reserved for gathering late corn and storing hickory nuts and walnuts. After the first frost, Mississippians carried large quantities of chestnuts and persimmons out of the surrounding forest in river-cane baskets. In late fall and early winter, the hunting of game and the gathering firewood for winter use intensified. Each season brought a new harvest and a new task to be performed by the larger community.

Cherokee Mountains

As carriers of fatal epidemic diseases, De Soto and the other Spanish explorers who visited the Appalachian region during the sixteenth century were directly responsible for the decline and eventual demise of the Mississippians. According to one estimate, for every twenty Native Americans present in the southern United States at the time of De Soto's *entrada* into the Blue Ridge, only one survived. The Spanish invasion therefore influenced the social and cultural formation of the Cherokees, the Native Americans most often associated with the southern Appalachians.

Within a century after Spanish contact, the Mississippian culture group known as Pisgah had been transformed into a culture group known as Qualla—the ancestral peoples of the modern Cherokee. For most of the seventeenth century, the Qualla Cherokees continued many of the cultural practices of their Mississippian ancestors, including wattle-and-daub building construction. The early Qualla Cherokees probably included survivors from the Spanish conquest as well as Mississippian culture groups from the surrounding Blue Ridge Mountains and South Carolina Piedmont. By 1700, there were permanent Cherokee settlements among the Blue Ridge Mountains of northeast Georgia and western North Carolina.

Because of widespread Cherokee occupation, the Appalachian region remained an obstacle to permanent frontier settlement until well into the eighteenth century. But neither the lofty mountain peaks nor the Cherokees themselves could stop the white traders and trappers who entered the region from newly founded settlements on the East Coast. Europeans from the

Carolinas and Virginia traded with the Cherokees as early as the 1670s, exchanging tools, knives, glass beads, cloth, and axes for skins and pelts. By 1716, regular trade occurred between the Cherokees and the Europeans on the East Coast. By the middle of the eighteenth century, the Cherokees were fast becoming dependent on European goods.

The Cherokees quickly became fascinated by manufactured goods, and their desire for guns and metal tools encouraged additional traders to settle in the region. Hunting and trapping for beaver soon became a preoccupation of Cherokee men, who believed European guns might give them an advantage over neighboring tribes. The original white traders brought to the Carolina and Georgia upcountry cattle, hogs, poultry, tea, sugar, salt, liquor, and a number of European herbs and grasses. In the gardens and orchards surrounding their settlements, traders planted fruit trees and grew vegetables more familiar to their own families and culture. Within decades of their first entry into the region, they had introduced into the mountains of the Blue Ridge apples, Irish potatoes, onions, turnips, cabbage, and sorghum.

Initially, the traders worked primarily to obtain skins for the fur trade. Having depleted the deer and beaver populations of the northeast US, Europeans found in the southern mountains a new source for leather and furs. In colonial days, fur transactions relied almost exclusively on credit, which placed both buyers and sellers in a financially tenuous position. In the beginning, however, neither party had any problem agreeing to the open exchange of goods. For example, the regulations drafted by the crown's Board of Commissioners and agreed upon by the principle Cherokee chief of the Lower Towns encouraged "a regular exchange of goods and peltries between Charleston and the [Cherokee] Nation."[1] Everyone also agreed upon a schedule of values: a gun was valued at thirty-five skins; one yard of stroud cloth, eight skins; one hatchet, three skins; a broad hoe, five skins; a calico petticoat, fourteen skins; an axe, five skins; and thirty bullets, one skin.

Soon demand was so high for salt, gunpowder, teakettles, and looking glasses that the board "fixed no price upon them, leaving the traders to exact

---

[1] Gary C. Goodwin, *Cherokees in Transition: A Study of Changing Culture and Environment prior to 1775* (Chicago: University of Chicago, Department of Geograpy, 1977) 97–98.

as much as the savages were willing to pay for them."[2] One of the earliest purchases of Cherokee peltry recorded by the board was received at Tugaloo, a trading post located in the northeastern Georgia mountains. On 11 June 1717, the crown's commissioners received at that post "nine hundred and one dressed deer skins, fifty-six raw, thirty beaver skins, and twenty one slaves...."[3]

The fur trade reached its peak in the 1750s. By that time many of the smaller Cherokee villages were already entirely dependent on European goods, while others resented that they were being neglected by traders who visited only the largest townships. To help remedy the situation, in 1751 South Carolina divided the nation into thirteen hunting districts, each with no more than one trader for every three townships. The board's attempts to control trading activities were largely unsuccessful. In many instances, traders cheated Native Americans by ignoring ordinances that required the use of uniform weights and measures when receiving and distributing goods.

After more than three decades of intense hunting and trapping, game in the mountain region became increasingly scarce. By 1760, buffalo and elk, the largest and most valuable animals of the southern Appalachians, began to disappear entirely from the mountain forests. Bear and deer populations also suffered greatly due to indiscriminate hunting practices and the increasing number of open-range hogs and cattle, which competed with native animals for mast such as acorns, hickory nuts, and chestnuts.

Not did the fur trade have a significant impact on mammal populations in the southern mountains, but several native plants like American ginseng also saw dramatic declines in the eighteenth century, particularly after the full entry of the Cherokees into world trade. Ginseng, a valuable commodity on the global market since the mid-eighteenth century, grew abundantly in the rich deciduous forests of the southern Appalachians, particularly on northern-facing slopes above 1,000 feet. The Cherokees were already familiar with the plant since they, like the Chinese who readily purchased the root, believed it had medicinal qualities. In fact, the Cherokees used

---

[2] John H. Logan, *A History of the Upper Country of South Carolina from the Earliest Period to the Close of Independence* (Charleston SC: S. G. Courtney and Company, 1859) 241.

[3] Ibid., 348.

ginseng for a variety of ailments, including headaches, "weakness of womb and nervous infections."[4]

Although the trading of the root began slowly at first, American ginseng was by far the most important plant of the mountain forest. In the mid-1740s, ginseng was still bringing a relatively small price in the markets of Charleston and Williamsburg, partly because Native Americans did not dry the root according to strict standards. In fact, a trader living in North Carolina sadly told James Adair, one of the first whites to live among the Cherokees, that he could "not get from any of the South Carolina merchants, one shilling sterling a pound, though his people brought it from the Alegany and Apalache mountains, two hundred miles."[5]

Ginseng did not become a significant commodity in the southern Appalachians until the 1750s, after the Chinese begin to lose faith in Canadian suppliers. The Chinese turned to southern markets in order to fill the void, and the Cherokees immediately took advantage of the situation. In the interim, white traders, or the Cherokees themselves, had received instruction about proper methods of gathering and drying the root, as English merchants were soon shipping ginseng acquired from Cherokees living in the mountains of north Georgia and the Carolinas "halfway around the world."[6] By the end of the eighteenth century, however, ginseng was so scarce in the Blue Ridge that John Drayton, governor of South Carolina (which then included north Georgia and North Carolina), commented that "ginseng had been so much sought by the Cherokee Indians for trade, that at this time it is by no means so plenty as it used to be in this state."[7]

The most conspicuous change as a result of early frontier settlement and trade on the mountain landscape was the loss of the region's many canebrakes. River cane was valuable as a livestock food source since few native grasses could survive year-round in the shaded understory (trees and shrubs growing close to the ground) of the upland forest. An evergreen

---

[4] James Mooney, "Myths of the Cherokees," in *Nineteenth Annual Report of the Bureau of American Ethnology, 1897–98* (Washington, DC: US Government Printing Office, 1900) 425.

[5] James Adair, *History of the American Indians* (London: 1775) 389.

[6] Timothy Silver, *A New Face on the Countryside: Indians, Colonists, and Slaves in South Atlantic Forests, 1500–1800* (New York: Cambridge University Press, 1990) 83–84.

[7] Margaret B. Meriwether, ed., *The Carolinian Florist of Governor John Drayton of South Carolina, 1766–1822* (Columbia: University of South Carolina Press, 1943) 109.

plant, river cane made excellent fodder for livestock, so traders used canebrakes to sustain their horses, cattle, and hogs.

The introduction of large herds of livestock into the mountain forest resulted in the clearing not only of canebrakes but also of other forest ground cover. Within decades of the first European settlement, wild pea-vines, hog-peanuts, and the wild strawberry were eliminated from vast areas of the forest floor. The pea-vine, which once grew "as high as a horse's back," was rarely seen in any great profusion after the American Revolution.[8] The hog-peanut, a low twining vine that produces a small root eaten by hogs, was also largely eliminated from areas of the forest by foraging livestock. Wild strawberries, which once carpeted large areas of the Blue Ridge Mountains, became scarce, transforming large strawberry fields into small, scattered colonies of individual plants.

The changing composition of the mountain ecosystem no doubt had a profound effect on Cherokee culture. Prior to the fur trade, the Cherokees relied on the flesh of deer, elk, buffalo, bear, and even beaver as dietary staples. Skins of these animals provided essential clothing. For example, buckskin leather was originally the basic article of dress for the Cherokees. As animals became more valuable in the peltry trades and scarcer in the surrounding forests, the Cherokees slowly began to adopt the use of European clothing.

The Cherokees began to prefer smooth cotton broadcloths in various colors or calico prints. To make this clothing, Cherokee women gradually began to use steel needles, scissors, and common thread rather than bone needles, sinew, and buckskin. By 1800, the dress of a significant number of Cherokee men resembled more closely that of a southern gentleman squire. No longer self-sufficing natives, many Cherokees were now dependent on the European trader for literally putting clothes on their backs.

From 1800 until removal in 1838, the Blue Ridge Mountains remained an integral part of Cherokee culture. By the early nineteenth century, however, many of their agricultural practices involved the use of numerous domesticated plants and animals, the outcome of their adoption of European farming methods in general. Not all that was native was forgotten or lost, however. Just as they had acquired European practices, Cherokees also shared their knowledge of the mountain environment with trappers, traders, and first mountain settlers.

---

[8] Logan, *History of the Upper Country*, 25.

For example, one of the Cherokees' most enduring contributions to Appalachian culture was apple cultivation. Although apple trees were initially introduced to the region by British fur traders, the Cherokees made them central to mountain horticulture. The mountain environment was ideal for apple orchards because of plentiful rainfall and "thermal belts," frostless and dewless zones on mountain slopes caused by an unusual meteorological phenomenon known as temperature inversion. Although it is not widely known, the Cherokees were directly responsible for keeping apple-growing alive in the Southeast, as the practice among Anglo-Americans was in rapid decline by the 1830s.

Mining the Blue Ridge

The nation's first major gold rush occurred in north Georgia when gold was discovered somewhere in present-day Hall, Habersham, White, or Lumpkin counties between 1826 and 1828—depending on the account. As thousands of gold-seekers flooded the area, the existing conflict between whites and Native Americans intensified. The area's first gold-boom town, Auraria, was soon displaced by Dahlonega in Lumpkin County as the center of gold-mining activity.

Gold mining, especially a technique called hydraulic mining, forever changed the landscape. This method of mining produced more gold than traditional panning methods. After the trees were cleared from a mountainside, engineers dammed a high source of water and channeled the water down to water cannons, building pressure in large hoses. Then they shot the water onto the cleared mountainside, washing away the earth that contained the gold. The dirt ran down a series of flumes that trapped the finer pieces of gold and sent larger pieces down to the mill to be crushed. In Lumpkin County alone, a 33-mile-wide aqueduct system carried water resources to the mining operations. Another mining method, load mining, involved sinking shafts into tunnels and blasting out the gold using dynamite.

By the 1840s, after a decade of mining that produced $20 million in gold, the Lumpkin mines began to close. Miners known as the twenty-niners became the forty-niners of the California gold rush. In 1849, Georgia State geologist Matthew Stephenson pleaded with the men to stay, saying "there's millions in it," the phrase that was later corrupted into "there's gold in them thar hills."[9]

By the 1840s, much of the Blue Ridge was occupied by whites who had settled the region as a result of the gold rush and subsequent land lotteries, which had awarded white settlers 40- and 160-acre tracts of mountain land. Those living outside Cherokee territory had occupied their homesteads prior to 1840 as a result of federal land grants that had been awarded to Revolutionary War soldiers and their widows. Many of these individuals were of Scots-Irish, German, or English descent, and most were originally from North Carolina, South Carolina, or middle Georgia.

The majority of the first occupants of the Blue Ridge Mountains initially owned 160 to 320 acres, since many were able to purchase adjoining land lots for as little as two dollars. The better land along the main watercourses was settled first and immediately put under cultivation. However, most of the property was left forested—as much as three-fourths according to the federal census records of 1850. Major crops included corn, oats, rye, and wheat, but minor crops like sweet and Irish potatoes, peas, beans, flax, tobacco, and sorghum molasses were also commonly grown in the mountains.

The climate and soil of the Blue Ridge made growing southern cash crops like tobacco and cotton difficult, relegating them to a position of relative insignificance to the agricultural economy. Faithfully committed to animal husbandry, Blue Ridge farmers raised hogs, sheep, horses, mules, oxen, and numerous beef cattle. Of less economic importance, but still acutely vital to the household economy, were the kitchen gardens, milk cows, and poultry yards—each the responsibility of women and all influential in shaping mountain life and culture.

Drovers and Herders

Livestock herdsmen, then known as drovers, also worked in the Blue Ridge Mountains. The widespread availability of hardwood mast such acorns and chestnuts was a boon to Blue Ridge cattle and hog drovers, who turned their stock out in the fall to feast on the abundant chestnuts. In his travels through the Blue Ridge in 1856, Frederick Law Olmsted reported

---

[9] David Williams, *The Georgia Gold Rush: Twenty-niners, Cherokees, and Gold Fever* (Columbia: University of South Carolina Press, 1993) 45.

that swine observed in the Blue Ridge Mountains were of "superior taste" and looked better than he had seen anywhere else in the South.[10]

The rise of the importance of livestock herding in the southern Appalachian mountains was due not only to the existence of a favorable ecological niche, which included the availability of a vast open range and grazing commons, but also to internal improvements such as the building of interstate toll roads and rail lines. During the antebellum period, regional population growth and expanding cotton and tobacco markets on the Atlantic coast also contributed to the rise of livestock production in the mountains. As more land was converted into cotton fields in the Deep South, planters had to rely increasingly on upland farms for meat and produce.

Many of these agricultural products were destined for cities like Atlanta, where the terminus of the Western and Atlantic Railroad was completed in 1842. Annual reports of the W & A Railroad reveal large quantities of upland freight being shipped to the station. While a portion of these goods were no doubt shipped down the rails to be sold on plantations or exported to foreign ports, a significant share of mountain agricultural products remained in southern cities, consumed by an ever-growing urban population. During fiscal year 1852/1853, no less than 29,193 hogs; 6,754,552 pounds of bacon, lard, and tallow; 239,302 bushels of wheat; 18,795 barrels of flour; and 510,923 bushels of corn and oats arrived at the terminal from Chattanooga.[11] In some areas of the Blue Ridge along the Georgia/Tennessee state line, it was easier for farmers to use the Ocoee River to ship goods west to Chattanooga than it was to go south over the mountains to Atlanta.

The proliferation of hogs and cattle throughout the mountains was not without important environmental consequences. Across the uplands, particularly in areas going through natural secession or recovering from timber cutting, grazing livestock suppressed the growth of young saplings and herbaceous plants. Over time, particularly in areas of heavy livestock use, the result was an open, park-like effect, with great distances between standing trees. In many of the disturbed areas, nonnative plants such as

---

[10] Frederick Law Olmsted, *A Journey in the Backcountry, 1853–1854* (1860; repr., New York: Ben Franklin, 1970) 22.

[11] Western & Atlantic Railroad reports cited in James Russell, *Atlanta, 1847–1890: City Building in the Old South and the New* (Baton Rouge: Louisiana State University Press, 1988) 23, table 7.

privet, multifloral rose, and mullein, to name only a few, rapidly replaced native vegetation. In drier locales, particularly along higher ridge tops, it became necessary to burn annually the woodlands in order to "green up" the forest floor, sprouting new growth for hungry livestock. In areas receiving the heaviest use, cattle herding even had an important impact on soil productivity. The repeated trampling of the woodlands by cattle and hogs contributed to soil compaction, higher surface runoff, and increased soil erosion.

Although their importance to mountain agriculture has been grossly underestimated in historical literature, sheep were second only to hogs in actual numbers in the Blue Ridge Mountains. The gradual decline of wolves and mountain lions, along with cooler temperatures and the clearing of additional woodlands for pasture and grasslands, made the mountain environs an ideal grazing area for these animals. Olmsted went so far as to say that "sheep raising and wool growing should be, I think, the chief business of the mountains."[12] An English cultural tradition, sheep herding was practiced on a fairly important scale throughout the Blue Ridge Mountains before 1840. On the eve of the Civil War, north Georgia farmers were already becoming known as exceptional shepherds. On only 267 farmsteads, Rabun County herdsmen kept a total of 7,824 sheep—an astounding average of 29 animals per farmstead.[13]

The primary purpose of raising sheep was to produce wool, the raw material used for woolen fabrics and coverlets. As more looms made their way into mountain communities, the art of dyeing and weaving flourished among women, becoming in some areas a small cottage industry. Carding mills also sprung up in many areas, giving those who could afford it the option of exchanging freshly sheared wool for finished and dyed yarn.

For the majority of mountain women, knowledge of local floral and fauna and their various chemical properties was essential to the art of weaving. Native plants, routinely gathered from surrounding fields and woodlands, were the principal mordants and coloring agents used to dye their yarns and fabrics. Pokeweed berries created rose dyes; staghorn sumac or bloodroot produced red ones; wild indigo or blue ash produced blues; and walnut hulls produced browns or tans. The palette of the experienced dyer was virtually unlimited.

---

[12] Olmstead, *Journey in the Backcountry*, 225.
[13] US Bureau of the Census, *Agriculture of the United States in 1860* (Washington, DC: US Government Printing Office, 1864) 23, 104, 154, 196, 210.

Crop production interested mountain men most or at least kept them busy around the homestead. A successful agriculturalist needed large grain supplies to feed his many horses, hogs, cattle, and poultry. Because it served as a food to both livestock and humans, Indian corn, as it was then called, remained the principal mountain crop. Growing corn took a substantial amount of land, although few farmers tilled more than 20 acres for that purpose. On average, corn production took up only about one-tenth of the farmer's land.

Corn was not only used as a primary foodstuff; it was also central to mountain subsistence culture. Corn was ground into meal and made into whiskey, and its husks and leaves were woven into hats, dolls, mops, and chair bottoms. Corn cobs served as primitive toilet paper, fire starters, bowls for tobacco pipes, and hog and cattle fodder. The harvesting of corn also greatly influenced social relations, bringing neighbors together for fall corn-shuckings.

Corn-shuckings, or "frolics" as they were often called, were yearly events in which community members assisted neighbors in the gathering and preparation of the corn harvest. On the day of the event, the ears of corn were gathered in the fields, loaded onto a wagon, and brought to the site of the corn-shucking. There the corn was unloaded, stacked, and arranged into equal piles upon the ground. Participants, which included men, women, and children, divided into teams and worked enthusiastically to finish shucking their pile of corn first. Sometimes a red ear was hidden among the piles, and the lucky finder received a special prize. Singing, dancing, drinking, and speech-making often accompanied the corn frolics, which generally ended with the eating of a large meal prepared and served by women.

As important as corn was to the typical mountain farmer, a variety of other grains and vegetables, including wheat, rye, beans, barley, peas, beans, squash, and pumpkins, was also grown on the typical Blue Ridge homestead. Additionally, other grains like sorghum and buckwheat were planted on the nineteenth-century mountain farm. As a whole, farmers in northern Georgia, eastern Tennessee, and western North Carolina cultivated far more of these two grains than did farmers in the Deep South, who had long abandoned such crops for the exclusive production of cotton and corn. In many ways, mountain agriculture resembled northern US agriculture in that emphasized crop diversity as well as the production of home-manufactured goods like wool, butter, beeswax, and honey.

The spread of home vegetable gardens, orchards, and corn, wheat, and rye fields across the Appalachian landscape contributed significantly to environmental change. More farms meant more improved land, more free-ranging cattle and hogs in the surrounding countryside, and fewer virgin forests. Within decades, the largest farmsteads were even beginning to exhibit the effects of soil loss and erosion. By the eve of the Civil War, crop yields had decreased dramatically enough in some areas that growers were forced to abandon their farms entirely. Soon, sedge grasses and exotic weeds were flourishing in bottomlands that had for decades yielded 50 bushels of corn to the acre.

Despite these changes, a significant amount of land in the region was still left untouched by human settlement, particularly areas owned by land speculators or industrialists interested in mining the large copper reserves. For areas that might have missed the axe and the plow, the Civil War brought additional environmental changes, accomplishing in a half-decade what had taken a half-century elsewhere. After the Civil War, recovery in the mountains was slow. The uplands of Georgia, Tennessee, and North Carolina sent many soldiers into battle, and many did not return home. Some counties in the Blue Ridge Mountains supplied as many men to Union companies as they did to Confederate service.

Farming in the Blue Ridge suffered greatly during the Civil War, with notable reductions in improved acreage and crop production. Survivors mined the dirt floors of smokehouses for grains of precious salt. Pines, sweetgums, and sassafras trees invaded untended fields, were corn and wheat had once grown thick and tall in the warm sunlight. Cash grew scarce and political revenge frequent. Into this social and economic vacuum entered a new wave of entrepreneurs, land speculators, and timber barons—northern industrialists who had an eye for transforming the mountain region into a private domain of capital and wealth.

The Forest for the Trees

Land speculation, initiated by northern industrialists, escalated to new heights in the mountains after the Civil War. By the early 1870s, politicians, businessmen, and prominent journalists were promoting the entire Appalachian region as a New South Mecca, encouraging northern capitalists to exploit the area's remaining mineral and timber reserves. Wealthy industrialists bought land sight unseen, often without knowledge of its actual worth or an intended use in mind. Acquisitions included lands held previously in speculation and also tax-delinquent properties and mountain lands that local landowners believed too hilly to cultivate. These latter properties were generally acquired by skilled land agents who convinced owners to sell them for as little as one dollar per acre, or in a few cases for a single hog, rifle, or shotgun.

One of the first industries to exploit the natural resources of the Blue Ridge Mountains was the copper industry, which became centered in the great copper basin of north Georgia and southeast Tennessee. The first mine opened in 1850 near McCaysville, Georgia, but the extreme remoteness of the mine severely restricted copper production and transport, the nearest railroad line being some 30 miles away in Dalton, Georgia. The narrow wagon road to Dalton was passable only during summer months, forcing mining companies to build a new roadbed along the Oconee River to Cleveland, Tennessee. Although local residents opposed the building of the road, it was finished in 1853 for the then-incredible sum of $22,000, a price paid exclusively by the mining companies. The new road allowed the copper mines to operate year-round, drawing hundreds of new mine operators to the copper basin area.

Copper production was devastating to the mountain environment, largely because of the many steps required in processing the mineral. First, the raw ore was placed on enormous piles of cordwood that were set on fire. After several weeks of continuous burning, the roasting piles released large amounts of sulfur, iron, zinc, and other undesirable contaminants known as sulfurettes. The sulfur gases killed all surrounding vegetation, beginning a desertification process of the area that continued well into the twentieth century. Interestingly, one of the first environmental lawsuits in the United States was *Madison et al. v. Ducktown, Sulphur, Copper & Iron, LTD*, a lawsuit that in 1904 pitted Georgia residents angry over the devaluation of their property against the one of the largest mines operating in the copper basin. The Georgia residents lost the suit, as the judge ruled that they had been justly compensated for their property losses.

Other steps in copper processing contributed to the devastation of the mountain environment. After roasting, the copper ores were placed into large iron smelters, furnaces fueled by charcoal. Three hundred bushels of charcoal a day were required to operate the furnaces, placing huge demands on local timber supplies. Woodchoppers advertised their services in local papers, while other residents made charcoal from private woodlots, selling the fuel directly to the mines. Records reveal that one company alone consumed more than 500,000 bushels of charcoal, roughly the equivalent of 12,500 cords of wood, in a single year. In order to secure adequate supplies, the mines eventually were forced to purchase timber well outside the copper basin.

By 1875 most of the basin's trees were already gone, and sulfuric gas emissions from the roasters prevented new growth of vegetation. The area's heavy rainfall made matters worse, washing away tons of topsoil and causing severe sheet and gully erosion. Stripping some 1,500 acres of mature timberland each year, by 1876 the Union Consolidated Mining Company was recovering wood from as far away as Morganton, Georgia. By 1878, 47 square miles of timber had been virtually eliminated from the forests surrounding the copper basin. Union Consolidated stripped some 18,000 acres while the Burra Burra Copper Company and the Polk County Copper Company consumed 6,000 acres each.

Because of local wood shortages, timber cutters began floating logs greater distances down the Toccoa and Oconee rivers, destroying community fish traps and severely impairing stream flows. Despite local opposition to the use of the river for floating timber, the Georgia legislature sided with the timber companies, passing a bill making it unlawful to obstruct "by the erection of fish traps or otherwise the main current of the Toccoa River in Fannin county to a width of thirty feet, so as to interfere with rafting of floating timber."[14]

Of course, not all of north Georgia and southeast Tennessee was effected by the copper industry. However, much of what remained untouched by the copper mines soon became the domain of large timber companies, who by the 1880s had begun moving to the southern mountains. By the turn of the century, the timber boon was in full swing in north Georgia and adjoining western North Carolina, and teams of sawyers began moving the biggest and oldest trees from the mountain forest.

As with the copper industry, the environmental effects of large-scale timbering practices in the mountains were immediately felt. Erosion, fires, and flooding increased significantly, damaging prime cropland along streams and destroying wildlife habitat. As early as 1892, Gifford Pinchot, who had accepted the important task of introducing sustainable forestry practices to the Blue Ridge Mountains of north Georgia and western North Carolina, wrote that "if forest management is successful in producing profit off this

---

[14] R. E. Barclay, *Ducktown Back in Raht's Time* (Chapel Hill: University of North Carolina, 1946) 263.

burned, slashed, and overgrazed forest, it will do so on almost any land in this part of the country."[15]

The increasing environmental destruction was due not only to the mere cutting of trees but also to the use of new and more technologically efficient logging methods. With the arrival of railroads to the remoter sections of the southern Appalachians, it was no longer necessary for logging operations to be confined to the vicinity of larger streams. Narrow-gauge railroads, then called dummy lines, could now be laid along the contours of steep hillsides once thought inaccessible by lumbermen.

From these dummy lines, logs of all sizes were skidded by cable across steep slopes to awaiting railroad cars for loading and transport. The end result of this logging method was, in effect, a devastating clear-cut since the skidded logs destroyed everything in their path. The skid trails that remained as a result of these logging activities created such severe erosion that the cutover landscape often took decades to heal. Accompanying the severe erosion were widespread forest fires that further denuded mountain slopes and hillsides. No doubt local herdsmen, who continued to burn the woods to promote the growth of new browse for cattle and sheep, started some of the fires. Many of the fires, however, were the direct result of careless lumbermen who routinely left behind large piles of brush and downed treetops at logging sites. Wood-fired locomotives, which spewed sparks out their great smokestacks, also caused fires.

The most controversial and widely debated topic surrounding early industrial logging in the mountains was soil erosion and flooding. By the early 1880s, there was already a consensus among observers that standing timber played an important role in preventing, especially after heavy rains, excessive water runoff and the loss of fertile topsoil. By 1900 there could be little doubt that injudicious lumbering and forest fires resulted in widespread loss of forest topsoil, which served as a natural sponge for water runoff during heavy rains. A year later, President Theodore Roosevelt, who placed the destruction of southern Appalachian forests squarely on the shoulders of the logging industry, stated that the preservation of the mountain forests could no longer be left to "the caprice of private capital."[16]

---

[15] O. C. Goodwin, "Eight Decades of Forestry Firsts: A History of Forestry in North Carolina, 1889–1969" (Raleigh: North Carolina Forest Service, n.d.) 34.

[16] Theodore Roosevelt, Message from the President of the United States, A Report of the Secretary of Agriculture in Relation to the Forests, Rivers, and

Only in 1907, when tragic floods occurred in West Virginia and Kentucky, did government involvement in the protection of mountain forests become a reality. After hearing considerable testimony from engineers, industry spokesmen, and conservationists, Congress finally passed the Weeks Act on 1 March 1911, officially authorizing the federal purchase of "forested, cut-over, or denuded lands with the watersheds of navigable streams."[17]

Among the first attempted land acquisitions in the southern Appalachians—indeed the entire United States—included lands in north Georgia, an area that had received considerable attention and study from Gifford Pinchot and others involved in the forest preservation movement. According to official government records, one of the initial acquisitions was a 31,000-acre tract sold to the newly created National Forest Service Reservation Commission (which would soon become the National Forest Service) by the Gennett Brothers of the Gennett Land and Lumber Company of Atlanta, Georgia. The Gennett purchase was, in fact, the first tract in the US to receive formal approval for purchase by the federal agency after the passage of the Week Act. The land—which included pieces of Fannin, Union, Lumpkin, and Gilmer counties—was officially acquired 29 August 1912.

In the short-term, the acquisition of public lands for conservation did little to benefit local residents, which helps to explain their relative indifference to the creation of the national forest preserve system. Most of the land being acquired had already passed into control of the timber and mining companies who, after taking much of the timber, topsoil, and minerals from the mountains, had left little for local residents to appreciate. With the establishment of game and fish regulations, fence laws, and woods-burning restrictions, the residents' ability to use the lands as a grazing, hunting, and trapping commons was severely limited. At the same time, the mountaineers' lack of a positive response to national forest acquisitions should not be equated with a lack of concern for the mountain environment or for conservation practices in general. Many mountain residents simply saw the federal purchases as another way for timber barons to rid themselves

Mountains of the Southern Appalachian Region, 1901 (Washington, DC: Government Printing Office, 1902) 34, note 21.
    [17] US Department of Agriculture, *Mountaineers and Rangers: A History of Federal Forest Management in the Southern Appalachians, 1900–1981*, Forest Service History Series 380 (Washington, DC: US Department of Agriculture, 1983) 13.

of cutover, useless lands and to profit even more from their speculative endeavors.

While corporate logging did much to alter the landscape of the Blue Ridge Mountains, industrial logging also had an important impact on the subsistence economy and culture of the region, removing much-needed farmland from the community land base as well as eliminating from the forest the many native plants and animals on which mountain families had long depended for their survival. Indeed, numerous testimonies from mountain residents provide evidence that white-tailed deer, turkeys, black bear, and other important game animals showed significant declines after peak periods of timber operations. Ginseng, goldenseal, mayapple, galax, and other plants seasonally traded at the mountain store for supplies or cash also underwent population decreases.[18]

The extent of land acquisition by timber companies was indeed staggering, so even if the land was not immediately logged, its continued use by local residents was limited. By 1930, only 40 percent of all privately owned timberlands in north Georgia was held by individual farmers, which left the ownership of the remaining 60 percent to industrial organizations. What is today the Cohutta Wilderness Area in north Georgia—65,000 acres (more than 100 square miles)—was owned by a single logging company, the Conasauga Lumber Company of Cincinnati, Ohio.

With the influx of timber and mining companies in the region, speculation on mountain lands increased dramatically, driving up prices and forcing many to pay off property taxes that in some communities had gone uncollected since the Civil War. Farmers failing to show proof of ownership could be driven off their land, sometimes even at gunpoint. Removed from their ancestral homes, mountaineers and their families ironically found refuge in the many lumber camps that increasingly dominated the mountain economy after 1900. These lumber camps provided shelter for the average mountaineer but seldom paid more than a subsistence wage.

Another result of the consolidation of land into large private and federal timber holdings included dramatic decreases in farm size. As fathers found it more difficult to acquire new lands for their sons and daughters or to maintain a modicum of productivity on their own lands, they often either sold off portions of their property to pay local taxes or leased it to younger

[18] US Department of Agriculture, *Mountaineers and Rangers*, 551; William Hall, "To Remake the Appalachians: A New Order in the Mountains that is Founded on Forestry," *World's Work* 28 (July 1914): 321–38.

tenants who would sharecrop the land. By 1910 the average farm size in the Blue Ridge Mountains had dropped to less than 100 acres, which left little forested land to be used for grazing hogs and cattle, collecting firewood, or any other subsistence activities that involved forest cover. Unfortunately, this trend continued for several more decades. Between 1910 and 1920, for example, farm sizes decreased an additional 39 percent in Rabun County, Georgia, and 22 percent in Fannin County.

By 1930 the average farm in the Blue Ridge Mountains covered less than 80 acres. The small, marginally self-sufficient mountain homestead of the 1930s, often celebrated in publications like the *Foxfire* series, was more accurately the byproduct of shifting social and economic patterns created, in no small part, by the wanton destruction of our native mountain forests. Owned now by private and federal timber interests, the surrounding forest was no longer the woodland commons that had for centuries been used and shared by a variety of mountain peoples for a number of different land-use and cultural activities. On those lands, the mountain farmer had not only herded cattle; he had also gathered chestnuts, picked berries, hunted, fished, and dug ginseng. To the original inhabitants of the Blue Ridge Mountains, the surrounding forest was much more than board feet on the stump. The mountain woodlands were a living matrix of plants, animals, and shared memories—a critical if not vital part of mountain life and culture.

Chapter 14
Razing Appalachia

On a mountaintop in southern West Virginia stands a machine 20 stories high. From the air, it resembles a child's Tonka toy in a sandbox. Despite its incredible size, it moves with remarkable speed and precision, its dragline pulling a 53-cubic-yard scoop large enough to remove, in a single swath, more than 130 tons of earth. From the ground, any sentimentality for the technological behemoth quickly vanishes: it is creating a moonscape out of beautiful mountains. The machine never stops, running twenty hours a day, and even supplies its own power and lighting system to illuminate the broken and sterile landscape after dark. The two dozen or so workers on the site refer to the machine as "Big John."

Big John symbolizes the latest technological advance in the surface-mining of coal—mountaintop removal. Mountaintop removal is a method of strip-mining of such enormous scale that it defies the imagination. One must see it firsthand to appreciate truly its full environmental impact on the Appalachian landscape. Entire mountains are literally moved by dozer and dragline in order to expose rich coal deposits hundreds of feet below the surface. The spoil or overburden is then dumped into adjacent coves and stream courses with little regard for the Clean Water Act or other federal regulations designed to protect our nation's waterways.

A recent study by the US Fish and Wildlife Service estimates that mountaintop removal projects have filled enough streams to stretch the length of the Ohio River. According to the published report, 470 miles of streams have been buried or approved to be buried in West Virginia alone. In Kentucky, permitted fills have submerged more than 355 miles of watercourses. Some individual valley fills measure more than 100 million cubic yards and bury 2 miles or more of a single tributary. In Mingo

County, West Virginia, more than 8,000 acres are scheduled for mountaintop removal projects, including Blair Mountain, the site of a historic coal war in 1921. Kentucky's highest peak, Black Mountain (elevation 4,139 feet), is another target of mountaintop mining, a fact that has sparked student protests in nearby Middlesboro, Kentucky.

Strip-mining is nothing new to Appalachia. Since the 1950s, coal has been excavated from rich seams using a similar, albeit less intensive method of scraping away the overburden earth to get at the black gold. Since the late 1980s, however, new mega-technologies—gigantic dump trucks, bulldozers, drilling machines, and draglines—have made mountaintop removal a much more profitable and cost-efficient enterprise. That, along with EPA regulations that mandate the burning of high-quality, low-sulfur coal, have made entire areas of West Virginia, eastern Kentucky, Virginia, and Pennsylvania a renewed target of the multibillion-dollar coal industry.

To add insult to environmental injury, there is considerable evidence that the burning of this same coal by the utility industry is killing forests from Maine to Georgia. Despite new EPA emission standards, coal-burning power plants are contributing to tree mortality across the entire eastern United States. Coal-fired power plants produce 70 percent of all sulfur dioxide emissions and are the primary cause of acid rain, which has resulted in unprecedented tree death, especially at higher elevations. On Mt. Mitchell, North Carolina, for example, moisture in the clouds is frequently 1,000 times more acidic than natural rainfall. The results have been catastrophic. Visitors to Clingman's Dome in the Great Smoky Mountains National Park now see great expanses of dead and dying trees.

Mountaintop removal, in all its phases, is destroying our native mountain ecosystems. It is also devastating the lives of local residents, who must daily confront the noise and fouled water created by blasting and erosion, not to mention the inevitable loss of their cultural commons. Dozens of communities in Appalachia have fallen victim to mountaintop removal projects, despite heroic efforts by local residents to educate public officials about the mega-technological practice.

Author's Note: In summer 2005, dozens of citizen activists were arrested after directly trying to stop mountaintop removal projects in Virginia, West Virginia, and Tennessee. Despite hunger strikes, rallies, direct-action protests, and a multi-media ad campaign, mountaintop removal mining continues in the Appalachian coalfields.

Chapter 15

A New Beginning

December 10

Wednesday evening. For the first time in more than a dozen years, I am alone. I share my bed with no one. I speak to empty rooms; my voice is heard only by a small tortoise-shell cat, Iris, and a much too energetic Brittany spaniel named Aggie.

To fight the loneliness, I tell myself, I will keep a diary of sorts, a personal journal documenting my search for redemption and self-worth. For an entire year I will immerse myself in my natural surroundings. Nature will be my solace and savior, and I will write daily about her secrets. As a child of a rural upbringing, the natural world has never betrayed or abandoned me, remaining perhaps the only constant in my life. My new life partner will ostensibly be the Gordon County environs that surround my wooded northwest Georgia home.

My place on earth is 7 acres of land surrounded by more than 2 square miles of fields and forests. Like Thoreau, I will live an uncrowded life. I have only a single neighbor within shouting distance of my front porch. The property is thickly wooded, containing a small portion of old-growth American beech and white oak. A small creek flows along its northern boundary.

My home, a modest circa 1929 bungalow, sits atop a small knoll overlooking Johns Mountain, a long narrow ridge to the west. Nearby is the 65,000-acre Armuchee Ranger District of the Chattahoochee National Forest. Wildlife abounds in the area, especially deer, turkey, geese, squirrels, raccoons, and bobwhite quail. Wildflowers are also abundant. The Cherokee word *armuchee*, local historians tell us, means "land of flowers."

As a professor at a small, two-year liberal arts college, I will have more time than most to stroll among the stately beeches and oaks, to gaze at majestic sunsets, and to ruminate on the foibles and follies of modern human existence.

January 7

Tuesday. Tonight, as I write for only the third time in my diary, wood logs lay neatly arranged on the brick hearth, their coarse grain shining brightly across their smooth ends. The various shades in the small stack signify a diversity of tree species: white oak, red oak, American beech, and sugar maple. There's also winged elm, which nineteenth-century woodsmen called "wahoo," a small tree with stiff, flat limbs that appear to have grown wings.

Outside on the porch, the wood is stacked high, ready for the cold January blast expected later in the week. My home is heated exclusively with wood, so gathering, stacking, hauling, and splitting wood is a necessary preoccupation of mine. This evening, I happily reap the benefits of a busy autumn in the wood lot. My warm stockinged feet rest atop a handmade Guatemalan chest that doubles as a makeshift coffee table. I sip herbal tea and watch the yellow flames dance wildly behind the clear glass of the coal-black wood stove.

Though seasonably cool now, the month started off unseasonably warm temperatures in the upper 60s and low 70s, bringing out the delicate blossoms of birds-foot violets, northwest Georgia's earliest blooming flower. Usually, I see the violets in late February along the steep roadsides of John's Mountain, where they bloom in small clumps of lavender or blue, the exact hue depending to a large degree on the pH of the soil. Purple blossoms signify acidity; blue ones are a clear sign that a more alkaline pH is present. The warm temperatures have brought them out early, perhaps too early, as the predicted bitter cold of the weekend will surely kill their gay and colorful blossoms.

The stove crackles and pops and I am reminded that Iris, my small tortoise-shell cat, has not returned from her evening hunting. It's getting late and I am beginning to worry about her. The worry may be totally unnecessary, I remind myself, as she often returns late, and usually with a shrew, vole, or, as on one occasion a few weeks ago, a Northern flying squirrel. She proudly dropped the prey on the front porch, its velvet fur stretched delicately over its arms and legs. Though its eyes were already cloudy and gray from the cold, I imagined the small mammal taking flight just hours before, gliding effortlessly among the broad limbs of white oaks and tall pines. Caught unexpectedly on the ground, the squirrel was not likely to be eaten by Iris. It was foremost a gift for me, so I half-heartedly thanked her.

January 8

Wednesday. Sunrise this cold January morning was breathtaking, looking like a sunset after a summer storm, but more ominous and foreboding. The gray clouds high above the eastern horizon were stamped with fish-scale-like crescents of blue and white. Below, in stark contrast to the black-blue sky resting heavily overhead, was a narrow band of yellow along the horizon.

Tonight is cold and rainy—a few degrees colder and we will certainly have sleet or snow. Lighting flashes in the distance and is followed by thunder, a rarity for early January, even in temperate northwest Georgia. Iris has still not returned and so I am afraid that a great horned owl or perhaps a coyote has found her in the nearby woods. If she has not returned this weekend, I will go searching for her. The cold and pouring rain will be hard on her tonight, and I try to convince myself that she is curled up in a nearby hayloft.

Moments ago, I opened my deceased Aunt Virgie's diary for this date: January 8, 1956. Written more than forty years ago, entirely in pencil, the worn and tattered ledger reads as a testament to a different time and place. I am sure I will be consulting it many times this year, for inspiration or simply to compare notes. "Today's" entry begins: *It is still cold & windy today.* Besides weather, she also duly recorded the number of hen eggs she daily gathered—*6 hen eggs, 4 pullet eggs.* Aunt Virgie was quite the poultry fancier; in fact, much of her income was derived from her daily gathered eggs or from the hens, which she sold to neighbors for frying or stewing.

January 9

Thursday. Another cold and dreary day and Iris has still not returned. The woodpile along the hearth is getting low, which means a few more trips to the woodshed. Unfortunately, there is largely yellow pine left there, wood that cannot be regularly burned in my delicate, state-of-the-art wood stove.

Outfitted with a catalytic converter that virtually eliminates all smoke and ash, the stove is actually a small furnace, routinely burning hotter than 1,100 degrees. I have become an expert at building and tending fires in this efficient little stove, whose burn time of six hours often requires that I rise at 5:00 A.M. to stoke the dying embers.

There is talk of accumulating snow tomorrow. The wind blows stiffly outside, causing the tinkling of cowbells, the sound imitated by a large clay wind chime that hangs from my covered front porch.

January 10

Friday evening. Snow flurries blow softly outside and begin to accumulate lightly, but still no sign of Iris. I miss her already. Tomorrow I will go looking for her, weather and health permitting. I am ill with bronchitis and feel pretty weak in my legs. Tonight, I relax in my grandmother's century-old Queen Anne chair, listening to bluegrass musician Kenny Baker and other virtuosos of the folk violin. The fiddle has a nice soothing rhythm and complements the lightly falling snow and the leaping fire that burns brightly in the wood stove.

Aggie, my Brittany spaniel, has also found a warm spot in front of the fire, occasionally glancing my way to see what I am doing. Tonight will be cold for northwest Georgia—18 degrees—and so I must get the fire burning hotter before bedtime. I even turned the light on in the well house to keep the pump from freezing. A single 60-watt bulb warms the 5-by-4-foot room nicely, enough to keep the temperature well above the all-important 32-degree mark.

I am surprised at how therapeutic writing in this diary has become for me. Almost every other waking moment is consumed of thoughts of separation, the divorce, and my next phone conversation with Margaret. Writing has become a healthy distraction, an elixir of sorts, calming and soothing my wounded heart.

January 11

Saturday. A cold but clear day. Jimmy and Kathy Drennon, good friends and my closest neighbors, called early this morning with well and water problems. The temperature dropped to 12 degrees last night, freezing their well pump and interrupting Saturday morning baths and showers. I suggested placing a small heater in his pump house to warm frozen pipes. After fifteen minutes, the strategy apparently worked, and so Jimmy and

Kathy returned the favor by inviting me over for a delicious home-cooked meal.

Tonight there is still no sign of Iris. I looked for her by car today, still too ill to do much walking in the cold outdoors. I did walk down to the beaver dam, which has not seen much activity this week. The water level is, however, noticeably high in the small pond behind the dam.

A doe came to the house in the afternoon, stopping to eat white clover sown in the front yard this summer. I took several photographs, mostly because of the unusual light, not because deer are a rarity here. Wild deer routinely wander into the yard, often coming to the bird feeder where they hungrily eat sorghum and other nutritious seed scattered over the ground. This one was a dark buff color and seemed not as cautious as the usual four-legged visitors. The deep freeze has probably made browsing difficult for the deer, forcing them into generally avoided areas near homes and human habitation.

The birds were certainly happy that I bought more birdseed and filled the feeders. Cardinals, Carolina chickadees, tufted titmice, white-throated sparrows, white-breasted nuthatches, and slate-colored juncos were my most frequent visitors today. The stove is burning brightly, and now I think about Aggie, who ran away again today on one of her periodic furloughs. I searched for her after giving her a head start of several hours, but had no success. Tonight I listen for the faint click of her toenails on the back porch and periodically look out the window for her darting shadow across the lawn. Maybe she, too, is looking for Iris.

The stars shine brightly tonight and the moon is a tiny thin crescent, a waning cradle perched low in the western sky.

January 12

Sunday evening. Another clear and cold day. Late afternoon light was beautiful as usual this time of year, reflecting mysteriously off the numerous bare trees in the yard and nearby woods. Lots of activity at the bird feeder outside my kitchen window: purple finches have been especially frequent visitors today. Several deer browsed in the yard, including "Cocoa," a young, dark-haired buck that appeared yesterday at the feeder. He looked hungry, and his right eye has a severe infection that seems to have impaired his vision. I took several photographs of the deer as they foraged for birdseed freshly scattered for the juncos and white-throated sparrows. Food is getting scarcer, forcing the deer to feed during daylight hours.

The water froze in the kitchen drain well below the sink, but thawed in the afternoon when temperatures rose above freezing for the first time in several days.

The room seems darker than usual where I write, even though I have lit a kerosene lamp and several beeswax candles, including one especially for Iris, who did not return again today. Collectively, the three candles seem to recall her warmth and bright spirit. She first arrived here several years ago when the irises were in bloom, giving new life into this house. A lovable cat, she is also my alarm clock, each morning pressing her wet nose hard against my sleepy face. Her purring, loud and incessant, is even annoying at times. I miss her terribly.

Fortunately, Aggie returned as expected last night, so I am thankful for her continued presence.

My illness has not improved much. I am, however, grateful for my home and the few things I have here. Nature has been kind with her blessings.

January 13

Monday. Another beautiful clear and cold day. Bright blue skies interrupted only with white streaks of jet stream crisscrossing the inside shell of a robin's egg. I bought cracked corn for the deer today and scattered it in the side yard around the bird feeder. Afterward, I walked down to the beaver pond, which has become a daily ritual of late. As I topped the hill to walked down the narrow worn trail to the creek, there were four white-tailed deer standing alertly above the dam. They saw me coming but stood to watch me approach, perhaps to see if I was friend or foe. They acted as if they were on their way to feast on the newly scattered corn, and I had interrupted their approach. They moved slowly at first before bounding off in a wide circle toward the large lake above the property boundary.

After I brought in the night's wood and fed Aggie, who was tethered outside near the car shed, a large doe walked deliberately out of the woods in a direct line toward the bird feeder. Aggie saw her too and began barking furiously as though she were an army of men about to set fire to the house. When she saw me standing in the window, she stopped, sat down, and looked at me as if to say, "Don't you see it? A deer! A deer!" She then looked directly at the deer, who was largely ignoring her. The doe's unconcern could be measured by its flicking white tail, which further teased Aggie as if to say, "I dare you to chase me."

Seconds later, the doe raced forward past the corner of the house, immediately out of Aggie's line of sight. Within minutes, she found the cracked corn and was hungrily picking it up with a nimble tongue. Fifteen minutes later she was joined by Cocoa, the young yearling who visited the yard yesterday. After sundown and the fall of complete darkness, they finished the corn together.

As I close the journal tonight, the stars again shine brightly in the winter sky. A near-quarter moon casts faint white beams across the front porch and living room windowpanes. A pair of barred owls cackle loudly down below the spring branch, disturbing the otherwise calm of a cold winter evening.

Author's Note: Iris did return, but was nearly starved to death. She lived with me for another five years before being killed by a car in Dalton, Georgia.

Chapter 16

Medicinal and Cultural Uses of Native Plants in the Southern Appalachians

Appalachia. The word itself comes from a Native American tribe, the Apalachee, who did not actually live in the southern mountains. By all historical accounts, the Apalachee Indians lived within a 40-square-mile area of the central Florida panhandle, from the west bank of the Aucilla River to the lands just west of the Ochlockonee River. How then did the province of the Apalachee become associated with a mountain region 500 miles to the north? Scholar David Walls credits French artist Jacques Le Moyne, traveling with a Huguenot expedition to Florida in 1564, as first designating the mountain region as the "Montes Apalatchi."[1] Le Moyne's map, "The Province of Florida in America," first published in 1565, locates a village called Apalatchi near the headwaters of the Chattooga and Tugaloo Rivers in northeast Georgia. The map's legend also describes the general area as "a place of great mountains," where, as the map shows, "arise three great rivers."[2]

---

[1] David Walls, "On the Naming of Appalachia," in J. W. Williamson, ed., *An Appalachian Symposium: Essays Written in Honor of Cratis D. Williams* (Boone NC: Appalachian State University Press, 1977) 58; also see Richard Drake, "Appalachian America: The Emergence of a Concept, 1895–1964," *Mountain Life and Work* 40 (Spring 1965): 6–9; John Hann, *Apalachee: The Land between the Rivers* (Gainesville: University of Florida Press, 1988) 160–80.
[2] Le Moyne quoted in W. P. Cumming, R. A. Skelton, and D. B.Quinn, *The Discovery of North America* (New York: American Heritage Press, 1971) 187.

Le Moyne's "Montes Apalatchi" is more accurately a reference to the Blue Ridge Mountains of northeast Georgia near an improbable Apalachee town site and not to the larger mountain chain that we call the Appalachians. Today, the Appalachians are geographically depicted as the chain of mountains that extend from New York to north Georgia, forming, in essence, the geographic backbone of the eastern half of the United States. Southern Appalachia is, by obvious geographic convention, the southern half of that same range, which includes those mountains from western Virginia to northeastern Alabama.

Ecologically speaking, the southern Appalachians is one of the most biologically diverse areas in all of North America, if not the entire planet. The area contains an estimated 80 species of amphibians and reptiles; 175 species of terrestrial birds; 65 species of mammals; 2,250 species of vascular plants; and more than 25,000 species of invertebrates. The southern mountain region supports 130 species of trees, as many as in all of Europe. Elevation ranges from 1,000 feet to 6,500 feet, giving rise to numerous ecological niches and a varied array of soil and moisture conditions. Hardwoods, mainly oaks, are the dominant tree species, although the American chestnut was the most important tree in the forest prior to the 1930s. Although much of this land has been developed for residential homes and industry, a large part of the region is still rural, and more than 3.5 million acres are found within the boundaries of national forests or national parks.

History of Plant Use

Medicinal plants have been used in the southern Appalachians since prehistoric times, but historical accounts document the Native American practice of using such plants to the early eighteenth century. American ginseng (*Panax quinquefloius*), a valuable commodity on the world market since at least the early eighteenth century, grew abundantly in the deciduous forests of southern Appalachia, particularly on northern-facing slopes. The Cherokees were familiar with the plant, believing it to have important medicinal qualities. In fact, the Cherokees used ginseng for a number of ailments, including "weakness of the womb," and as a general tonic.[3] Seneca snakeroot (*Polygala senega L.*), another common plant of the southern

---

[3] James Mooney, "Myths of the Cherokees," in the *Nineteenth Annual Report of the Bureau of American Ethnology, 1897–98* (Washington, DC: US Government Printing Office, 1900) 426.

mountains, was also gathered by the Cherokees, who found it to be an excellent remedy for poisonous snakebite. English and French apothecaries purchased snakeroot in great quantities, and, like ginseng, it became a significant trade item during the eighteenth century. The Moravians of North Carolina, who settled on the eastern border of the Appalachian frontier, reported that Native Americans routinely helped gather hundreds of pounds of the plant, which they later shipped to European merchants.[4]

American ginseng was by far the most important plant in Appalachia, though the trading of the root got off to a relatively slow start. In the mid-1740s, ginseng was still bringing a fairly small price in the markets along the east coast, partly because Native Americans were not drying the root according to Chinese standards. In fact, a trader living along the upper Yadkin settlements of North Carolina told James Adair that he could not get more than one shilling sterling a pound from South Carolina merchants. Adair, convinced of its importance to the region, wondered if some "public-spirited gentleman" might inform the region's inhabitants about "how to preserve the ginseng, so as the give it a proper colour; for could we once effect that, it must become a valuable branch of trade."[5]

Ginseng became a significant commodity in the southern Appalachians only after the Chinese lost faith in Canadian suppliers during the 1750s. French Jesuits living in Canada discovered the plant in 1716, and they were the first North Americans regularly to supply the Chinese with the root. Soon afterward, tons of North American ginseng was being shipped to China, which led to its over-harvesting. As Peter Kalm noted of the Iroquois in 1749,

> the trade which is carried on with here is brisk; for they gather great quantities of it, and send them to France, from whence they are brought to China.... The Indians of this town were likewise so taken up by this business that the French [Canadian] farmers were not able during that time to hire a single Indian to help in the harvest. Many people feared lest but continuing for several successive years to collect these plants without leaving one or two in each place to propagate their species.

---

[4] Timothy Silver, *A New Face on the Countryside: Indians, Colonists, and Slaves in South Atlantic Forests, 1500–1800* (Cambridge: Cambridge University Press, 1990) 83.
[5] James Adair, *History of the American Indians* (London: Edward and Charles Dilly, 1775) 389.

So great was the demand for the root, adds Kalm, that it "obliged the Indians…to go far within the English boundaries to collect [the root]."[6]

The growing demand and resulting scarcity of ginseng in the northeast forced traders to look to the southern Appalachians as a new source for the plant. Moreover, in 1752, the Chinese discovered that an enormous amount of the root from Canada had been dug out of season (the highest-grade ginseng is dug in the fall) and improperly dried in ovens. As a result, the Canadian export in ginseng dropped from about $100,000 to $6,500 in a single season before ceasing entirely in 1755.[7] Turning to southern markets in order to fill the void, the Chinese soon had new suppliers among the Cherokees, who had apparently received instruction from white traders about the proper methods of harvesting the root. In 1761 Henry Timberlake saw it among the Overhill Cherokees, who sold large quantities to local traders as well as used it in their native medical practice. Apparently, the Cherokees did not limit their trade to the Chinese or white men, as they also sold the root to Florida natives dwelling near the Atlantic coast.[8]

As in the case of ginseng and snakeroot, Cherokees shared much of their knowledge about the mountain environment with fur trappers, with traders, and later with mountain settlers. Even after their forced removal in 1838, the remaining Cherokees of the Qualla Boundary and Snowbird Mountains in North Carolina stayed in close communication with white mountain communities. Without question, their close contact with whites facilitated "exchanges in ecological knowledge between the two groups" and eventually helped shape southern mountain culture.[9] In fact, upon their first arrival to the region, European settlers adopted many Cherokee ways—some out of sheer necessity, others simply due to their practical utility. In the mountains of North Carolina and southwest Virginia, for example, ginseng was gathered from the eighteenth century forward by

---

[6] Peter Kalm, *Travels in North America*, vol. 2 (London: T. Lowndes, 1772) 436–37.

[7] M. G. Kains, *Ginseng; Its Cultivation, Harvest, Marketing and Market Value, with a Short Account of Its History and Botany* (New York: Orange and Judd, 1914) 5.

[8] Samuel Cole Williams, *Lieutenant Henry Timberlake's Memoirs, 1756–1765* (Johnson City TN: Watauga Press, 1927) 70–71; William Bartram, *The Travels of William Bartram*, ed. Mark Van Doren (1791; repr., New York: Dover Publications, 1955).

[9] John Witthoft, "Cherokee Indian Use of Potherbs," *Journal of Cherokee Studies* 2 (Spring 1977): 250.

settlers who must have learned of the plant's medicinal properties from Cherokees. The Cherokees believed the plant to be a sentient being, and so upon digging it, they dropped a single seed of the plant in the ground as repayment "to the plant spirit."[10] Even though most white settlers used it sparingly because of its high market value, ginseng was "reputed to cure anything from cough to a boil to an internal disorder." In the north Georgia mountains, frontier settlers generally boiled two or three roots in a pint of water and then gave them to children as a cure for colic.[11]

Among other native plants, both the Cherokees and white mountain settlers gathered wild leeks or "ramps" (*Allium tricoccum*) from late fall to early spring, and the plants' abundance in the mountains helped convince whites of their value as an important food source. Like the Cherokees, the settlers transplanted ramps near their homes to flourish in a semi-cultivated state. Pokeweed (*Phytolacca americana*), referred to on the frontier as "Cherokee sallet," became another green regularly eaten by frontiersmen. The fruit of the pokeweed, sometimes considered poisonous by contemporary mountaineers, was believed to have important medicinal properties as well. The Cherokees also ate young shoots of the green-headed coneflower or sochan (*Rudbeckia laciniate L.*) and used them for a variety of medicinal purposes. "Sochan," an actual corruption of the Cherokee word for the plant, was cooked and consumed by mountain settlers, as were a number of other native plants.[12]

The Crude-drug Industry

Without question, the Cherokees influenced medicinal plant use in the mountains. Not only did they educate settlers to the medicinal properties of native plants, but they also facilitated the mountaineer's participation in the trade and sell of these plants to extra-local markets. In fact, root and plant digging in the mountain region has provided an important source of income to mountaineer farmers since at least the early nineteenth century. The War Between the States actually increased the cultivation and digging of many

---

[10] Wilma Dykeman, *Highland Homeland: The People of the Great Smokies* (Washington, DC: National Park Service, 1978) 52–55.

[11] Eliot Wiggington, ed., *The Foxfire Book* (Garden City NY: Double Day, 1972) 235.

[12] Paul Hamel and Mary Chiltoskey, *Cherokee Plants: A 400 Year History* (Sylva NC: Herald Publishing Company, 1975) 50; Witthoft, "Cherokee Use of Potherbs," 252.

native plants by mountaineers: one of the first crude-drug houses in North Carolina was in fact established in Lincolnton during the height of the conflict.

After the war, the "crude-drug" industry, as it was then called, became concentrated in the southern Appalachians, particularly in Tennessee, North Carolina, Virginia, and Kentucky. By the end of the nineteenth century, the enterprise was fast becoming an important source of supplemental income for individuals who otherwise lived on subsistence agriculture. By the turn of the century, the collection of plants for medicinal uses became important enough that the United States Department of Agriculture developed the Bureau of Plant Industries around 1903. The Bureau of Plant Industries produced numerous publications describing in detail American medicinal leaves and herbs, root drugs, medicinal barks, and weeds used in medicine. These publications were designed as guides and reference books for farmers, drug collectors, druggists, students, or others who "may be interested in one way or another in the collection of medicinal flora."[13]

Although medicinal plants were collected in the wild in the mountains, many were cultivated as supplemental agricultural crops. In fact, the bureau's publication, "American Medicinal Plants of Commercial Importance," gave specific instructions on the collection and preparation of plant material for the crude-drug market. Throughout the bulletin, the economic importance of collecting medicinal plants for the crude-drug market is strongly emphasized, and some plants were commonly sold in quantities ranging from "a few tons to fifty tons." To ensure potency and quality, many of the larger firms claimed adherence to provisions found in the Pure Food and Drugs Act of 1906, one of the first American laws designed to regulate the marketing and distribution of medicinal herbs.[14]

Another early publication of the bureau discusses the popular herb goldenseal, which it began seriously investigating in spring 1899. The publication includes a two-and-a-half-page description of the plant showing diagrams of both the first and second season's growth and the rhizome that is medically important. The section on collection and preparation is characteristically detailed: "The root should be collected in autumn after the plants have matured seed. Spring-dug root shrinks far more in drying and always commands a lower price than the fall-dug root. After the roots are

---

[13] Penelope Lane, "The History of Crude-drug Use in the Southern Appalachians," unpublished manuscript, n.d., 5.
[14] Ibid., 4–8.

removed from the earth they should be carefully freed from soil and all foreign particles. They should then be sorted, and small, undeveloped roots and broken pieces may be laid aside for replanting."[15]

Interestingly, it is clear from the description that the individuals cultivating and/or collecting these plant materials were quite knowledgeable about their product and about the importance of protecting and preserving it for future generations. The Bureau of Plant Industries provided additional relevant and useful information about cultivating the plant, illustrating detailed construction drawings of drying sheds and elaborate lathe-work designed to provide artificial shade for commercially grown plants.

By the end of the first decade of the twentieth century, the southern Appalachians had attracted numerous drug buyers to the region, many who soon opened processing facilities and collection points for growers and gatherers. One such collection point was the S. B. Penick & Company, which had offices in Asheville and Boone, North Carolina, and St. Louis, Missouri. Penick contracted with enterprising small farmers and local businessmen to collect medicinal plants ranging from bloodroot (*Sanquinaria canadensis*) to wild sarsaparilla (*Aralia nudicaulis*). These businessmen often operated community stores and would purchase materials from individuals in the community to satisfy market demands. A few decades later, Penick contracted with a company in Roan Mountain, Tennessee, C. R. Graybeal, who in turn provided J. P. Morgan with a truck that he would drive around country roads to collect materials from isolated farmers.[16]

By the late 1920s, Penick was a major supplier of crude drugs to the world market, a market that was now largely dependent upon the southern Appalachian region. In fact, in a company price list and manual published in 1929, Penick claimed that in "the Piedmont District" (southern Appalachia), 85 percent of all American drugs were gathered and prepared for the drug market and that Asheville, North Carolina, was "the center of this collecting section." A close competitor to Penick was the Wilcox Drug Company, established in Boone, North Carolina, in 1900 by General Grant Wilcox. According to company records, the Wilcox firm purchased roots, herbs, and

---

[15] Bureau of Plant Industries, *Manual of Use, 1899* (Washington, DC: US Department of Agriculture, 1899) 2.
[16] Edward T. Price, "Root Digging in the Appalachians: The Geography of Botanical Drugs," *Geographical Review* 50 (January 1960): 11–15.

bark from across the entire southern Appalachian region, with most sales "carried out through New York brokers."[17]

The extensive collecting activities of such firms and individuals may have contributed to the decline of many medicinal plants in the mountains, several of which are presently listed as endangered or threatened species. Dr. Edward Price, who in the 1960s published an important article on the geography of botanical drugs in the southern Appalachians, claimed that these collection centers greatly encouraged the depletion of the forests. While it is true that one firm collected some 13,000 pounds of ginseng in a single year, by the late 1960s most of the major crude-drug houses established in the mountains earlier in the century had moved to other regions of the United States, leaving only the Blue Ridge Drug Company at West Jefferson, the S. S. Penick Company in Asheville, and the Wilcox Drug Company in Boone. Although smaller collectors in the mountains continued to trade regularly in medicinal plants, their work became much more seasonal, providing an important, albeit supplemental income for mountain families.

Collecting or Conserving?

Despite the fall of southern Appalachia from the position of regional cornerstone of the American plant-medicine industry, the mountains today remain an importance source for numerous commercial botanicals. Goldenseal and ginseng from the southern mountains continue to contribute a considerable portion of the world market for these two plant species. Numerous other species are still widely collected in the mountain region, including black cohosh (*Cimicifuga racemosa*), mayapple (*Podophyllum peltatum*), boneset (*Eupatorium perfoliatum*), Seneca snakeroot (*Polygala senega L.*), Indian pinkroot (*Spigelia marilandica*), and witch-hazel (*Hamamelis virginiana*). Wilcox Natural Products (formerly Wilcox Drug), one of the region's largest botanical suppliers, buys more than fifty plant varieties from local collectors, processing them at their headquarters in Boone, North Carolina. Two smaller though no less important buyers are Morgan Herbs and Metals of Roan Mountain, Tennessee, and White Brother's Fur and Ginseng of north Georgia, both of which buy considerable amounts of native plants for the herbal products and pharmaceutical industries.

---

[17] Ibid., 14–15; S. B. Penick & Company, *Price List and Manual of Crude Drugs* (New York: S. B. Penick & Company, 1919) 3.

To their credit, Wilcox Natural Products, a private corporation now owned by the Zuellig Group of North America, a Swiss firm, is also actively involved in the commercial cultivation of native mountain plants. According to Chuck Wanzer, general manager of the Boone, North Carolina, facility, as much as one-fourth of their annual production is now derived from locally cultivated plants. Presently, Wilcox maintains a 30-acre facility strictly devoted to the growing and harvesting of native plants as well as to assisting other local growers with on-site consultations. Interestingly, one of Wilcox's most lucrative products is the saw palmetto berry (*Serenoa repens*), collected not in the mountains but in Florida, where it grows wild. According to Wanzer, one of the largest purchasers of saw palmetto berries is Pierre Fabre Industries, a well-known French pharmaceutical and cosmetics firm with worldwide distribution.[18]

Of native mountain plants, goldenseal remains the Zuellig Group of North America's most important species. Although a federally protected plant, native goldenseal is still collected in southern Appalachia in considerable quantities, especially in states like West Virginia and Kentucky where the habitat is ideal. According to one reputable source, more than 300,000 pounds of goldenseal are annually collected in North America, with only 20,000 pounds coming from cultivated sources. Wilcox Natural Products is responsible for nearly half of all cultivated goldenseal in the United States, making it a corporate leader in the conservation of this unique and rare native species. Goldenseal, an endangered species in the US, is also protected internationally by the Washington Convention on International Trade in Endangered Species of Wild Fauna and Flora.

The digging of native plants for the ever-growing natural foods supplement and botanicals industry begs the question of conservation. Do the high prices currently paid for native species like ginseng and goldenseal encourage over-harvesting, and, if so, to what extent? Historically, one can place blame on the crude-drug and multinational pharmaceutical companies and their collection practices for the decline in some species of mountain plants. Today, however, the problem is a much more complicated one of simply collecting verses not collecting. In the last two decades, more habitats (and thus more native plants) in the southern Appalachians have been lost to suburban and industrial development than in the past two centuries. In West Virginia alone, more than 300 square miles of mountain lands are in the

---

[18] Author's telephone interview with Chuck Wanzer, 26 May 1999.

process of being permanently destroyed by mountaintop removal, a state-of-the-art coal-mining technique that literally decapitates entire mountains and the lush biologically diverse habitats they have supported for centuries.

Modern industrial logging has also been responsible for permanently destroying the fragile understories of mountain deciduous woodlands. At present, extensive clear-cutting for the voracious appetites of industrial chip-mills is increasing at an alarming pace, threatening to destroy the tens of thousands of acres of the region's remaining hardwood forests. Chip-mills grind trees into quarter-sized chips for paper and particle board, and in the process they are destroying more than 1.2 million acres of forests in the southeastern United States. The average chip-mill, which generally employs only six to eight men, devours 8,000 to 10,000 acres of hardwood forests annually, yielding more than 300,000 tons of chips. Recent ecological studies have shown that herbaceous understories never recover from such logging practices, including many of the species that are dug for pharmaceutical and botanical industries.[19]

"Wildcrafting," on the other hand—a term used for the practice of local populations harvesting native plants—often involves the sustainable use of the forest. In southern Appalachia where there are many cultural and historical uses of plants, over-gathering is generally tempered by the long-term benefits gained by conserving a commercially valuable plant species. More often than not, wildcrafters belong to a multigenerational tradition of plant gatherers who seek to regenerate the plants they routinely harvest. Judy Touchstone of northwest Georgia, for example, has dug ginseng from "wild" populations her father started from seed more than forty years ago. In some cases, harvesting plants can actually assist in plant proliferation. In fact, scientific studies of ginseng harvesting have shown that as many as one-forth of all plants in a single community may be annually gathered without significant detriment to the long-term health of the stand. Ginseng diggers who selectively gather only mature plants and routinely replant seeds from these same plants are actually ensuring the long-term viability of the species.[20]

[19] David Cameron Duffy and Albert J. Meir, "Do Appalachian Herbaceous Understories Ever Recover from Clear-cutting?," *Conservation Biology* 6 (June 1992): 196–201.

[20] P. Nantel, D. Gagnon, and A. Nault, "Population Viability Analysis of American Ginseng and Wild Leek Harvested in Stochastic Environments," *Conservation Biology* 10 (November 1996): 608–21.

For many in southern Appalachia, as Library of Congress folklorist Mary Hufford has pointed out, the mountain forest has historically been perceived as a commons by which all members of a community benefit.[21] The current environmental abuses by coal and timber companies, local residents argue, is a far greater threat to forest biodiversity and may result in not only the extinction of entire populations of medicinal plants, but also in the loss of a cultural tradition going back more than two centuries. Commercial buyers of mountain plants have an obligation to ensure that they are gathered legally and to promote local and responsible cultivation of native species, but they alone cannot solve the problem of conservation. We as a society must also recognize the numerous health benefits of preserving native forest ecosystems and act accordingly. A much more comprehensive and politically aggressive preservation plan is needed for biologically unique places like the southern Appalachians. The biological heritage of the region may be worth saving for its own sake, but its value to the health of future generations makes it doubly imperative that we begin solving the truly devastating problem of habitat loss.

---

[21] Mary Hufford, "Weathering the Storm: Cultural Survival in an Appalachian Valley," in Harvard Ayers et al., eds., *An Appalachian Tragedy: Air Pollution and Tree Death in the Eastern Forests of North America* (San Francisco: Sierra Club Books, 1998) 126–59.

Chapter 17

A Whole World Dying

Few single events in North American environmental history compare with the loss of the American chestnut tree. Chestnut trees once comprised roughly 20 percent of the entire forest in the southern mountains, and in specific areas they accounted for as much as one-third of all trees. William Ashe reported seeing locales where the trees "occur pure or nearly pure over areas as large as 100 acres." In 1901, he and Horace Ayers estimated that their southern Appalachian study area contained more than 884,000 acres of chestnut timber.[1] The tree was largely confined to the Blue Ridge Mountains and Cumberland Plateau, where they commonly grew at altitudes between 1,000 and 4,000 feet. The Ridge and Valley province had a few important stands of chestnuts as well, but these were found only on the slopes of the highest ridges where richer soils and heavier rainfall predominated. A reconstruction of nineteenth-century forests in northwest Georgia found chestnut trees comprising no more than 6 percent of the area, with hickories and oaks, the most dominant tree species, making up 45 percent of the total forest.[2] William MacDonald, professor of plant pathology at West Virginia University and a leading expert on the tree,

---

[1] Ayers and Ashe, *The Southern Appalachian Forests* (Washington, DC: Department of the Interior, US Geological Survey, 1905) 30, 52–53.
[2] Gayther Plummer, "18th Century Forests in Georgia," *Bulletin of the Georgia Academy of Science* 33 (1975): 7.

estimates that chestnut-dominated forests once covered more than 200 million acres of land from Maine to Georgia.[3]

The death of the American chestnut was due to an exotic blight introduced into the United States from Japanese chestnut nursery stock just after the turn of the twentieth century. A forester at the New York Zoological Park first reported the disease in 1904 after observing an immense number of dead and dying chestnut trees on park lands under his supervision. Five years later, the first scientific bulletin appeared about the disease, which was determined to be a fungus later named *Endothia parasitica*.[4] Only a year after the bulletin's publication, an editorial in the *Southern Lumberman* referred to a "mysterious blight" that had recently been observed in Pennsylvania and New York. "Large timbered sections of [Pennsylvania] are already and in an alarming manner affected by the disease," stated the report.[5] By 1912 all the chestnut trees in New York City were dead, and the chestnut blight had reached no fewer than ten states. Scientists in Pennsylvania launched a vigorous control program that included burning dead trees, monitoring the disease's advance, and spraying infected trees. This effort, a scientist later commented, was a little like using toy swords to battle an enemy equipped with atomic bombs. Yet foresters told the public that "the control and ultimate extermination of [the chestnut blight]…will sooner or later become a real accomplishment."[6]

The disease spread relentlessly southward at an astounding rate of some 50 miles per year. Aided by woodsmen who carried it on their shoes and axes, the blight first entered North Carolina near Stokes and Surry counties about 1913. Shady Valley, in upper east Tennessee, was hit by 1915. By 1920 the American chestnut in the Great Smokies was ultimately doomed, though there were few visible signs of the blight there before 1925.[7] North Carolina lumbermen even used the imminently encroaching disease as a last-ditch effort to defeat the proposed Great Smoky Mountains National Park. "Certainly nothing could be more unsightly than the gaunt

---

[3] Quoted in Donald E. Davis and Margaret Brown, "I Thought the Whole World was Going to Die: The Story of the American Chestnut," *Now and Then* (Spring 1995): 31.

[4] G. F. Gravatt, *Chestnut Blight*, USDA Farmer's Bulletin No. 1641 (Washington, DC: US Government Printing Office, 1930) 1–3.

[5] Anonymous, *Southern Lumberman*, 6 August 1910, 38C.

[6] Davis and Brown, "I Thought the Whole World was Going to Die," 30.

[7] William E. Cole, *Tales from a Country Ledger* (Acton MA: Tapestry Press, 1990) 105.

and naked trunks of these dead trees, standing like skeletons in every vista which the eye turns," they wrote.[8] By the 1930s, the blight had reached much of north Georgia, and by 1940 there was scarcely a tree in the entire region that was not dead or did not show some sign of being infected with the disease.

Although few people alive today remember what the southern Appalachian forests looked like before the blight devastated the region, those who did provide indisputable testimony to the significance of the chestnut tree to the mountain environment. "This is an unbelievable thing, how many chestnuts there were," remembered Paul Woody, who grew up near Cataloochee, North Carolina.[9] Gifford Pinchot himself recalled seeing chestnut stands with individual trees 13 feet across and with crowns spreading more than 120 feet above the forest floor.[10] Charles Grossman, one of the first rangers at the new Great Smoky Mountains National Park, recorded a chestnut tree 9 feet, 8 inches in diameter at a point 6 feet off the ground. "The hollow portion is so large that [an adult] could stand up in it," wrote Grossman after discovering the tree. "This hollow runs more than 50 feet up the trunk and at its narrowest point is not less than 3 feet. This must be the tree of which I heard. A man lost some stock during a snowstorm and later found them safe in a hollow chestnut tree."[11]

Due to their abundance and enormous size, the American chestnut ranked as the most important wildlife plant of the eastern United States. The largest trees could produce 10 bushels or more of nuts. Reports of layers of chestnuts 4 inches deep on the forest floor were not uncommon in the southern mountains. Many of the wildlife species mountain people thought of as game—squirrels, wild turkey, white-tailed deer, bear, raccoon, and grouse—depended on chestnuts as a major food source. "The worst thing that ever happened in this country was when the chestnut trees died," said Walter Cole of east Tennessee. "Turkeys disappeared, and the squirrels

---

[8] Western Carolina Lumber and Timber Association, "Report of Committee Appointed by Western Carolina Lumber and Timber Association," manuscript, Forest History Society, Durham NC, 25 July 1925, 4.

[9] Paul Woody, interview by Katherine Manscill, 1973, transcript, Oral History Collection, Great Smoky Mountains National Park Archives, Sugarlands Visitor Center, Gatlinburg.

[10] David Wheeler, "Where There Be Mountains, There Be Chestnuts," *Katuah Journal* 21 (Fall 1988): 3.

[11] Ibid.

were not one-tenth as many as there were before."[12] Will Effler, who grew up on the West Fork of the Little River in what is today the Great Smoky Mountains, recalled shooting a wild turkey that held no fewer than ninety-two chestnuts, "still in the hulls and undigested," in its swollen craw.[13] Other non-game animals were equally dependent on the chestnut, including several unique insect species that relied upon chestnut trees as their principal food course. Paul Opler of the US Fish and Wildlife Service has estimated that at least seven native moths became extinct in the southern Appalachians as a result of the chestnut blight.[14] The loss of the chestnut also slowed the recovery of wildlife populations already suffering from loss of habitat by logging operations. Former Randoph-Macon College biologist James M. Hill ascribes the slow recovery of deer, wild turkeys, goshawks, Cooper's hawks, cougars, and bobcats in the mountains to habitat destruction directly caused by the chestnut blight.[15]

Of course, humans seasonally ate chestnuts too, making them an important dietary supplement when the trees dropped their nuts after the first major frost. Each October, children living in the mountains scooped up chestnuts by the sackful, hanging their cloth bags on nails outside the door until December when the nuts would begin to get "wormy." Cherokees made more use of the nut, which they frequently added to cornmeal dough that "was boiled or baked."[16] Some families gathered bushels of chestnuts, taking them by wagon to urban markets. John McCaulley, whose family foraged for chestnuts in the Great Smoky Mountains around 1910, remembered seeing in one mountain cabin a "hundred bushels of chestnuts, piled up there, and about four men packing off, every day." McCaulley

---

[12] Walter Cole, interview by Charles Grossman, 1965, transcript, Oral History Collection, Great Smoky Mountains National Park Archives, Sugarlands Visitor Center, Gatlinburg.

[13] Vic Weals, *Last Train to Elkmont* (Knoxville: Olden Press, 1991) 128.

[14] Paul Opler, "Insects of the American Chestnut: Possible Importance and Conservation Concern," *Proceedings of the American Chestnut Symposium* (Morgantown: University of West Virginia, 1978) 83–85.

[15] James M. Hill, "Wildlife Value of Castanea dentata, Past and Present, in Mark Double and William McDonald, eds., *Proceedings of the International Chestnut Conference*, West Virginia University College of Agriculture and Forestry, Morgantown, 10–14 July 1992, 190.

[16] Mrs. Birgie and Johnny Manning, interview by Glenn Cardwell, 22 April 1980, Everts Cove, Sevier County TN, transcript, Oral History Collection, Great Smoky Mountains National Park Archives, Sugarlands Visitor Center, Gatlinburg.

himself recalls gathering as many as 7 bushels of chestnuts in a single day's outing. These he said were taken to Knoxville on mules where they were sold for "four dollars a bushel."[17] Chestnuts were also routinely shipped by rail to major cities on the eastern seaboard. In 1911, West Virginia reported that one railroad station alone shipped 155,000 pounds of chestnuts to destinations along the train's northerly route.[18]

Another important use of chestnuts in the mountain region was as food for hogs. For a month or two each fall, hogs ran loose in the woods to feast on chestnuts and other mast littering the forest floor. Martha Wachacha, recalling the scene around her home in Cherokee, North Carolina, said "there were about a hundred pigs when I first moved here. Pigs and hogs were so fat. There was plenty of chestnuts back then."[19] In late November, or as soon as the weather got cold enough, mountain residents rounded up the fattened hogs for slaughter. Chestnut-flavored pork hung in the smokehouse all winter, where it continued to be the primary source of protein for most families. A Virginia farmer commenting on the role of chestnuts in mountain agriculture noted that it "didn't cost a cent to raise chestnuts or hogs in those days. It was a very inexpensive way to farm. The people had money and had meat on the table too."[20]

As a building material, chestnut wood was unsurpassed. It was highly rot-resistant, making it an ideal for fences, shingles, and furniture. The tree was a valuable source of tannic acid used in the leather industry, and chestnut bark and rough chestnut cordwood were other important sources of income for mountain residents. In Tennessee alone, 50,000 cords of wood were yearly cut to supply those tanneries in operation before 1912. This "tanbark" or "acid wood," as it was called locally, was taken largely from trees already cut for other purposes or small defective trees that were not of nut-bearing age.[21] Commercial operations were also heavily engaged in the

---

[17] Donald Davis and Margaret Brown, "Trail History Notebook," unpublished manuscript, Great Smoky Mountains Natural History Association, Sugarlands Visitor Center, Great Smoky Mountains National Park, Gatlinburg, 1992, 147.

[18] N. J. Giddings, *Untitled Report on Chestnut Blight in West Virginia* (Harrisburg: Pennsylvania Chestnut Blight Conference, 1912) 173–74.

[19] Maggie Wachacha, interview by Lois Calonehuskie, Earl Davis, and Tom Hill, *Journal of Cherokee Studies* 9 (1989): 50.

[20] Stephen Nash, "The Blighted Chestnut," *National Parks* 62 (July/August 1988): 16.

[21] William Ashe, "Chestnut in Tennessee," *Forest Studies in Tennessee, Bulletin 10* (Nashville: Baird-Ward Company, 1912) 5.

harvesting of chestnut trees for tanbark and cordwood. One observer remarked in 1931 that even though chestnut timber was once cut by lumbermen for the bark alone, "very little waste of this kind is now noted."[22]

As might be expected during the era of industrial logging, the blight did not slow the harvest of chestnut trees; in fact, the cutting actually increased after the initial introduction of the disease. Most lumber barons were harvesting the largest chestnut trees even before the blight was officially observed in the mountain region. Early on, lumbermen even doubted the potential devastation of the disease, believing the fast-going trees would eventually regenerate across the mountain landscape. Moreover, they knew that a chestnut tree was worth money dead or alive, since foresters soon determined that it was possible to manufacture lumber from standing dead chestnuts for up to ten years after the death of the tree. For acid wood, the salvage period was even longer: Reuben Robertson, president of the Champion Fibre, estimated that the company cut chestnut trees for pulp and tannin twenty years after the blight first arrived in North Carolina.[23]

The chestnut was therefore responsible for bringing another major industry to the upper South—leather tanning. By 1930, there were no fewer than twenty-one chestnut-fueled plants in the southern Appalachians, producing more than one-half of the US supply of vegetable-based tannins. Within a decade, almost all evidence of chestnut trees had vanished from the mountains as the growing tanning industry, the "largest consumer of chestnut," had found ways to use every part of the tree.[24] After 1940, with the development of synthetic replacements in the production of tannin, the demand for the chestnut greatly diminished, leaving only a few ghost-white skeletons to stand lone sentry over the once great forest. The dead and dying chestnut snags were painful reminders to mountaineers that the mountain landscape, including an entire way of life, was all but gone. "Man, I had the awfulest feeling about that as a child, to look back yonder and see

---

[22] E. H. Frothingham, *Timber Growing and Logging Practices in the Southern Appalachian Region*, USDA Technical Bulletin No. 250 (Washington, DC: US Government Printing Office, 1931) 12.

[23] Reuben Robertson, interview by Jerry Mander, 1959, transcript in vertical files, Forest History Society, Durham NC.

[24] Gravatt, *Chestnut Blight*, 14, fig. 12.

those trees dying," recalled Joe Tribble, a native of eastern Kentucky. "I thought the whole world was going to die."[25]

Mountain residents were right to mourn the lost of the chestnut. The chestnut tree was possibly the single most important natural resource of the Appalachian South, providing inhabitants with food, shelter, and, in the early twentieth century, a much-needed cash income. In fall and winter, chestnuts could be boiled or roasted over an open fire or traded at local stores for supplies. Having the greatest durability of available native woods, chestnut timber was crafted into long-lasting boards, posts, shingles, and split-rail fences. The tender and abundant sprouts could even be pulled from the ground and fed to cattle as fodder. As a wildlife food, the chestnut was unsurpassed and helped keep local game populations at their highest levels. In a memoir written shortly before his death, Shady Valley, Tennessee, native William Cole summed up the extraordinary value of the tree to mountain residents. "A favorite outing for me and my friends was to go to the ball ground on Sunday to collect chestnuts," wrote Cole. "The chestnut tree was a great tree, chestnut wood was a great wood, and chestnuts a good food."[26]

Now more off the farmstead than on it, the food and folkways of the region's inhabitants began to change conspicuously. By the early 1930s, mountain families were utilizing less buttermilk and more whole milk, less rye and wheat breads and more light breads, and consuming more processed sugar and less maple syrup and honey. While there were some dietary constants throughout the region, such as the consumption of cornbread and biscuits, the use of canned and other "storebought" foods increased significantly during the first three decades of the twentieth century.[27] For those who remained exclusively farmers, the use of crop monoculture became a more common way to farm. Family size dropped by more than two individuals, from 10 family members per household in 1910 to 7.62 per household in 1934. Home-building techniques changed as well. "Boxed" houses—that is, frameless structures made exclusively with sawn planks and boards—gradually replaced log cabins as residents working seasonally for lumber companies had less time, or the necessary extra help, to build

---

[25] Tribble quoted in Nyoka Hawkins, "Building Community through Grassroots Democracy," *Local Voices* 10 (February/March 1993): 7.

[26] Cole, *Tales from a Country Ledger*, 104.

[27] Lester R. Wheeler, "Changes in the Dietary Habits," *Tennessee Academy of Science* 10 (July 1935): 169.

traditional log homes. The number of working outbuildings on the homestead also diminished, including the smokehouse, springhouse, and separate kitchen facility. Furniture was no longer homemade, and looms and spinning wheels largely became items of the past.[28] Needless to say, everything from architecture to social relations was altered by the separation of the mountain environment from the mountaineer.

In many ways, the death of the chestnut symbolized the end of a waning, albeit vital subsistence culture in the Southern Appalachians. The loss of the tree no doubt gave additional advantage to the forces of industrialization that were gaining a stronger foothold on the regional and local economy. No longer able to range hogs and cattle in the woodland commons, trap fish in free-flowing streams, or gather chestnuts on the hillsides, the rural mountaineer increasingly looked to the mill town and urban center for economic salvation. The environmental abuse of the mountains, along with their permanent removal from the traditional land base, made it difficult for mountaineers to continue a semi-agrarian and intimately forest-dependent way of life. With the death the chestnut, an entire world did die, eliminating subsistence practices that had been viable in the southern mountains for more than four centuries.

---

[28] Lester R. Wheeler, "A Study of the Remote Mountain People of the Tennessee Valley," *Journal of the Tennessee Academy of Science* 9 (January 1935): 34–36.

Chapter 18

The Land of Ridge and Valley

Unique to the upper south are the northwest Georgia mountains. Known by geographers as the "Armuchee Ridges," these picturesque mountains are part of the Ridge and Valley physiographic province of the southern Appalachians. Taylors Ridge, Johns Mountain, and Rocky Face Mountain comprise a significant portion of the region, although numerous smaller ridges are considered part of the geographic area as well.

Popular recreation areas such as Lake Marvin, the Pocket, and Redwine Cove are found within the boundaries of the northwest Georgia mountains, sites frequented by weekend visitors and local residents alike. The Armuchee Ranger District of the Chattahoochee National Forest comprises no fewer than 66,000 acres of public land in the area, incorporating portions of six northwest Georgia counties.

From an ecological perspective, the Armuchee Ridges are truly distinctive. The mountains are at a biological crossroads, containing numerous plant species from the northern and southern ends of their range. Because of its diverse ecology and natural beauty, the area received attention from the US Congress who, in 1992, temporarily stopped all logging activities in many portions of the Armuchee Ranger District.

Not only does the northwest Georgia mountain region display a unique geology and natural history; it is also rich in human history. This corner of north Georgia was also the heart of the former Cherokee Nation, which had its capital at New Echota near Calhoun. Pioneer settlers also worked the land, leaving their own cultural imprint on the landscape. Later in the century, mine prospectors and their employees dug deep into the mountains, uncovering thousands of tons of precious ores for the insatiable engines of commerce and industry.

In the area's wide and rich river valleys, cotton truly became king during the late nineteenth century, promoting the development of the selling and manufacturing of a whole array of cotton products in the area, including tufted linens and bedspreads. While few signs remain of these previously vital industries, abandoned homesteads and mining sites can still be seen throughout the mountain region, marking a way of life almost forgotten.

Cherokee Georgia

In 1831, northwest or "Cherokee" Georgia was surveyed by order of the governor into four sections, and these sections were further subdivided into land districts 9 miles square. Those grid quadrants were subdivided into sixty districts, and then laid off into 160-acre "landlots." Georgia residents subsequently drew these lots in a public lottery for a fee ranging from two to eighteen dollars. Landlots never claimed later became known as "wild lands," and those still occupied by Cherokees were later surveyed and evaluated so that "just compensation" could be granted before their removal.[1]

Despite their noted influence on mountain life and culture, nineteenth-century Cherokees utilized the surrounding countryside in much the same way as did white settlers. By 1820, most Cherokees valued the surrounding landscape more for its ability to grow corn, wheat, or cotton, or to provide pasture for their grazing livestock than as a home to native plants and animals. In northwest Georgia, most Cherokees also made daily use of the wheel, loom, and plow and wore Anglo-style clothing. Several even found themselves among the planter elite, owning both slaves and large plantations.

James Vann was one of several prominent Cherokee planters and merchants who rose to social and economic prominence in the area during the early nineteenth century. Recognizing the necessity of roads in the Tennessee Valley for stimulating commerce, Vann also initiated the building of the Federal Road, the first route to bisect the Cherokee Nation. Completed in 1807, the road connected Nashville, Tennessee, to Augusta,

---

[1] Douglas Wilms, "Agrarian Progress in the Cherokee Nation Prior to Removal," *Studies in the Social Sciences, West Georgia College* 16 (1977): 1–3.

Georgia. At the major Cherokee toll gates, the rates were fairly typical of the period: wagon and team, one dollar; two-wheeled carriage, fifty cents; man and horse, twelve cents; hogs, sheep, and goats, one cent per head. Traces of the Federal Road can still be seen in some isolated locales. Years of horse, foot, and wagon travel have carved narrow, yet visible swaths through the countryside, leaving an important historical legacy for future generations to map and preserve.

After the forced removal of the Cherokees in 1838, white settlers began pouring into the northwest Georgia mountains, settling lands won in the land lottery. Among the first whites in the northwest Georgia mountains were livestock drovers who ranged cattle across fertile woodland valleys and along ridge tops. The proliferation of hogs and cattle throughout the mountains was not without important environmental consequences, as grazing livestock suppressed the growth of young trees in the forest understory. Cattle drovers also burned the woods annually in order to sprout new growth for the ranging animals.

Waters of Life

By the 1840s, the growing white population brought the need for improved commercial transport in the area, which made the region's largest rivers important arteries for commerce and trade. Creeks and rivers were essential to the settlement of the region, as waterpower was needed to drive the ever-important grist- and sawmills. Gristmills were also the focal point of community life, as hardly anyone lived more than a half-day horse-and-buggy ride away from the local miller. Millponds were also favorite spots for fishing, picnics, and group baptisms. Gristmills harnessed the energy of the area's swift-moving streams and turned corn and wheat into nutritious meal and flour. Gristmills also attracted other important enterprises, and so a visit to the local millhouse was a monthly, if not weekly, outing.

Early travel in the mountains was indeed dependent upon the flow of water; high waters from spring or summer freshets severely limited excursions beyond a creek's swollen banks. Of course, one could always float down the river in a kneel boat or canoe, an excursion made less arduous after the invention of the outboard motor in the 1920s. Water levels directed traffic in other ways as well since fords were always dug at the most shallow point in the creek or river.

Riverboat traffic was also not uncommon on northwest Georgia major rivers, especially after the Civil War. Steamboats regularly made their way up the Coosawattee, Conasauga, and Oostanaula rivers, especially during high-water season from November to May. Steamboats came upriver to load cotton, lumber, wheat, and oats, which were shipped to markets in Rome and major ports further downstream. Several steamboat companies were formed in the region before 1880, and the boats themselves were given names that reflect the local character of the enterprises. Boats making regular trips upstream included *Hill City*, *Sport*, *Dixie*, *Mitchell*, *Resaca*, and the *Coosawattee*.

The Conasauga River, the fastest flowing of the rivers mentioned above, has a unique and interesting history. In the nineteenth century, it was known locally as the "Slave River" because of the great number of slaves who manned flatboats along its waters. The Conasauga was a major artery for transporting mountain furs and peltry to the Gulf of Mexico, and early eyewitnesses recall hearing the slaves' voices "in songs, shouts, or murmuring...far beyond the river's banks."[2]

Sawmill operations also sprang up everywhere along the Conasauga River at that time, including a large one at a community known as Tilton that was owned and operated by Wiley J. Ault. Mr. Ault took advantage of the well-wooded bottomlands along the banks of the river, cutting down enormous trees that had been standing for more than 100 years. The trees were often floated down the river in large rafts to a point were they could be safely extricated from the water's edge and then sawn into boards. Log rafts were not uncommon sights on northwest Georgia's rivers, particularly during the heyday of industrial logging, which peaked sometime during the 1920s.

Mineral springs were also abundant in the northwest Georgia mountains and drew numerous visitors from across the South. In fact, the "taking of healthful waters" had developed into a popular ritual for most southerners prior to the Civil War. During the warm summer months, people would visit as many mineral springs as possible, taking advantage of their tonic and soothing effects. Water "cures" were also popular among physicians of the era who would prescribe the drinking of various mineral waters for such illnesses as dyspepsia, gout, and skin disorders. Chemists routinely tested the composition of mineral waters, and their various properties were published routinely in popular books and magazines of the period.

---

[2] Donald E. Davis, *The Land of Ridge and Valley: A Photographic History of the Northwest Georgia Mountains* (Charleston SC: Arcadia Publishers, 2000) 39.

Perhaps the land of Ridge and Valley's most well-known basin of mineral water was Catoosa Springs near the Keith community in Catoosa County. At that time there were more than fifty-two visible springs on the site, almost all with varying mineral properties. During the 1850s, a large hotel and several row cottages were built to accommodate guests. During the Civil War, Catoosa Springs became the site of several Confederate hospitals. Many sick soldiers were able to return to duty after drinking or bathing in the mineral waters.

In decades past, mineral springs were favorite gathering places for families and friends, especially during warm summer months when such places served as weekend retreats for local residents as well. Mineral springs were therefore more than a source for water; they served as a place where people could nourish and replenish their bodies and reflect in the quiet serenity and beauty of the grounds. They were, indeed, "waters of life."[3]

Mining the Mountains

While general farming and agriculture had a significant effect on the mountains and valleys of northwest Georgia, industry also left an indelible mark on the area. Underneath the northwest Georgia mountains lay an abundance of valuable minerals: talc, bauxite, shale, and the numerous ores for making iron. The mining of these mountains is a little-known chapter in the history of the Appalachian region and is perhaps illuminated for the first time in this essay. In fact, the original discovery of bauxite in North America was made at Hermitage in Floyd County in 1887, and this mine provided much of the US domestic supply for more than a decade.

Iron forges and furnaces were among the earliest industries to locate here, and collectively they had a tremendous impact on the mountain landscape. Among the first iron operations in northwest Georgia was the Stamp Creek Furnace, erected in Bartow County in 1837 by Moses and Aaron Stroup. Others soon followed, making the area around Cartersville, in Bartow County, a major iron-producing center. Of the four furnaces erected along the Etowah River, the largest, the Etowah Furnace, employed more than 500 hands at peak production during the 1850s.

Nineteenth-century iron manufacturing required vast quantities of natural resources, all of which could be readily found in the northwest Georgia mountains, including an unlimited supply of hardwood trees. The

---

[3] Ibid., 38.

trees were needed for the production of charcoal, the only fuel hot enough to melt the various ores used in the iron-making process. Because the mountains of northwest Georgia possessed large stands of mature oak, hickory, beech, and maple, not to mention an abundant water supply, it became a prime location for the nineteenth-century iron master.

During the antebellum period, iron manufacturing involved two distinct operations: blast furnaces and bloomery forges. One of the earlier blast furnaces was erected before the Civil War by Doah Edmondson in Walker County near the foot of John's Mountain. This furnace, which took two years to complete, was 20 square feet at its base and more than 20 feet high. The more numerous and smaller bloomery forges used charcoal for fuel but still required considerable amounts of timber. Most bloomery forges in the northwest Georgia mountains, such as the one operating on the Conasauga River in Murray County, produced what was then known as "hollow-ware"; that is, kettles, pots, and pans as well as stove plates, wrought-iron bars for nails, tools, wagon rims, mill gears, and plow points.

By the 1850s, the iron industry was having a noticeable effect on the mountain landscape. Clear-cutting of timber left surrounding hillsides devoid of vegetation and topsoil, making them less desirable for other agricultural pursuits. The continued use of specific sites for charcoal production drastically decreased soil fertility, resulting in sterile patches of ground that for decades supported little or no plant life. Of course, there were numerous environmental effects resulting from iron production. Most furnaces were nearly always located near creeks and rivers since a great deal of water was needed to operate them. In order to direct the greatest volume of water into the furnace operations, small dams were constructed next to the forge, resulting in the flooding of the surrounding countryside. The environmental impact of the iron industry was not limited to charcoal production, the building of dams, or general forge operations. There was also the clearing of roads for employee housing, especially at the largest facilities, such as the Etna Furnace in Polk County.

By far the greatest environmental impact from iron ore mining came after the first introduction of steam shovels to the industry, which allowed for the excavation of enormous quantities of earth at each mine site. This new technology was used widely in northwest Georgia, from Sugar Valley in Gordon County to Cartersville nearly 40 miles away. As a result, the scale of mining expanded exponentially after the turn of the twentieth century and left deep and lasting scars upon the mountain landscape.

Iron ore was only one of a dozen or so minerals excavated in northwest Georgia during the nineteenth and early twentieth centuries. Large pockets of manganese and talc were also recovered, and mine sites from those excavations are still visible today. For the first three decades of the twentieth century, numerous state geologists continued to search the mountains for new pockets of ores, photographing potential mine sites, mineral springs, and other sites of interest as they explored the rural countryside. With the exception of talc mining, the mining of minerals in northwest Georgia had nearly ceased by the end of the 1930s. Seven decades of mineral excavation had completely exhausted most mine sites, forcing industrialists to look elsewhere for their raw materials.

A National Forest

By the 1870s, the forests of northwest Georgia were the target of much land and mineral speculation, initiated largely by northern industrialists seeking to acquire tracts of unsettled lands for mining and timbering. These lands were acquired slowly, as railroad lines were needed to take full advantage of the yet untouched natural resources. Large-scale timbering often preceded mining operations, as standing trees were major obstacles to mineral ore extraction.

Historically, northwest Georgia forests were comprised almost exclusively of hardwoods, with oaks and hickories being the most dominant of the tree species. Species composition varied with elevation, however, and south-facing slopes often harbored stands of shortleaf pines. At higher elevations, American chestnut trees could be found in scattered groves, at least until the 1940s when the valuable tree was exterminated by a deadly Asian blight.

The diary of Moravian missionaries Steiner and Gottlieb Byhan, who lived at Spring Place in Murray County, provides one of the earliest descriptions of northwest Georgia forests. "The all-purpose woods," they wrote in 1801, "are hickory, black, white, and other oak, chestnut, walnut, poplar, sourwood, and many others. In the low places are maple, beech, elm, sweetgum...sassafras [and] sumach." Trees in the native hardwood forests of northwest Georgia were apparently of exceptional size and quality, as evidenced by the comments of M. H. Bunn, who traveled through the region in 1844: "In afternoon I left Mr. Price's [home] and reached Mr. Henry's [home] higher up in Broomtown Valley in Walker County. Passed through a beautiful section of fertile land. Never saw a section more heavily timbered. Red oak, chestnut, and poplar, etc., remarkably tall and straight, stood thick, forming almost a complete shade."[4]

Almost none of the forests were completely un-cut in northwest Georgia, as mountain lands had been cleared for agriculture since well before the eighteenth century. Trees in the wide river valleys were the first to see the axe, and gradually more timber was cleared along hillsides and accessible slopes. Most nineteenth-century farmers left more than half of their farmsteads in woodland as the trees provided them with food, firewood, and forage for their ranging livestock.

The 1920s was the heyday of industrial logging in the area, which involved elaborate harvesting and transport systems to get the tall timber to the local mill. Cable "skidders" were sometimes used to drag fallen logs to the rail lines, which were loaded with a steam-powered engine and winch. From there, Shay locomotives often transported the logs to the sawmill. Perhaps the most extensive of all logging operations in northwest Georgia were those of Conasauga Lumber Company, which owned more than 70,000 acres in Murray, Fannin, and Gilmer counties. The Cincinnati, Ohio-based company moved into the region after 1912 and logged extensively in what is today the Cohutta Wildernesss Area, as well as the northwest corner of Murray County, including the headwaters of Holly Creek. By 1925, the Conasauga Lumber Company employed more than 700 men, making it one of the area's largest employers.

As a result of many of the environmental abuses of industrial logging, the National Forest Service was formed during the second decade of the twentieth century to help acquire cutover lands and return them to timber productivity. One of the first tracts of land bought in the area included 23,000 acres purchased in 1930 from the Conasauga Lumber Company. These lands became part of the Chattahoochee National Forest and later the Cohutta Wilderness Area, the largest protected tract of public land in the eastern United States. The Chattahoochee National Forest was officially established by presidential proclamation on 9 July 1936, with a combined area of 1,165,000 acres.

The lands to be purchased for the Armuchee Ranger District, which lay far to the west and south of the Cohutta Mountains, were also purportedly cut over, burned over, and of little economic value. During the 1930s, members of the Civilian Conservation Corps planted trees and built

---

[4] Ibid., 81.

several recreation areas to help rejuvenate the mountain landscape. Fish and game were also stocked into the national forest, including white-tailed deer, which had been virtually eliminated from the northwest Georgia mountains by 1940. By the 1960s, land acquisition efforts in the Armuchee Ranger District had been largely suspended, leaving the total acreage at around 65,000 acres. Despite its smaller size, the Armuchee Ranger District contains some of the largest contiguous stands of hardwoods found in the entire Ridge and Valley province of southern Appalachia. It also contains rare stands of "transmontane," or high-elevation long-leaf pines. Botanist Eliza Frances Andrews was among the first to draw attention to these unusual trees and wrote about their extraordinary ability to resist fire in a 1917 article published in the *Botanical Gazette*.[5] Today the Chattahoochee National Forest serves as an important recreation area, attracting visitors from across the state. Efforts to protect the Armuchee Ranger District from logging have been relatively successful, even though more than 40,000 acres of the area is still included in the timber base.

High Cotton

For nearly two centuries, northwest Georgia has been a region of small agricultural communities comprised of individuals with strong ties to the land. For the first half of the nineteenth century, both whites and Cherokees practiced small-scale mixed farming agriculture, growing everything from wheat and oats to sweet potatoes and beans. Most farm families grew what they ate and made a large amount of their clothing. Many farmers in the region resisted large-scale, cash-crop agriculture, as transportation to outside markets was poor. Few plantations existed in the northwest Georgia mountains, but those that did rivaled the ones of the Deep South.

With the coming of the railroad to the region in 1847, an economic boom resulted. Dalton, in Whitfield County, temporarily became the economic center, and its depot became an important shipping point for commercially minded farmers seeking to supply grains to seacoast plantations. As a result, wheat became a more important crop in northwest Georgia, ranking second only to corn throughout much of the 1850s.

The Civil War devastated farms and farming in the land of Ridge and Valley, sending it into an economic depression that would last for another half-decade. By the 1870s, with the return of important railroad lines,

---

[5] Ibid., 82.

commercial agriculture was once again on the upswing. Fertilizer, in the form of commercial guano, also became readily available, which made the growing of cotton a profitable enterprise. By 1880, cotton production had more than doubled in the region, making towns like Dalton and Rome important collection points for the popular commodity.

Cotton growing became the lifeblood for many northwest Georgia residents and remained so through the Great Depression. In Bartow County, for example, 22,000 acres of cotton were under cultivation in 1879; by 1920, 55,000 acres of cotton were being grown. Most cotton lands yielded between 1/2 to 1 bale of cotton per acre, but these yields diminished after cotton was grown on the same fields year after year. Cotton growing had an important impact on native soils that would eventually help undermine the region's potential as a major agricultural area.

With cotton fields came cotton mills. Industrialists in the post-war era believed prosperity hinged on manufacturing, and cotton textile production was cheap and the raw material readily available. Among the first textile mills in the region was the Crown Cotton Mill, established in Dalton in 1885. It was undoubtedly the largest enterprise in the city and attracted labor from Whitfield County and surrounding communities. The Crown Cotton Mill was neither the largest or first such establishment in the region, however, as the Trion Manufacturing Company was founded in 1847 in Chattooga County. By 1891, the Trion mill was one of the largest in northwest Georgia. Outfitted with 22,000 spindles and 630 looms, it employed more than 500 individuals, including 300 young girls.

Initially millwork did not appeal to local residents, especially the men, who were more content with farming as long as crops could be successfully harvested and annual debts paid. During the 1890s, more farmers in northwest Georgia became less rather than more self-sufficient. Tenancy was also on the rise and poverty more widespread. For many, working for wages in a mill was seen as a necessity brought on by increasing landlessness, fluctuating cotton prices, and debt-peonage.

With the cotton mill came the cotton-mill village, and after the turn of the century, the typical cotton mill supplied modest homes for employees, which were leased to them for a percent of their wages. The mill village was almost always immediately adjacent to the factory and had a unique character. Although almost all the homes were of identical design, the employees were encouraged to take individual pride in their dwellings and were sometimes offered prizes for the best-kept yards and homes.

In most mill villages, mill workers were never fully severed from their rural roots and so brought the values of the countryside with them. Some families even kept residences in the countryside and simply sent their children to work in the mills. Initially, the mill-village worker often continued to grow a vegetable garden, raise chickens, and pen hogs, and so the factory did not immediately destroy time-honored rural traditions. During the 1920s and 1930s, however, as more mill-village homes became electrified and furnished with indoor plumbing, mill villagers began to make clear distinctions between village folk and country folk, and many saw their country cousins as having a backward character.

By the mid-1940s, the mill village was itself on the wane, although the textile industry was still vitally important to the area. The ability of workers to purchase their own homes and the growing centrality of the automobile in people's lives made mill-village life far less attractive.

By 1950, the cotton-mill village was all but obsolete in northwest Georgia. With the help of local investors and new technological innovations, carpet manufacturing began to replace traditional textile production in many northwest Georgia communities. Because synthetic fibers are largely used in the manufacturing of carpet, the importance of cotton production fell precipitously. Cotton, and the agriculture economy that supported it, was no longer king.

Today, northwest Georgia has retained much of its rural character, but the growth of Chattanooga to the north and Marietta to the south has required the building of numerous housing developments. Much of the more remote mountain landscape remains preserved in national forests, and annual festivals such as those at Prater's Mill in Whitfield County continue to celebrate the area's rural past. Agricultural pursuits play only a small part in the lives of most northwest Georgia residents, however, so it is likely that the forces of urban growth and development will continue to shape the Ridge and Valley landscape in the coming decades.

Chapter 19

The Great Smokies

With a potential market of 10,000,000 people—the number of annual visitors to the area—publishers are forever taking chances on books about the Great Smoky Mountains National Park. Indeed, a recent Amazon.com web search of books about the "Great Smoky Mountains" yielded more than 166 exact titles. The University of Tennessee Press also maintains a long list of books about the national park and its surrounding environs, including this latest by Daniel S. Pierce. Dr. Pierce, who teaches in the department of history at the University of North Carolina in Asheville, has honed and tweaked his doctoral dissertation in order to bring us what ostensibly is a revision of Carlos Campbell's *The Birth of a National Park in the Great Smokies*, the standard history of the national park's creation for more than three decades.

Pierce tries to differentiate this work from Campbell's and others by (1) emphasizing the natural environment of the park as historical agent and (2) revealing the many disparate voices of those promoting the park. Of course, Pierce begins the book with a discussion of the mountain landscape and those who originally inhabited it prior to European settlement. Sadly, there is little in this first chapter about the Woodland or Mississippian people and their rich and varied interaction with the southern Appalachian environment during the pre-contact era. Furthermore, little is mentioned about the role of elk or buffalo in altering the forest landscape prior to the nineteenth century. While Pierce's discussion is generally well argued, he makes interesting claims regarding Native American land use in the Smokies. On the formation of grassy balds, for example, Pierce argues that many were created by "Indian burning," though he gives us little convincing evidence that this was the case. Indeed, there has never been an eyewitness historical account of high-altitude woods burning by the Cherokees, which isn't surprising given the fact that most of their incendiary activities occurred along major river bottoms at elevations well below 1,000 feet.

The strength of the introductory chapter is the section on logging, which receives the greatest attention by the author—and rightly so, as the industrial-railroad logging did by far the most damage to the mountain environs prior to the park's official dedication in 1940. Archival photographs nicely augment this section, and collectively they illustrate the wanton destruction of some of the largest tracts of old-growth timber in the eastern United States. Readers learn that the area that would later become the most visited national park in the eastern US was at one time mostly owned by no fewer than ten absentee logging companies that, as Pierce more aptly demonstrates in chapter 5, not only were responsible for long-term environmental damage to the region but also greatly complicated the land-buying process for the park during the 1930s.

Because Pierce moves through more than 500 years of environmental history in less than 34 pages, there is little wonder that he only superficially delves into the more interesting aspects of human-nature relationships in the Smokies. The American chestnut tree, for example, arguably the single most important tree species in the Great Smoky Mountains, gets fewer than two pages of treatment in the entire book. For that discussion, the reader should consult Margaret Brown's recently published *Wild East: A Biography of the Great Smoky Mountains National Park* or my own book *Where There Are Mountains: An Environmental History of the Southern Appalachians*. Both of these works pay considerably more attention to the role the natural habitat played in the formation of mountain subsistence culture in the southern Appalachians.

Where Pierce clearly succeeds in this book is his treatment of the individual boosters and corresponding political forces that championed the cause of the Great Smoky Mountains National Park. Here we find both original research and a carefully crafted analysis of the political wrangling that occurred during the park's early formation. According to Pierce, one of the earliest and most influential park boosters was Horace Kephart, whose major work *Our Southern Highlanders* (1913) introduced thousands to the Great Smokies. But as Pierce himself notes, local natives were as influential as Kephart in bringing national attention to the area, including the husband-

and-wife team Willis and Ann Davis, who worked tirelessly to promote the Great Smokies preserve during the 1920s. Colonel David C. Chapman, a prominent Knoxville businessman, is also rightly portrayed by Pierce as the most important spokesperson for the entire park movement, a fact hard to deny given the energy and enthusiasm he brought to the cause for more than a decade.

For the bulk of the book, Pierce takes the reader through the many turns, setbacks, and state and federal maneuvers to secure lands for the park. His narrative is strictly chronological, well documented, and full of interesting anecdotes regarding the actions of the major players. Of special note is the fistfight that occurred between David Chapman and governor aid George Dempster after a disagreement regarding the amount of money spent for land acquisition by the Tennessee Great Smoky Mountains Park Commission in 1932. Chapman, after circulating a statement arguing that the commission had acquired only 1/4 acre of land for the park after spending more than $11,000, was called a "goddammed liar" by Dempster, and a battle quickly ensued. Chapman, the smaller of the two, apparently received the most blows, evident by the official injury report that describes a "missing front tooth, back-eye, cut lip, and two broken ribs" (Pierce, 130).

Throughout the text, Pierce focuses primarily on the major proponents of the park, which often causes him to overlook the many who vehemently opposed it. Pierce's oversight is perhaps not surprising given his dependence on local newspapers for his primary sources. Although the people's words may have never made it into local print, the oral history collection housed at the national park archives contains the voices of numerous individuals who wanted fair and just compensation for their land and personal property. Most of these mountain residents sold out to federal land buyers only when threatened with the prospect of condemnation proceedings, which they knew would be next to impossible to challenge without expensive legal assistance, especially during the Great Depression when money was scarce.

Equally disturbing for habitual readers of *Appalachian Journal* will be the author's seemingly unbalanced treatment on the whole question of removal. As the author himself notes, the Great Smoky Mountains were far from being a sparsely settled landscape; the creation of the national park required the expulsion of nearly 5,000 people, many of whom lived in organized communities containing churches, stores, schools, and post offices. But as an apparent park apologist, Pierce tries to justify the exodus by proclaiming that the economics of the people of the area was already "increasingly precarious," which made the coming of the park an economic godsend by allowing local residents to "buy new land at a time of low land prices" (p. 169). He also uncritically cites the demographic data of Crandall Shiftlett, who claims that the Appalachian region was in a "population crisis" in the early twentieth century, in order to make the argument that mountain residents could never hope to bolster more than an economically marginal livelihood in the Great Smokies. The best and only option therefore was to sell their land to the federal government and move to where land was more fertile or into town where jobs paid a more livable wage.

Not only are there disturbing Malthusian overtones to Pierce's analysis, but he also clearly fails to understand that the "population crisis" was created in part by the coming of the large timber companies to the region. These companies artificially created land scarcity by purchasing tens of thousands of acres of mountain lands and then virtually enclosing these areas to prohibit local use or ownership by mountain residents. Only after the lumbermen had made much of the Smokies unusable by clear-cutting the forest—and thus destroying a viable ecosystem that had evolved over thousands of years—did most mountaineers began to question their highly forest-dependent way of life and consider other economic options that would take them far away from their mountain homelands.

Despite these important shortcomings, Pierce's *The Great Smokies* will probably become the standard history on the formation of the national park. The prose is exceptionally readable and keeps the reader's interest throughout. The inclusion of numerous archival photographs and political cartoons enhances the text. At first glance, the bibliography appears sparse, but this is due in part to the author's heavy use of primary sources. A concluding chapter summarizes the more recent controversies surrounding the park's management, reminding the reader that the story of the Great Smoky Mountains continues to unfold, even as the lived experience of former residents is becoming forever lost to memory.

Chapter 20

Mountains of Culture: Environmental History and Appalachia

Human society is a part of a larger structured whole, so an individual cooperates with more than the members of his human group. Every aspect of nature, plants and rocks and animals, colors and cardinal directions...have a cooperative share in the maintenance of the universal order.
    —Dorothy Lee, *Freedom and Culture*

In recent decades, many scholars have tried to restore the natural world to a more equal position in the story of the past. These individuals, representing a number of different though not entirely unrelated academic fields, have made their intellectual project the study of natural history, its objective effects on people, and humanity's role in transforming the natural environment. The most visible of these scholars belong to a discipline commonly known as environmental history, which, as one leading practitioner forcefully states, "rejects the common assumption that human experience has been exempt from natural constraints, that people are a separate and uniquely special species, [and] that the ecological consequences of our past deeds can be ignored."[1] Defined in the vernacular, adds Donald

---

[1] Donald Worster, "Transformations of the Earth: Toward an Agroecological Perspective in History," *Journal of American History* 76 (March 1990): 1088.

Worster, environmental history "deals with the role and place of nature in human life."[2]

William Cronon's pioneering study *Changes in the Land* was exemplary of the methodological approach used by environmental historians writing more than a decade ago.[3] In his analysis of the evolution of Native American subsistence patterns in colonial New England, Cronon demonstrates the inherent relatedness of ecological and social systems. For Cronon, ecology and culture are inexorably intertwined, thus "ecological history begins by assuming a dynamic and changing relationship between environment and culture."[4]

Timothy Silver, another environmental historian using Cronon's methodological approach, similarly demonstrated how the environment affected the settlement and development of South Atlantic forests. In his book *A New Face on the Countryside*, Silver discusses Native American, Anglo-European, and African cultures as well as each culture's unique influence on the environment.[5] Cronon's and Silver's contributions are important not only because they emphasize the role of the environment in shaping North American history, but also because they demonstrate the cultural diversity of the colonial frontier. Because the colonization process required an exchange of subsistence practices among all the inhabitants of a region, the result was multiculturalism. In the colonial frontier, no single group remained culturally homogenous.

Carolyn Merchant, who maintains that environmental history "reasserts the idea of nature as historical actor," forcefully shows how humans and the environment are interdependent agents of social and environmental change. Her important study, *Ecological Revolutions*, employs social, economic, and ecological analyses in order to show how human consciousness, the local environment, and human communities evolve over

---

[2] Ibid., 1089.

[3] For a more specific discussion about the environmental history's theories of interpretation and methods of analysis, see Kendall E. Bailes, *Environmental History: Critical Issues in Comparative Perspective* (Lanham MD: University Presses of America, 1985); Barbara Leibhardt, "Interpretation and Causal Analysis: Theories in Environmental History," *Environmental Review* 12 (Spring 1988): 23–36.

[4] William Cronon, *Changes in the Land: Indians Colonists, and the Ecology of New England* (New York: Hill & Wang, 1983) 13.

[5] Timothy Silver, *A New Face on the Countryside: Indians, Colonists, and Slaves in South Atlantic Forests, 1500–1800* (New York: Cambridge University Press, 1990).

time.[6] Of critical importance in Merchant's analysis is the role gender plays in environmental change. In subsistence economies, women have a direct impact on nature through crop production, whereas men are more involved with environmentally destructive activities, such as hunting large animals, cutting down forests, and plowing fields.[7] By documenting the different effects men and women had on the environment, says Merchant, environmental history offers "a more balanced and complete picture of past human interactions with nature."[8]

As Merchant suggests, we can never fully uncover the complexity of the social order without understanding the environmental context in which it occurs. Arthur McEvoy, a legal historian who studied the California fisheries of the nineteenth and twentieth centuries, also found that environmental factors were central to the economic and cultural development of that region. McEvoy carefully documents the importance of salmon to the California natives, who were directly dependent upon the fish for their livelihood, as well as the fish's importance to the modern commercial fishing industry, a multibillion-dollar enterprise.[9] As William Cronon has noted, McEvoy's study is important because it effectively demonstrates how a region's political economy, its natural ecology, and the environmental attitudes of its residents are all significant determinants of environmental and cultural change.[10]

Although the writings of Worster, Cronon, Silver, Merchant, and McEvoy represent only a portion of available literature in the environmental history field, these authors are most responsible for developing the

[6] Carolyn Merchant, *Ecological Revolutions: Nature, Gender, and Science in New England* (Chapel Hill: University of North Carolina Press, 1990) 7.

[7] See, for example, Sandra Marbug, "Women and Environment: Subsistence Paradigms, 1850–1950," *Environmental Review* 8 (Spring 1984): 7–22; Vandana Shiva, *Women, Ecology, and Development* (London: Zed Books, 1988); Vandana Shiva, "Resources," in Wolfgang Sachs, ed., *The Development Dictionary: A Guide to Knowledge as Power* (London: Zed Books, 1992) 206–18; George P. Murdock, "Comparative Data on the Division of Labor by Sex," *Social Forces* 15 (May 1935): 551–53.

[8] Carolyn Merchant, "Gender and History," *Journal of American History* 76 (March 1990): 1121; idem, *Major Problems in Environmental History: Documents and Essays* (Lexington MA: D. C. Heath, 1993).

[9] Arthur F. McEvoy, *The Fisherman's Problem: Ecology and Law in the California Fisheries, 1850–1980* (New York: Cambridge University Press, 1986).

[10] William Cronon, "Modes of Prophecy and Production: Placing Nature in History," *Journal of American History* 76 (March 1990): 1123, n. 4.

environmental history discipline.[11] It should be noted, however, that non-historians trained as sociologists, geographers, or even biologists have produced a substantial body of work in the field.[12] While environmental historians have only recently sought to reorient their discipline toward a more holistic ecological perspective, cultural and historical geographers have for a much longer period made the environment a central concern of their scholarly enterprise. Influenced by the scholarship launched by Carl Ortwin Sauer in the 1920s, geographers have made important inroads toward understanding how human groups and their environments interact to form "cultural landscapes"—the tangible byproduct of human-nature interactions over time. Sauer calls the interactive process by which cultures utilize, shape, and transform their natural surroundings "landscape morphology," and he and his students used the concept to illustrate the various ways in which cultural perceptions of nature have influenced land-use decisions on the North American continent.[13]

Utilizing the approach pioneered by Sauer, Terry Jordan and Matti Kaups, in *The American Backwoods Frontier*,[14] have created a theoretical and methodological framework from which to interpret both environmental and cultural change, something environmental historians have been hesitant to

---

[11] See also, for example, Alfred Crosby, *Ecological Imperialism: The Biological Expansions of Europe, 900–1900* (New York: Cambridge University Press, 1987); Roderick Nash, *Wilderness and the American Mind*, 3rd ed. (New Haven CT: Yale University Press, 1982); Joseph Petulla, *American Environmentalism: Values, Tactics, Priorities* (College Station: Texas University Press, 1977); and Stephen Pyne, *Fire in America: A Cultural History of Wildland and Rural Fire* (Princeton: Princeton University Press, 1982).

[12] For the role that agricultural crops played in the development of Western civilization, see Henry Hobhouse, *Seeds of Change: Five Plants that Transformed Mankind* (London: Sidwick and Jackson, 1985). For the importance of sugar to the development of slavery in the Caribbean and America, see Sidney Mintz, *Sweetness and Power: The Place of Sugar in Modern History* (New York: Penguin Books, 1986). For the relationship that existed between Native Americans and cultivated plants, see Gary Paul Nabhan, *Enduring Seeds: Native American Agriculture and Wild Plant Conservation* (San Francisco: North Point Press, 1989).

[13] Carl O. Sauer, "The Morphology of Landscape," *University of California Publications in Geography* 2 (1925): 19–53; Preston E. James and Geoffrey J. Martin, *All Possible Worlds: A History of Geographical Ideas* (New York: John Wiley and Sons, 1981) 321.

[14] Jordan and Kaups, *The American Backwoods Frontier* (Baltimore MD: John Hopkins University Press, 1989).

do in any substantive way.[15] The authors maintain that most cultural diffusionist studies, environmental determinist theses, and economic and sociological examinations cannot offer the full depth or breadth of explanatory understanding as a method that combines elements from each approach. Accordingly, Jordan and Kaups offer readers what they call an "ethnic and ecological interpretation" of social and cultural development on the Appalachian frontier. Their methodological approach attempts to marry cultural diffusionism with "particularistic" cultural ecology, an explanatory model that focuses, they claim, on the unique interplay between individual culture groups and their distinct physical environments.[16]

Particularistic cultural ecology, says Jordan and Kaups, "recognizes that more than one path of adaptation exists in a given environment and that the choice among them is a function of culture."[17] Culture, they argue, directs the appropriate adaptive strategy by helping individuals or social groups determine what resources are meaningful in a specific environmental setting. The Scots-Irish, for example, brought to the southern Appalachians a proclivity for cattle herding, of which they had considerable knowledge, but they knew little else, say the authors, about living in a vast wooded forest.[18] In order to survive in this unfamiliar terrain, the Scots-Irish had to turn to the Native Americans or Finns and Swedes for practical knowledge about hunting and gathering, growing crops, and constructing habitable dwellings. Thus, over time, the cultural diffusion process is determined by a culture's specific adaptive traits, such as cattle herding, and partially by the skills it borrows from other culture groups, such as log-cabin construction, in a

[15] For discussions concerning environmental history's "weak" methodological focus, see Richard White, "Environmental History, Ecology, and Meaning," *Journal of American History* 76 (March 1990) 1111–16; William Cronon, "Modes of Prophecy and Production: Placing Nature in History," *Journal of American History* 76, 1122–31; Donald Worster, "Seeing Beyond Culture," *Journal of American History* 76, 1142–47.

[16] Jordan and Kaups, *American Backwoods Frontier*, 32.

[17] Ibid.

[18] Ibid., 121. The cattle-herding heritage of the Scots-Irish is discussed in Ronald H. Buchanan, "Field Systems of Ireland," in Alan R. H. Baker and Robin Butlin, eds., *Studies of Field Systems in the British Isles* (Cambridge MA: Cambridge University Press, 1973); E. Estyn Evans, "The Scotch Irish: Their Cultural Adaptation and Heritage in the American Old West," in E. R. R. Green, ed., *Essays in Scotch-Irish History* (London: Routledge & Kegan Paul, 1969).

place-specific environment that also determines the range of adaptive possibilities.[19]

Within this dynamic framework, the cultural complex of the Appalachian frontier could be seen, particularly in the long view, as the product of a heterogeneous blending of cultural traits, a cultural matrix determined to a large degree by the ecological specificity of the mountain environment. Ironically, Jordan and Kaups actually warn against making such a conclusion. The central thesis of their book is that the *"American backwoods culture had significant northern European roots."*[20] That is, Jordan and Kaups see the Savo-Karelians, an eastern Finnish group that devised a well-developed forest colonization cultural complex in the fifteenth and sixteenth centuries, as "the most significant shapers of the American backwoods way of life."[21] In actual execution, Jordan and Kaups are not terribly interested in demonstrating significant cultural particularism on the American frontier. They do support the more commonly held view that the eastern Woodland Indians were "significant contributors to the backwoods pioneer adaptive system," but they argue persistently that the principal agents of cultural determination of frontier culture were the eastern Finns.[22]

In order to prove this highly revisionist thesis, the authors deemphasize or even deny the existence of reciprocal cultural diffusion or syncretism on the frontier. Their argument for the primacy of Finnish influence is further supported, they believe, by the fact that the frontier environment is similar to the "hardscrabble" habitat of northern Europe, where the Savo-Karelians developed their highly adaptive subsistence culture. In celebrating the presence of Savo-Karelian culture in the backwoods frontier, Jordan and Kaups do not, however, as they might have us believe, critically incorporate place-specific ecological influences into their analysis. To do so fully, they first would have to admit to the ecological heterogeneity of the frontier environment that does not in its entirety resemble the "hardscrabble" terrain of northern Europe.

There are of course significant ecological differences between northern Europe and eastern North America as well as notable differences between

---

[19] Jordan and Kaups, *American Backwoods Frontier*, 19–36. On preadaptation in the Upland South, see Milton Newton, "Cultural Preadaptation and the Upland South," *Geoscience and Man* 5 (10 June 1974): 143–54.

[20] Jordan and Kaups, *American Backwoods Frontier*, 36 (their italics).

[21] Ibid., 36–37.

[22] Ibid.

the environments of the Delaware Valley region and the Appalachians. Prior to European settlement, the Appalachians were a patchwork quilt of topographical environments comprised of level wooded land, large and small forest clearings, high sandy plateaus, steep rocky ridges, upland forests, mountain balds, swampy glades, and fertile creek and river bottoms often covered with thick and imposing canebrakes.[23] In many of these ecologically specific environments, cultural adaptations borrowed from the Finns or Swedes would be no more or less superior to those of other ethnic groups who settled the region in the eighteenth and nineteenth centuries.

The authors rightly give credit to the Woodland Indians for helping the backwoods pioneer with crop selection and farming practices in many of these local environments, but they are relatively undiscerning when discussing specific Native American groups, agricultural systems, or subsistence techniques other than to argue persistently that the *fundamental* cultural borrowings on the frontier "were achieved by the Delaware Valley Finns and Swedes as an outgrowth of their close association and harmony with the local Indians."[24] In defending their fundamental thesis, Jordan and Kaups are more accurately advancing another conventional diffusionist model of cultural inheritance that does not, in the main, see the environment as a primary agent of social and cultural change.

Jordan and Kaups's inability to make nature a primary agent of cultural change is not surprising given the fact that in the social sciences culture has traditionally been seen in *opposition* to nature. Even Arthur Kroeber, who argues that "cultures are rooted in nature, and can therefore never be understood except with reference to that piece of nature in which they occur," felt compelled to qualify his position by stating—in Durkheimian fashion—that "the *immediate* causes of cultural phenomena are other cultural phenomena."[25] However, if we assume that a dialectical relationship

---

[23] Karl Raitz and Richard Ulack, *Appalachia: A Regional Geography: Land People, and Development* (Boulder CO: Westview Press, 1984) 67–73; Nevin Fenneman, *Physiography of Eastern United States* (New York: McGraw Hill, 1938); Ann Sutton and Myron Sutton, *Eastern Forests* (New York: Alfred A. Knopf, 1985) 81–94.

[24] Jordan and Kaups, *American Backwoods Frontier*, 117.

[25] A. L. Kroeber, *Cultural and Natural Areas of Native North America* (Berkeley: University of California Press, 1963) 1 (his italics). Obviously, Kroeber is concerned that his work will be associated with the "old environmentalism," which, he says, "believed it could find the causes of culture in the environment." In using the term *old environmentalism*, Kroeber is referring to the nineteenth century school of thought (environmental determinism) that attributed the causes of human behavior

exists between the environment and society, then culture must always have an environmental component or at least be indirectly influenced by environmental forces. Regardless of the historical epoch, human beings never fully escape the limitations imposed by the ecology of their physical environments. In the 1920s, when the chestnut blight decimated the chestnut tree in the southern Appalachians, the residents of the region lost not only a major source of wood for housing and fencing, but also an all-important food source for themselves and their livestock.

In the Appalachians, the mountain environment and its unique ecology have driven numerous subsistence strategies. The practice of gathering ginseng, for example, is dependent upon a single plant species that grows in a specific upland forest ecosystem. More than two centuries ago, ginseng was being gathered in the mountains and dried and shipped to China, where the plant was highly valued as a medicine and general panacea.[26] Many trace the Appalachian practice of "sang" digging—as native mountaineers call it—to André Michaux, the French botanist who explored the mountainous region at the turn of the nineteenth century and who is said to have taught early settlers how to recognize, collect, and locate markets for the plant.[27] Ginseng, which brought $400 for a pound of the dried root in 2000,[28] was

---

to spatial or geographic factors and not, in the main, to influences found in dynamic and living ecosystems.

[26] M. G. Kains, *Ginseng: Its Cultivation, Harvesting, Marketing and Market Value, with a Short Account of Its History and Botany* (New York: Orange Judd Company, 1902) 1–5; Richard Heffern, *The Complete Book of Ginseng* (Millbrae CA: Celestial Arts, 1976) 21–38; Michael A. Weiner, *Earth Food: Plant Remedies, Drugs, and Natural Foods of the North American Indians* (New York: Collier Books, 1979) 18–19.

[27] Donald Culross Peattie, "Blue Ridge Wild Flowers," in Roderick Peattie, ed., *The Great Smokies and the Blue Ridge* (New York: Vanguard Press, 1943) 172–200; Wilma Dykeman and Jim Stokely, *Highland Homeland: The People of the Great Smokies* (Washington, DC: US Department of the Interior, National Park History Series, 1978) 52–55.

[28] In 1980 alone, some 48,000 pounds of wild ginseng was gathered in the mountains of Georgia, Kentucky, North Carolina, Tennessee, Virginia, and West Virginia at a commercial value of more than $13 million (330 ginseng roots make up a dry pound of ginseng) (Ronald Singer, "Federal Requirements for Exports of American Ginseng," in *Proceedings of the Second National Ginseng Conference* [Jefferson City: Natural History Section, Missouri Department of Conservation, 1980], 5). During 1981–1982, 5,658 pounds of ginseng were collected from the wild in North Carolina. At current prices, this represents more than $600,000 paid to collectors (Robert Sutter, "The Ginseng Monitoring Program in North Carolina," in

also used by the Cherokees for medicinal purposes, and they themselves dug the root in the eighteenth century for export to Asian markets.

A truly ethnic and ecological interpretation of ginseng gathering, I believe, should ask the following questions of this long-standing cultural practice: (1) Who was responsible for first introducing the practice to settlers in the region—the Chinese, Michaux, or Native Americans? (2) How and when did the practice of digging the root become diffused throughout the southern mountains? (3) Do all ginseng gatherers use the plant themselves or believe in its medicinal powers? (4) What kinds of cultural or ecological knowledge is required in gathering and preserving the plant? (5) How did market forces influence its harvest and continued use? (6) In what ways has the practice changed over the past centuries, given ginseng's increasing scarcity in the wild?

In answering these kinds of questions, environmental historians can demonstrate how specific environmental influences affect the development of a culture and regional landscape without resorting to ethnic survival theses like those promoted by Jordan and Kaups and other scholars writing culture-inertia histories of the Appalachian frontier. Ginseng gathering, like most subsistence practices in the Appalachian Mountains, owes its existence to several cultural traditions, though it is clearly dependent on a specific ecological environment that permits the plant's growth. From my own perspective, the natural environment is a leveling factor that discriminates equally against all culture groups.[29]

If a single group deserves special attention in the context of southern Appalachia, it would certainly be the Native Americans, who for centuries prior to pioneer settlement coexisted in relative harmony with the North American landscape. Although Native Americans no doubt "altered the landscape to suit their needs, adapting techniques and technology...to the peculiarities of local climates and topography," their overall impact on the environment was, comparatively speaking, minimal when compared to landscape change during the twentieth century.[30] At the same time, as the

---

Proceedings of the Fourth National Ginseng Conference [Lexington: University of Kentucky College of Agriculture, 1982] 117).

[29] This is Donald Worster's point in his defense of making environmental history "more than social or cultural history" (Worster, "Seeing Beyond Culture," 1144).

[30] Silver, *A New Face on the Countryside*, 5. In recent years there has been a renewed interest in the Indian practice of fire burning, which is said to have dramatically altered the physical environment of North America. Stephen Pyne

first permanent inhabitants, the Native Americans developed unparalleled knowledge of the plants and animals of their environment.[31]

When different social groups colonize an environment, no single culture gains absolute hegemony. John Mack Faragher takes a similar position when he asserts that "frontier history is the story of the contact of cultures, their competition and their continuing relations. It cannot be the story of any one side."[32] This is not to suggest that elements of a particular culture cannot or do not persist unchanged, nor that all cultures share an equal power base. In overemphasizing cultural continuity in Appalachian history, scholars falsely presume that culture is the product of homogenous, functionally integrated social groups. In this traditional view of culture and cultural change, writes sociologist Ernest Gellner, there can be "no syncretism, no doctrinal pluralism…no dramatic conversion or…holding of alternative belief systems"[33]

The myth of cultural continuity remains strong in anthropology, sociology, and social history. As Margaret Archer points out in her elegant study of culture and social theory, there is a common and erroneous tendency for all social theorists (grounded partly in their debt to German historicism) to see culture as a unified, integrated whole. The penchant for defining cultures as "coherent patterns," "cultural systems," or the product of a "single, symbolically consistent universe"[34] results in a fairly naive view

---

argues that much of the eastern United States was once an open savannah created by Indians. However, it is doubtful that the fires of the Indians were intense or frequent enough to do much damage to the larger woodland environment. See Stephen Pyne, *Fire in America: A Cultural History of Wildland and Rural Fire* (Princeton: Princeton University Press, 1982) 75.

[31] The ecological knowledge of Native Americans will never fully be known. Attempts at reconstructing their use of North American plant life include Melvin Gilmore, *Uses of Plants by the Indians of the Missouri River Region* (Lincoln: University of Nebraska Press, 1977); Gary Paul Nabhan, *Enduring Seeds: Native American Agriculture and Wild Plant Conservation* (San Francisco: North Point Press, 1989); William H. Banks, "Ethnobotany of the Cherokee Indians" (Master's thesis, University of Tennessee, Knoxville, 1953).

[32] John Mack Faragher, *Women and Men on the Overland Trail* (New Haven CT: Yale University Press, 1979) iv.

[33] Gellner quoted in Margaret S. Archer, *Culture and Agency: The Place of Culture in Social Theory* (Cambridge: Cambridge University Press, 1988) 9.

[34] Ruth Benedict, *Patterns of Culture* (New York: Houghton Mifflin, 1934); Florian Znaniecki, *Cultural Sciences: Their Origin and Development* (Urbana:

of culture that takes into account neither cultural ambiguities nor the important role changing physical environments play in influencing both the rate and direction of cultural change.

In fact, there is almost always a diversity of cultural approaches to resource use. An Alpine cattle herdsmen will use and preserve the environment for different reasons than will a Quechuan potato grower of the Andes—though neither individual will likely do irreparable environmental damage since both rely heavily on their physical surroundings for their immediate sustenance. Before contact with the Europeans, the Cherokees of the southern mountains practiced a land tenure system that gave all members of the community relatively equal access to available natural resources. As Douglas Hurt describes it, "North American Indians usually did not think of private poverty as an absolute right or consider land as a commodity that could be bought, sold, or permanently alienated in some fashion…. The community owned the uncultivated land, while the individual created a control or use claim by cultivating a specific field or plot or land." The practice of communal property rights by the Cherokees not only helped the community maintain a more harmonious and egalitarian social order; it also helped them preserve the ecological integrity of their local environment.[35]

In Appalachia, the relationship between culture and environment has long been an enigmatic one. Attempts to find environmental influences on southern Appalachian culture have generally resulted in a crude geographic determinism in which the "isolation" or "severity" of the mountains is said to be the fundamental cause of the "primitive" or "frontier-like" behavior of the mountain people. Ellen Churchill Semple, for example, writing at the turn of the century, argued that cultural persistence in eastern Kentucky was a direct result of social isolation created by the rugged mountain

---

University of Illinois Press, 1952) 296–329; and Mary Douglas, quoted in Archer, *Culture and Agency*, 3.

[35] Douglas R. Hurt, *Indian Agriculture in America* (Lawrence: University Press of Kansas, 1987) 74. In communal property, "the natural resource is held by an identifiable community of users who can exclude others and regulate use." The continued practice of communal property regimes throughout the modern world calls into question Garret Hardin's "tragedy of the commons" thesis, which unfortunately has convinced most of the modern world that communal environmental management is not socially possible (F. Berkes, D. Feeney, B. J. McCay, J. M. Acheson, "The Benefits of the Commons," *Nature* 340 (13 July 1989): 91–93.

environment. Writing three decades after Semple, J. Wesley Hatcher argues that it was not so much altitude as topographic relief that determined the cultural conditions of "Appalachian America."[36] Hatcher gave more agency to specific soil types and physical land forms, which, he argued, varied greatly from place to place. Hatcher believes residents of the region belonged to one of three social classes ranks each class according to the topographic characteristics of the local environment.

The first class is found, writes Hatcher, in "the valleys of the creeks and rivers, where the soil is richest, exposure to the sun is fullest, vegetation rich, water supply abundant and sweet, and lines of communication relatively easy and many." The second class, Hatcher believes, are "pushed up the streams where the valleys are narrower, the hills and mountains are higher and steeper, the soil is poorer and thinner." The third group are "shunted to the starvation points, where slopes are steepest, soil is poorest and thinnest, exposure to sun least favorable, water supply worst, easy accessibility impossible." It is this third group, he says, that most people perceive when they think of mountaineers.[37]

Hatcher does acknowledge important class distinctions present in the mountain region, but he falls short of demonstrating how environmental factors affect the cultural activities of the area. A closer look reveals that his ranking system was created to prove the cultural superiority of one class over another. He maintains, for example, that "the more vigorous and alert [mountaineers] manage to get possession of the vantage points, while the less highly endowed were shunted off to the less desirable locations." Hatcher is really only telling us that the "genetic characteristics" or "social standing" of the mountain residents determine habitation patterns in the mountains.[38]

To correct the environmental determinism of Semple, Hatcher, and others and still to explore the impact of the environment on Appalachian regional culture, several things must be done simultaneously. First, consideration must be given to the social development of all three terrain types representative of the Appalachian landscape. By critically comparing

---

[36] Ellen Churchill Semple, "The Anglo-Saxons of the Kentucky Mountains: A Study in Anthropo-Geography" (New York: Henry Holt, 1911) 588–623; J. Wesley Hatcher, "Appalachian America," in W. T. Couch, *Culture in the South* (Chapel Hill: University of North Carolina Press, 1935) 374–402.

[37] Hatcher, " Appalachian America," 382, 386, 387.

[38] Ibid., 382.

the development of the Ridge and Valley, Blue Ridge, and Cumberland Plateau provinces, one can obtain a more complete picture of the variety of cultural practices that prevailed in the region throughout the area's history. Far too many scholars continue to make generalizations about the entire Appalachian region based on what are more correctly studies of Appalachian subregions, or in some cases individual communities within subregions. Second, comparisons should be made between cultural practices found in the southern mountains and those found outside the region in other rural areas of the South. A few scholars are just beginning to recognize—and admit—that mountain culture historically shares much in common with rural culture elsewhere. If cultural practices are truly unique to the region, they should not readily occur outside the southern Appalachians.

That nature influenced culture in the southern Appalachian mountains should be a historical given. Mississippian and Cherokee societies evolved in direct relationship to the Appalachian environment, a physical environment very different from the one we know today. By reconstructing that environment, we better understand the previous culture as well as its relationship to our own. By studying the environmental history of the southern Appalachians, it is possible to see, perhaps for the first time, the full impact of early human settlement on the mountain landscape. It is also clear that, over the *longue durée*, ecological forces did retain considerable agency over the course of human action in the Appalachia region.

Epilogue

When writing about Appalachia, one must always consider the role of home and place in the lives of mountain residents. The fact that the terms "home" and "place" in Appalachia are collapsed into a single word—"homeplace"—speaks volumes about the role of the mountain landscape in shaping Appalachian identity. For rural Appalachians, to be separated from their natural surroundings is to be removed from the very thing that makes them who they are as individuals. In Appalachia, mountains and home are synonymous.

In the opening essay, I discussed the destruction of my own homeplace, a phenomenon that unfortunately is occurring elsewhere in the mountain region. Despite heroic efforts to stop the practice, mountaintop removal projects continue to transform vast areas of the Appalachians. In many locales, urban growth and development is transforming the rural countryside in ways that may be irreversible. What does this mean for Appalachia? The simple answer is that the Appalachia of the twenty-first century will be vastly different from anything we have witnessed before. Some scholars even believe Appalachia will simply cease to exist—not as a geographic area, obviously, but as a rural place where individuals live in relative harmony with their natural surroundings.

Of course, much of Appalachia can still be preserved. Presently there are hundreds of individuals working toward protecting the mountains and the rural communities still scattered across the region. All who care about the future of rural America should support and celebrate their difficult work. In fact, my own career, as reflected in the essays in this volume, has been an attempt to bear witness to the ongoing environmental struggles of the Appalachian region.

Since penning the closing essay of *Homeplace Geography*, I have continued writing about Appalachia and the many environmental threats currently facing the region. For several years, I worked as coeditor of the environment section of *The Encyclopedia of Appalachia* (Knoxville: University of Tennessee Press, 2006), a massive project that involved compiling and editing entries from more than twenty-five authors. More recently, I finished a 10,000-year environmental history of the American South (Santa Barbara: ABC-CLIO, 2007), a book that also features new materials about Appalachia not found in my previous work.

Among my proudest accomplishment to date, however, has been my work with the American Chestnut Foundation. In 2004, I helped establish a Georgia chapter of this foundation, a nonprofit organization incorporated in the state of Georgia. Since its formation, chapter members have discovered numerous blooming American chestnut trees in the mountains of North Georgia and have already pollinated several of those trees with blight-resistant pollen taken from the American Chestnut Foundation's research farms in southwest Virginia. Because of work being done by the Georgia chapter and others in the mountain region, it is possible that the American chestnut tree will once again reign supreme over the Appalachian forest.

If and when this occurs, there will be new hope for Appalachia. As I wrote in chapter 17, "A Whole World Dying," the loss of the chestnut tree made it virtually impossible for rural Appalachians to maintain their self-sufficient, forest-dependent way of life. With the return of the American chestnut to the mountain region, perhaps a whole world, an entire native landscape, could be restored to its original splendor. Healthy chestnut trees in the Appalachian forest would certainly create real economic possibilities for all mountain residents, providing yet another reason to protect and defend our mountain homeplace.

Index

Wilderness, Society, The, 46, 47.
wild strawberries, 141.
wild turkeys, 130, 157, 179, 180.
Williamsburg (Virginia), 140.
Wilson, Larry, 60.
wool, 145, 146. *See also* sheep.
world economy, 123.
Worster, Donald, 201-202.

Yellow Creek Concerned Citizens
    (YCCC), 59-61.
Yokum, Dwight, 21.

Zuellig Group of North America,
    173.

DATE DUE